CW01335757

Liverpool 1660–1750

Liverpool 1660–1750

People, Prosperity and Power

Diana E. Ascott, Fiona Lewis
and Michael Power

LIVERPOOL UNIVERSITY PRESS

First published 2006 by
Liverpool University Press
4 Cambridge Street
Liverpool
L69 7ZU

This paperback edition published 2010

Copyright © 2006, 2010 Diana E. Ascott, Fiona Lewis and Michael Power

The right of Diana E. Ascott, Fiona Lewis and Michael Power to be identified as the authors of this work has been asserted by them in accordance with the Copyright, Designs and Patents Act, 1988.

All rights reserved. No part of this book may be reproduced, stored in a retrieval system, or transmitted, in any form or by any means, electronic, mechanical, photo-copying, recording or otherwise without the prior written permission of the publishers.

British Library Cataloguing-in-Publication Data
A British Library CIP Record is available

ISBN 978-1-84631-007-2 cased
      978-1-84631-503-9 limp

Typeset in Plantin by Koinonia, Bury
Printed in the UK by Marston Digital

To Michael
in fond memory, with thanks

Contents

List of Figures   viii
List of Tables   ix
List of Abbreviations   xi
Preface   xii

Introduction   1

1   Contexts: The Emergence of an Early Modern Port   8

2   Population and Demography   32

3   Occupation: Structure, Mobility and Succession   68

4   Family and Friends: Inheritance Strategies in a Mobile
    Population   106

5   Government   138

6   Politics   162

    Conclusion   190

Appendices
1   Sources and methods   195
2   Probate listing   211
3   Overall sample sizes   215

Bibliography   216

Index   236

List of Figures

1.1	Liverpool in the 1660s	10
1.2	Liverpool in the later Stuart Period	11
1.3	Liverpool in 1725	12
1.4	Liverpool in 1765	13
2.1	Baptism, burial and marriage totals from parish registers, 1661–1760	36
3.1	Occupational classification scheme	72
3.2	Occupational groups derived from parish registers, 1660–1750	73–75
3.3	Occupational classification of testators (male and female)	77
3.4	Occupational groups – maritime classification	83–85
3.5	Short family linkage	96
3.6	Webster family linkage	98
4.1	Clieveland family linkage	126
4.2	Danvers family linkage	128
4.3	Pemberton family linkage	130
Appendix 1 Sources		197

List of Tables

1.1 Tonnages to and from major English ports, 1709, 1751,
     1790   16
1.2 Liverpool merchants involved in major trades in 1707   18
2.1 Liverpool Hearth Taxes 1663, 1664, 1666 and 1673   33
2.2 Population estimates from Hearth Tax totals   34
2.3 Sex ratio at burial (males per 100 females)   39
2.4 Infant mortality rates per 1,000 live births – some
     comparisons   42
2.5 Infant and child mortality rates and expectation of life
     at birth from model life tables, sexes combined, by
     occupational group   44
2.6 Mean birth intervals in months (number of cases):
     1701–1750   49
2.7 Pre-nuptial pregnancy (percentage of all marriages
     with children) Liverpool 1701–1750   50
2.8 Residence of marriage partners, where origin of both
     partners known, expressed in percentage terms   53
2.9 Percentage baptism and burial links based upon family
     reconstitution histories with baptism of two or more children 59
3.1 Testators in port-related occupations expressed as
     percentage within period cohorts   86
3.2 Decedents in port-related occupations (percentage terms)   86
4.1 Relationship of beneficiaries to testator, 1661–1760,
     expressed as percentage of total number of wills (1,451)   114
4.2 Relationship of beneficiaries to testatrix, 1661–1760,
     as percentage of total number of wills (318)   115
4.3 Division of realty among children under wills from period
     cohorts, by testator's gender   116
4.4 Division of personalty among children under wills from
     period cohorts, by testator's gender   117
5.1 Liverpool Officers 1650–1750   142
5.2 Number of new councillors and aldermen in each decade   145

5.3 Occupational profile of Liverpool townsmen in government,
     1650–1750 (based on 29.4% with occupations identified)   148
5.4 Occupational profile of Liverpool townsmen in government
     in late seventeenth and early eighteenth centuries (%)   150
5.5 Changes in status ascriptions: Liverpool townspeople
     in government before 1700 and after 1700   151

Appendix 3 Overall sample sizes   215

List of Abbreviations

PRO   Public Record Office (now National Archives)
LRO   Lancashire Record Office
CRO   Cheshire Record Office
LplRO   Liverpool Record Office

CS   Chetham Society
EcHR   *Economic History Review*
EHR   *English Historical Review*
JEcR   *Journal of Economic History*
LPRS   Lancashire Parish Register Society
LPS   *Local Population Studies*
P&P   *Past and Present*
RSLC   Record Society of Lancashire and Cheshire
THSLC   *Transactions of the Historic Society of Lancashire and Cheshire*
TIBG   *Transactions of the Institute of British Geographers*
TLCAS   *Transactions of the Lancashire and Cheshire Antiquarian Society*

Preface

This book is based on a research project, 'The Liverpool Community, 1660–1750', and we are very grateful to the Leverhulme Trust for financial assistance in making the work possible. In addition to the help given by many members of the University of Liverpool secretarial and support staff, colleagues in the former Departments of History, and Economic and Social History (now the School of History) we would like to acknowledge and thank Julie Holbrook for keyboard inputting, Barbara Peers for research assistance and Brenda Lowndes for computing expertise.

To our families and friends within and without the University, thank you for your support.

To the staff at the Liverpool Record Office, Lancashire Record Office, Cheshire Record Office, St Helens Local History and Archives Library, the Merseyside Maritime Museum Archives and Library, the British Library, the Public Record Office (now National Archives), many thanks.

We are grateful to Liverpool Record Office for permission to reproduce the illustrations on pages 12 and 13.

Authorship of the volume is as follows: Chapter 1, D. E. Ascott and M. J. Power; Chapter 2, F. Lewis; Chapter 3, D. E. Ascott and F. Lewis; Chapter 4, D. E. Ascott; Chapters 5 and 6, M. J. Power.

Introduction

The emergence of Liverpool as a major port during the late seventeenth and early eighteenth centuries was one of the most striking economic developments in pre-industrial England. From a small mid-seventeenth town dependent on agriculture, fishing and a limited trade with Ireland, Liverpool grew into an important Atlantic port and a considerable processing and manufacturing centre by the mid-eighteenth century. At the beginning of the period, it did not rank among major provincial ports, but it grew in size and commercial importance to vie with them by the mid-eighteenth century and, in the longer term, to eclipse them. This book is an attempt to investigate some of the factors behind Liverpool's emergence and to develop an understanding of the town's growth by illuminating the dynamics of its population, economic structure, social networks and political establishment.

As such, it is a contribution to the growing volume of research into urban history, much of which has been synthesised into recent general surveys.[1] The period covered is the first half of the widely recognised 'long eighteenth century', the start of accelerating change in towns – in population distribution and density, in hierarchical reordering and altered focus. Domestically, urban population became a feature of the midlands and north as well as the south, while the burgeoning British urban system became re-oriented from the periphery of Europe to the centre of Atlantic commerce. Liverpool exemplified all aspects of this change. Despite escalating economic and demographic expansion, however, the later seventeenth-century town avoided the problems of extreme wealth and poverty that would emerge subsequently: the flexibility and stability of Liverpool's society were not yet overstretched.

Liverpool in 1660 was a very small town in which social contacts of family, neighbourhood and church were important. The gulf between rich and poor was not great among townsmen, though the local grandees, the Earl of Derby, Lord Molyneux and the Moore family, might have been perceived as living in another dimension. The portmoot court of Liverpool invariably ended its mid-seventeenth-century proceedings with the phrase 'We agree to all ancient laws and laudable customs', which suggests that tradition still held a central place. During the course of the eighteenth century the influx of immigrants, the development of trade and manufacture, and the emergence of big players in Irish and transatlantic trades and in property ownership made the town a large and altogether more complex place. Though still not a great town, it had become a major port, and was perceived by residents and outsiders alike as having a new significance. How Liverpool society adapted to rapid change and promoted economic growth rather than crisis are important questions. The achievement was greater because most of the population were newcomers. How immigrants settled down in their new town and adapted and built their fortunes is, of course, a recurrent theme in Liverpool's history, and as important in this earlier period as it was when Irish, Welsh, Scottish, Jewish, Chinese and African immigrants came in greater numbers in the nineteenth century.[2]

It is perhaps surprising that there has been little sustained analysis of Liverpool's early modern history. Much scholarly publication has been based on municipal records, with selections or transcriptions from the Town Books looming large.[3] The comprehensive work on civic structures and institutional development was written a century ago by Ramsay Muir and Platt, while Baines preceded that, in the mid-nineteenth century, with a focus on Liverpool's commercial wealth as foundation for the town's physical growth and international influence.[4] More recent published work on the early growth of trade is limited to monographs by Parkinson, and Hyde, and articles such as that of Clemens.[5] Unfortunately Parkinson's work is devalued by a dearth of source detail and a cavalier attitude towards the accuracy of citation. Hyde's commentary on the early modern centuries is just a prelude to his main focus on the modern era, the era on which other economic historians concentrate not least because of its relative wealth of source material.[6]

Work on the society of early modern Liverpool is sparse and the town's growth calls for a closer investigation of those responsible for it, individually and collectively. The people of Liverpool, and their origins and occupations, remain obscure. This book studies aspects of the Liverpool community in the first century of its rapid expansion in order to throw light on the reasons for and character of its growth. By linking records of individuals from a variety of sources, it has been possible to discover details of the lives and social relationships of a wide range of men and women who lived and worked in the town.[7] The work, painstaking and difficult for such a fluid population, has begun the process of systematically identifying the individuals, of high status and low, who were instrumental in the development of Liverpool. Some of the men and women who participated in the emergence of a great town can now be illuminated, both as individuals and members of a community.

Chapter 1 is a contextualising essay, outlining the development of Liverpool and in particular the growth of trade between 1660 and 1750, which is compared with that of rival port towns such as Bristol, Glasgow and London. A number of explanations for the growth of Liverpool are suggested: the rise of Atlantic trade and of consumer demand for colonial products; the fundamental importance of the town's location both seaward and landward; occupation structure in relation to the economic potential of the town; and Liverpool entrepreneurship. This chapter provides an essentially economic context to the substantive chapters on population, wealth and politics that follow.

Chapter 2 presents a demographic study of a type not previously attempted for a growing urban community with the additional population instabilities of a burgeoning port. The classic methods of historical demographers are applied to investigate the contribution of nuptiality, fertility and mortality to population growth, and to assess the scale and character of migration, both into and out of the town. Overall results are compared with the work of the Cambridge Group for the History of Population and Social Structure, and disaggregated to address the particular experience of the maritime sector. Despite the technical difficulty caused by the extreme geographical mobility of many in the population, the chapter provides the first comprehensive insight into the very particular characteristics of a port population.

Chapter 3 goes further to establish the economic structure of the port by constructing an occupational profile of the town. Evidence from a range of sources is utilised with analyses from parish registers and probate material, which offer complementary perspectives on employment patterns. Reference to other studies of port economies, large and small, for the pre-industrial period would indicate that shipping, sea-going and maritime activities warrant definition and identification in their own right.[8] Therefore particular emphasis is placed on revealing port-related occupations. The quantitative approach is further refined by qualitative investigation of the economic standing of women, often omitted from occupational studies. Given the transience of much of Liverpool's population, the town provides an important case study in occupational mobility and plurality of occupation, and the chapter also reveals the development of occupational dynasties even among ordinary working people often hidden from history.

Chapter 4 reveals an important aspect of social networks, the strategies for wealth transmission via marriage and family bequest employed by many in Liverpool. This is an important element in the broader question of how Liverpudlians worked together and capitalised on the opportunity of the times, and one that has received little attention in the standard histories of the town. While the role of key individuals in initiating trade, dock building and town development has long been stated, scant evidence has been provided for how such people used family connections and networks to promote change in the exemplary way attempted by Gordon Jackson for Hull.[9] How exactly did they build up resources to mount the enterprises that drove the growth of Liverpool? How did they co-operate or compete in developing their own and the town's fortune?

General comment on stratagems for familial provision has been made by Houlbrooke and an individual instance is provided by Macfarlane's work on the Josselin papers.[10] While rural customs have been analysed in a number of studies, both domestic and colonial, a comparison is more appropriate with other work on urban and metropolitan practice in the later medieval and early-modern eras.[11] Chapter 4 reviews the components of Liverpudlians' wealth; the various concerns for, and means of, its preservation; and the resulting patterns of bequest, all of which are compared with studies from elsewhere. It then moves beyond analysis of individual wills to exemplify the understanding gained by reconstructing the familial, social and economic circumstances which influenced testators' decisions at different levels of society. The chapter engages with the fundamental question of how Liverpudlians created and cemented social ties, an aspect not previously considered for any below a small elite.

The institutional context in which Liverpudlians lived and worked has been more adequately investigated by Muir and Platt. From their work on the charters of the town and a study of the town books, it is possible to build up a picture of a corporate town that tightly regulated the community but allowed maximum freedom of economic enterprise. Chapter 5 analyses the governance of the town in which traditional markets and order were tightly regulated, but to which new freemen were admitted and allowed complete liberty of trade.[12] Unlike London and Bristol, in which chartered companies held monopoly rights over sectors of trade, Liverpool entrepreneurs could enter whatever trade they wished, provided they had access to capital or credit, unconstrained by vested interests or traditional restrictions. Such freedom of economic activity implies competition but at the level of trade and merchanting there is more evidence of co-operation.[13] The degree of political consensus among the leading merchants and governors of the town is addressed in Chapter 6 which can be compared with Checkland's brilliant analysis of the divisions among the Liverpool elite at the end of the eighteenth century.[14] The political and religious tensions which split communities in cities such as London and Bristol did not seem to have the same force in Liverpool, where the need to promote a large-scale trade entrepôt perhaps put a premium on burying local rivalries in the national competition for markets.[15]

To seize on co-operation at council level in building a dock, or new churches, or promoting waterway improvements as indicative of a general level of close community in the town would, however, be misleading. Aside from political and religious differences, there were many other issues to divide the society. Liverpool's sudden growth transformed a small town in which face-to-face relationships were the norm to a larger, more anonymous society in which many were strangers. Incomers had to get to know each other, and learn to live and work together. Moreover, the growth of the big business of trade, especially concentrated in a few hands, created greater distance between rich and poor, employer and employed, property owner and tenant. It provided some general benefits too. Gauci has recently argued that the emergence of large-scale merchants in the late seventeenth century should not obscure the number of smaller dealers who shared in and benefited from the growth in trade. Economic opportunity in a fast-growing port provided a common interest among businesses large and small and created a common purpose.[16] Economic growth also had the benefit of increasing the demand for services and employment.

It would be misleading to argue that negative effects were greater than positive, or to look for evidence of anomie or class consciousness characteristic of large nineteenth-century cities. Even so, disagreements among the governing group of the town, an increasing provision for dependant groups such as widows, orphans and the sick, and censure of unruly behaviour on the streets, all suggest the problems of a fast-growing town.[17] Public disorder seems to have become a problem from the mid-eighteenth century, with election riots on 18 October 1757, and a larger scale seamen's riot in 1775.[18]

From the second half of the eighteenth century, therefore, there is increasing evidence of social conflict resulting from population growth and stratification, of the sort made familiar by the much larger historiography of urbanisation in the industrial age. The role of this book, however, is to explore the relatively unknown era of initial expansion in the largely mercantile economy of England's fastest-growing port town. In so doing, it offers alternative perspectives on some of the established narratives of early modern urban history, and in particular aims to set new standards for approaches to the study of complex and rapidly changing populations.

Notes

1. P. Clark, ed., *The Cambridge Urban History of Britain*, vol. ii, *1540–1840*, Cambridge, 2000; J. M. Ellis, *The Georgian Town 1680–1840*, Basingstoke, 2001; C. Chalklin, *The Rise of the English Town, 1650–1850*, Cambridge, 2001; R. Sweet,

The English Town, 1680–1840: Government, Society and Culture, Harlow, 1999.

2. C. Pooley, 'The residential segregation of migrant communities in mid-Victorian Liverpool', *TIBG*, 2, 1977, pp. 364–82.

3. For example, J. A. Picton, *Memorials of Liverpool*, London, 1873; J. Touzeau, *The Rise and Progress of Liverpool from 1551 to 1835*, Liverpool, 1910; G. Chandler, *Liverpool under Charles I*, Liverpool, 1960; M. Power, ed., *Liverpool Town Books 1649–1671*, RSLC, 136, 1999.

4. J. Ramsay Muir and E. M. Platt, *A History of Municipal Government in Liverpool from the Earliest Times to the Municipal Reform Act of 1835*, Liverpool, 1906; T. Baines, *History of the Commerce and Town of Liverpool, and of the Rise of Manufacturing Industry in the Adjoining Counties*, London, 1852.

5. C. N. Parkinson, *The Rise of the Port of Liverpool*, Liverpool, 1952; F. Hyde, *Liverpool and the Mersey: The Development of a Port 1700–1970*, Newton Abbot, 1971; P. Clemens, 'The rise of Liverpool 1665–1750', *EcHR*, 29, 1976, pp. 211–25.

6. For example, G. J. Milne, *Trade and Traders in mid-Victorian Liverpool: Mercantile Business and the Making of a World Port*, Liverpool, 2000.

7. See Appendix 1: Sources and Methods.

8. G. C. F. Forster, 'Hull in the sixteenth and seventeenth centuries', in *Victoria County History, York: East Riding*, ed. K. J. Allison, London, 1969; M. Reed, 'Ipswich in the seventeenth century', unpublished PhD thesis, University of Leicester, 1973.

9. G. Jackson, *Hull in the Eighteenth Century*, London, 1972, pp. 96–128.

10. R. A. Houlbrooke, *The English Family 1450–1700*, London, 1984, chapter 9; A. D. J. Macfarlane, *The Family Life of Ralph Josselin, a Seventeenth-Century Clergyman*, Cambridge, 1970.

11. M. Spufford, *Contrasting Communities: English Villagers in the Sixteenth and Seventeenth Centuries*, Cambridge, 1974; L. G. Carr and L. S. Walsh, 'Inventories and the Analysis of Wealth and Consumption Patterns in St. Mary's County, Maryland, 1658–1777', *Historical Methods*, 13.2, 1980, pp. 81–103; J. I. Kermode, *Medieval Merchants: York, Beverley and Hull in the later Middle Ages*, Cambridge, 1998; R. T. Vann, 'Wills and the family in an English town: Banbury, 1550–1800', *Journal of Family History*, 4, 1979, pp. 346–67; J. Stobart and A. Owens, eds, *Urban Fortunes: Property and Inheritance in the Town, 1700–1900*, Aldershot, 2000; P. Earle, *The Making of the English Middle Class*, London, 1989.

12. Power, *Liverpool Town Books*.

13. For a more detailed discussion, see M. Power, 'Creating a port: Liverpool 1695–1715', *THSLC*, 149, 2000, pp. 51–71.

14. S. Checkland, 'Business attitudes in Liverpool 1793–1807', *EcHR*, V, 1952, pp. 58–75.

15. G. S. de Krey, *A Fractured Society: The Politics of London in the First Age of Party 1688–1715*, Oxford, 1985; H. Horwitz, 'Party in a civic context: London from the Exclusion Crisis to the fall of Walpole', in *Britain in the First Age of*

Party 1680–1750, ed. C. Jones, London, 1987, pp. 173–94; J. Barry, 'The politics of religion in Restoration Bristol', in *The Politics of Religion in Restoration England*, ed T. Harris, P. Seaward and M. Goldie, Oxford, 1990, pp. 163–89.

16. P. Gauci, *The Politics of Trade: The Overseas Merchant in State and Society 1660–1720*, Oxford, 2001, pp. 59–60.

17. M. Power, 'Politics and progress in Liverpool', *Northern History*, 35, 1999, pp. 11–38; W. L. Blease, 'The poor law in Liverpool 1681–1834', *THSLC*, 61, 1909, pp. 97–182.

18. J. A. Picton, *Municipal Archives and Records from 1700 to 1835*, Liverpool, 1881, p. 149; R. Barrie Rose, 'A Liverpool's sailors' strike in the eighteenth century', *TLCAS*, 68, 1959, pp. 85–92.

1
Contexts: The Emergence of an Early Modern Port

Liverpool was a small agricultural and fishing settlement when King John promoted his new town there in 1207. He created a borough primarily as a port of embarkation for Ireland, a grant which did not lead to significant growth.[1] It is not surprising that the medieval town remained unimportant and developed little trade, since Liverpool was sited on a lee shore at the narrows of a bottle-shaped estuary subject to a great range of tides, and emptying into the Irish Sea through shifting sandbanks. It was for such reasons that the Royal Navy avoided the Mersey as a base.[2] Before docks were built, shipping had to ground on the shore or anchor in the tideway unless it could find shelter in the Pool, an inlet from the Mersey just south of the castle. Liverpool was over-shadowed as a port by Chester, with its long-standing importance recognised by its position as 'a county of itself', and by its creation as a diocese at the Reformation. As the Customs head port while Liverpool was its mere creek, Chester was pre-eminent in trade before the silting of the Dee coincided with development in Liverpool's hinterland. The overland communications to, and within, that poor hinterland were impeded by the mosses of south-west Lancashire and a paucity of roads not remedied until the turnpikes of the early eighteenth century. Indeed Liverpool did not have a stage-coach to London until 1760, the nearest connection to the main north to south road being some 20 miles east at Warrington.[3]

Sixteenth-century Liverpool had intermittent trade connections with the Iberian Peninsula and France, but not on a sufficient scale to be nationally significant, and such contact had died by the end of the century.[4] Its main trade was with the ports of the Irish Sea, a pattern interrupted and altered by the needs of transport and victualling armies engaged in Ireland through the Elizabethan years. Direct trade with Ireland flourished from the early seventeenth century but was again interrupted by the Civil War, after which the town petitioned parliament for reparations for the losses and significant damage of three sieges.[5] At the Restoration Liverpool's Irish trade recovered and, although still on a small scale, outstripped that of Chester.[6] Confirmation of Customs autonomy to the growing port reflected this.[7] Custom port status often lagged behind economic growth but was crucial to the effective management and administration of commerce.

Liverpool, with not much more than a thousand inhabitants, was still a small town at this date. Even in the context of its county it was smaller than Wigan or Preston, towns of standing in Lancashire with over 2,000 inhabitants each, and smaller even than Warrington which had some 1,600.[8] By comparison with other port towns, Liverpool seems even less significant: Hull was much larger, with about 6,000 people; Newcastle was larger again, with 12,000 inhabitants; and Bristol had some 20,000. Liverpool's growth after the Restoration began to close the gap. By the end of the seventeenth century its population was approaching 7,000 and by the mid-eighteenth century it reached about 22,000, overtaking Hull (12,000), catching up with Newcastle (29,000), closing on Glasgow (31,700) but still only half the size of Bristol (50,000).[9] In the century between 1650 and 1750 Liverpool grew much more quickly than Hull, Glasgow and Bristol. Indeed it had the highest cumulative growth rate, at 3.13 per cent per annum.[10]

Liverpool's rate of growth was high because it expanded from a tiny base. Its competitors had all emerged earlier: Hull had been an important medieval international port, Bristol and Glasgow were large towns in the sixteenth century with more complex functions than Liverpool, and Newcastle had developed rapidly in the sixteenth century on the fortunes of the coal trade.[11] Liverpool grew to challenge such ports only during the eighteenth century but by 1800 the town was as large or larger than most major provincial ports in Britain and Europe.[12] Its growth was principally due to in-migration, which Langton and Laxton estimate accounted for 80 per cent of the increase in population in the late eighteenth century.[13] Work by Rawling and by Lewis has transformed understanding of the demographic behaviour and movement of people into and out of Liverpool during the previous hundred years.[14] Thus the town emerges as one of the most mobile communities studied by historical demographers.

Population growth transformed the size and appearance of the town from the seven medieval streets of the 1660s through the infilling and expansion of the 1700s, to some 222 'streets, squares, lanes, and alleys … in 1753'.[15] The extent of development can be seen by comparing four maps: the first, a historical reconstruction of 1660s Liverpool, suggests its medieval shape and extent; the second encompasses the later Stuart period and reconstructs the town of the 1708 rate; the third, J. Chadwick's 1725 map, shows development following construction of the dock; the fourth, John Eyes' 1765 Plan, displays the larger and more complex town of the mid-eighteenth century.[16]

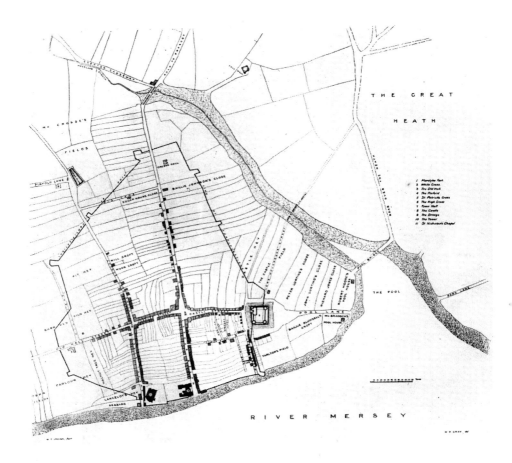

Figure 1.1 *Fergusson Irvine, Liverpool in Charles II's time by Sir Edward Moore 1667–8 (Liverpool 1899) facing p. 1. Special Collections, University of Liverpool SPEC Noble D.13.19.*

Castle	1	**Charity**		
Old Hall	2	Pool House	30	
Tower	3	*Almshouses :*		
Town Hall a) 4; b) 5		Poole's	31	
Crosse Hall	6	Richmond's	31	
Places of Worship		Warbrick's	32	
(St Mary del Key)	7	Charity School	33	
St Nicholas' Chapel/Church	8	**Law and Order**		
St Peter's Church	9	Stocks a) 34; b) 35		
Castle Hey Presbyterian Chapel	10	Pinfold	36	
Key Street Presbyterian Chapel	11	Pillory a) 37; b) 38		
Friends' Meeting House	12	Ducking Stool	39	
Baptist Meeting House	13	Cage	40	
Commerce and Industry		**Crosses**		
Granary	14	*Wayside :* St. Patrick's Cross	41	
Tithebarn	15	*Town :* High Cross	42	
Horse Mill	16	White Cross	43	
Horse Mill	17	**Sanctuary Stones**		
Middle Mill	18	Castle Street	44	
Middle Mill	19	Dale Street	45	
Paul's Mill	20	**Bridges**		
Salthouse	21	Townsend Bridge	46	
Sugar refinery	22	Pool Bridge	47	
Sugar refinery	23	Dry Bridge	48	
Sugar refinery	24	Lord Street Bridge	49	
Custom House a) 25; b) 26				
Tannery	27	Fall Well	50	
Dock	28			
Pot Works	29			

Figure 1.2 *Liverpool in the later Stuart period: 1660–1714*
Source: *S. M. Nicholson, The Changing Face of Liverpool 1207–1727, Liverpool, Merseyside Archaeological Society, 1981, Figure 10, p. 20.*

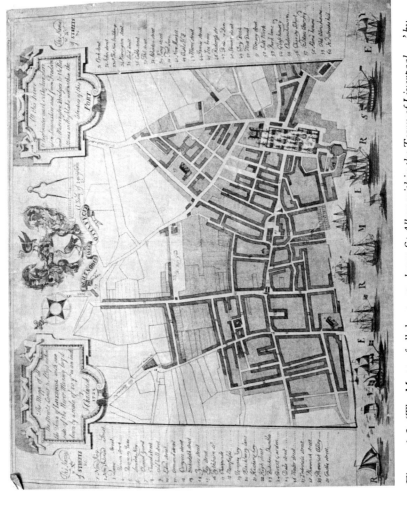

Figure 1.3 'The Mapp of all the streets, lanes & Alleys within the Town of Liverpool ...' by
J. Chadwick, 1725. Liverpool Record Office

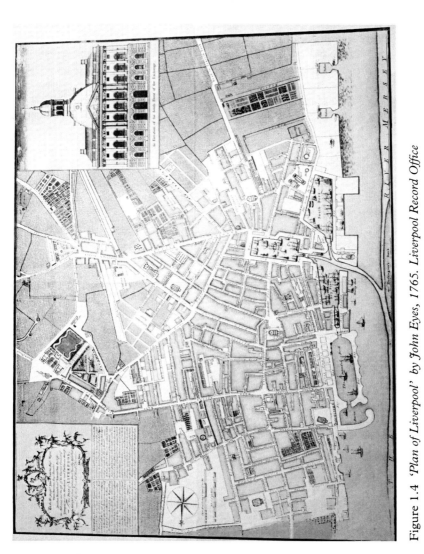

Figure 1.4 'Plan of Liverpool' by John Eyes, 1765. Liverpool Record Office

The innovative wet dock, commenced in 1709 and opened in 1715, inaugurated a dock estate that was to facilitate the great expansion of trade and become a blueprint for similar developments elsewhere.[17] A second dock was opened in 1753, the two structures precursors of a monumental line of docks which are the modern city's most characteristic landmark. Accompanying commercial growth there was considerable building of accommodation for living and working, often under the same roof. Places of worship and entertainment, and institutions for town government and trade, were also built.[18] Appreciable wealth was expended on several sets of almshouses, a Bluecoat School, an Infirmary and a Sailors' Sixpenny Hospital.[19]

The morphology of the town began to change as it physically expanded, encroaching upon the Common and Town Field, which came into Corporation control in 1672.[20] The seventeenth-century town had contained a heterogeneous mix of inhabitants within its original streets, and even in the eighteenth century the majority of merchants still lived in that central area in homes often integral with their commercial premises. Others were moving by mid-century to fine new houses in the south-eastern development of Hanover Street, Seel Street and Park Lane, and some even further afield to rural Everton or Toxteth Park, if not to landed estates. Not until towards the end of the century did social zoning begin, with a proliferation of court and cellar dwellings for the poor concentrated to the north of Tithebarn Street, between Whitechapel and Dale Street, south of the Old Dock, and along the waterfront.[21]

Contemporary comment reveals what impressed visitors during the period. In 1673 Richard Blome, the topographer, noted the current building at corporation expense of 'a famous town house placed on pillars and arches of hewen stone and underneath the public exchange for merchants' on whose West Indies trade he expressly remarked.[22] By 1698, Celia Fiennes reported a place which 'was a few fishermens houses', grown to 'a very rich trading town, the houses of brick and stone built high and even ...; there are abundance of persons you see very well dress'd ..., its London in miniature as much as ever I saw anything'.[23] Daniel Defoe, writing in the 1720s, gave the strongest impression of the dynamism of the town: reportedly twice as big at his first visit in 1680 as in 1660, much bigger by his second visit in 1690 and double that size by 1720 when his commercial eye noted that 'it still visibly encreases both in Wealth, People, Business and Buildings: What it may grow to in time, I know not.'[24] He remarked on the many improvements: the building of new churches; the development of 'New Liverpool', which grew around the new dock; the building of the dock itself, the well-built houses, the straight spacious streets, and the Exchange.

The town has now an opulent, flourishing and encreasing Trade, not rivalling Bristol, in the Trade to Virginia, and the English Island Colonies in America only, but is in a fair way to exceed and eclipse it, by encreasing every way in Wealth and Shipping.[25]

The prediction seemed to have been borne out by the mid-eighteenth century when Williamson's *Liverpool Memorandum* in 1753 described the town as:

Of late Years, the most flourishing Seaport (next to the Mother Port) in Great Britain. The Inhabitants are universal Merchants and trade to all foreign parts, but Turkey and the East-Indies. It shares the trade to Ireland and Wales with Bristol, and engrosses most of the Scotch Trade ... Ships of any burthen may come up with their full Lading, and ride before the town ... and Vessels of 18 Feet Draught of Water may go into the docks, which are not inferior to any in Great Britain. On the 14th September 1749, the first Stone of a new Exchange was laid, which is now near finished, and, for its size, is not to be paralleled in Europe.[26]

Allowing for a degree of local triumphalism, the impression of a town and port at the forefront of commercial activity is unmistakable. Liverpool had been transformed and was moving fast towards becoming the second port of the kingdom.

Trade

Defoe equated Liverpool's growth with its development as a port, and trade is usually the sector most associated with the town's economic development. There is no doubt that, in terms of an increase in the range of commodities and the opening of Atlantic trade, the period after the Restoration witnessed a revolution. Salt exports rose from 26,000 bushels per annum in the 1670s to 428,000 bushels in the early 1720s, a sixteen-fold increase; tobacco imports from 200,000 pounds per annum in the 1670s to an estimated annual 6,100,000 pounds in the years 1738–50, a thirty-one-fold increase; and sugar imports from 4,900 hundredweight per annum to an estimated 100,000 hundredweight over the same period, a twenty-fold increase.[27] In 1664–65 commodity trade with the Americas was only 2 per cent against 90 per cent with Ireland, but by 1708–09 the proportion was 30 per cent to 60 per cent.[28]

A useful context for Liverpool's trade performance in the early eighteenth century is provided by the import and export tonnage of other provincial ports (see Table 1.1). The annual Liverpool tonnage increased by 117 per cent between 1709 and 1751; Bristol's tonnage rose 41 per cent; Hull's grew by 186 per cent; Newcastle's improved 66 per cent – the large provincial ports were all doing well. More revealing

Table 1.1 *Tonnages to and from major English ports, 1709, 1751, 1790*

	1709	*1751*	*1790*
Bristol	41,016	57,732	134,402
Hull	13,870	39,592	147,022
Liverpool	30,210	65,406	479,001
Newcastle	47,833	79,557	131,984
London	—	408,212	876,617

Source: Board of Trade statistics quoted by Jackson, *Hull in the Eighteenth Century*, p. 67. Scottish ports were not included.

is the escalating rate of Liverpool's increase in tonnage in the following period, the late eighteenth century: it reached 479,001 tons in 1790, a massive increase of 632 per cent in volume of trade in forty years which left competitors far behind. Liverpool began to bear comparison even with London.[29] The commercial revolution, which had begun in Liverpool in the late seventeenth century, bore spectacular results.

The extent of that commercial revolution in Liverpool, which originated in the period 1660 to 1750, is clear enough and more details can be reconstructed of its chronology. After the interruptions of the Civil War and Interregnum even Irish trade was at a low ebb. Clemens estimates there were 140 merchants engaged in overseas trade at this date but they were all small-scale traders. Exports of salt and coal and imports of agricultural produce were modest, and Liverpool traders did not venture to Europe or engage in the Atlantic trade in sugar and tobacco.[30] The Irish trade recovered fairly rapidly and, by the customs year 1664–65, included 246 exported consignments of coal, salt, lead, iron and textiles, and 403 imported consignments of herrings, sheep, nags, cattle and linen yarn, which together made up 90 per cent of overseas trade in the year. There were a large number of traders, 389, but the scale of their business was small, averaging only 2.4 consignments each for the whole year. Some 66 traders were ships' masters trading on their own account and only 11 traders accounted for ten or more consignments.[31]

The first direct evidence for Liverpool's Atlantic trade dates from 1667, when the *Antelope* returned with sugar from Barbados.[32] This trade was not followed up in the early 1670s, perhaps due to the Dutch war of 1670–72 and an Act of 1670 which limited trade between Ireland and the colonies. Parkinson claims that transatlantic trade resumed in 1677 and that in 1679 six ships brought muscovado sugar from Barbados, St Christopher or Montserrat, or tobacco from Maryland.[33] The experience of the 1670s and 80s seems formative for Liverpool merchants. By the last decade of the century, the town's trading profile had been transformed by the increasing scale and geographical range of merchant enterprise, the growth of new staple commodities, the increase in ships, and above all the new-found confidence and ambition of the leading residents. In the words of the petition to make Liverpool a separate parish, on 4 January 1699, the town was

> [f]ormerly a small fishing town but many people coming from London in the time of sickness and after the fire, several ingenious men settled in Liverpool which caused them to trade to the plantations and other places, which occasioned sundry other tradesmen to come and settle there, which hath so enlarged their trade, that from scarce paying the salary of the officers of the customs it is now the third port of the trade of England and pays upwards of £50,000 per annum to the king.[34]

The increase in the merchant fleet is an obvious indicator that trade expanded fast at this time despite the interruptions of war during the reigns of William III and Queen Anne. Indeed William III could call on Liverpool ships to embark troops for Ulster to defeat the Jacobite and French threat in 1689.[35] By 1707 just over a quarter of the 170 ships in Liverpool were involved in the Atlantic trade.[36] The substantial proportion of overseas trade carried on by a small group of great merchants is the most striking aspect of the increase. There were 365 merchants listed in the port book for 1708–09 (fewer than the 389 traders in 1665) accounting for 2,143 consignments, an average of 5.9 each (compared to the average of 2.4 in 1665). Only 40 of the 365 traded on any scale, accounting for ten or more consignments during the year.[37] The number of major merchants was smaller still as Poole has established. From the port books of 1704, 1707 and 1711, her work identifies a select group of 13 great players in commodity trades: seven merchants dominated the import of tobacco, three of sugar, four of cotton wool, two of iron, and three of tallow; three merchants dominated the export of salt, four of coal, three of iron and two of linen.[38] Table 1.2 shows the total number of men involved in the four major import trades and seven major export trades in 1707, alongside the proportion of trade controlled by the caucus of great merchants. It is clear that this small group dominated long-distance import commodities, American tobacco, Caribbean sugar and Swedish iron, for which transport cost and purchase capital must have been high. They controlled exports rather less, except for coal and refined products such as rock salt and sugar, in which their dominance probably resulted from their control of the refining process.

Overseas trade most obviously demonstrates the change in ambition and scale of the major Liverpool merchants. Coastal trade was increasing too, and stray pieces of evidence give pause for thought about the true scale of maritime operations from Liverpool. A list of English clearances

Table 1.2 *Liverpool merchants involved in major trades in 1707*

	No. of merchants	% trade conducted by 13 chief merchants
Imports		
Tobacco	54	51
Sugar	53	57
Swedish iron	3	73
Tallow	26	39
Exports		
White salt	78	11
Rock salt	8	49
Coal	29	45
Refined sugar	9	47
Linen	59	30
Earthenware	70	10
Wrought iron	57	16

Source: Poole, 'Liverpool's trade in the reign of Queen Anne', appendix 1, pp. 151–264.

from Liverpool logged by the Customs House in 1715 is not much short of 400, including 266 to Ireland, 22 to the Isle of Man, 21 to the West Indies, 21 to North America and 45 to Europe.[39] The number of coastal voyages, steady in the thirty years to 1660, increased almost five-fold between the Restoration and the Revolution of 1688: by 1689/90, there were 145 inward and 116 outward voyages. In 1737, Liverpool's coast-wise shipments numbered 254, with 136 incoming.[40] Coasting vessels added significantly to the scale of commerce and to activity in and around the port, despite being small and generally carrying low-value commodities.

The maritime interest made a decisive breakthrough and began to dictate policy in Liverpool during the period from the late 1680s to the late 1710s.[41] The increase in trade and emergence of a small group of great merchants, engaged in large-scale and risky ventures, built up pressure for the town to improve its port facilities and resulted in the building of a pioneering wet dock between 1709 and 1715. This encouraged a continued growth in trade to the mid-eighteenth century: a doubling of tonnage carried between 1709 and 1751 made Liverpool faster growing than Bristol but slower than Hull (see Table 1.1). Even so, Hyde estimates the annual growth at a 'surprisingly low' 0.7 per cent per annum between 1716 and 1744, a rate that dramatically rose to 4.9 per cent per annum from 1744 to 1851.[42] Data on the ships using Liverpool in the early eighteenth century broadly support the steady increase: compared with the 170 ships engaged in overseas trade from

Liverpool in 1707, there were almost twice that number, 318, by 1753. More significant was the greater proportion involved in transatlantic trade by this date: 47 ships were in the West Indian trade, 36 in American and 88 in the African trade, altogether 54 per cent of the total, compared with 27 per cent in 1707.[43] The increased importance of transatlantic trade to Liverpool is underlined by the numbers of ships sworn as British in the Plantation Registers: some 263 ships were registered from Liverpool in the five years 1743 to 1748.[44]

What most contributed to Liverpool's success in Atlantic trade was that it engaged in all the main commodity trades and did not specialise in any one. It was less important than Bristol for sugar imports, and Glasgow for tobacco imports, though it challenged both towards the end of the eighteenth century.[45] Its most successful commercial initiative in the period was the slave trade, in which the first recorded Liverpool voyage was in 1700. At this date the London Royal Africa Company had a monopoly and interlopers had to pay the company a levy of 10 per cent.[46] When this monopoly was removed in 1712, Liverpool was still a marginal player, but Liverpool merchants began to engage regularly in the trade in the 1720s, when London merchants scaled down their involvement after the collapse of the South Sea Bubble. By 1730, 15 Liverpool ships were involved, by 1737, 33, and, by 1749, some 75 were listed as engaged in the African trade with space for 23,200 slaves.[47] By this date Liverpool had become the dominant slaving port.

A number of influences benefited overseas trade in general, and Liverpool in particular, during the early eighteenth century. Trade was encouraged by the coming of peace in 1713, and a government policy of reducing duties on imported raw materials and on exported manu-factures in 1721. Peace provided freedom from foreign privateers and opened trade to the Baltic, the Netherlands and to Portugal.[48] A depression in sugar and tobacco markets in the 1720s limited trade but an upswing in both commodity trades in the 1730s allowed Liverpool merchants to increase involvement in sugar, tobacco and slaves, and their share of transatlantic trade increased rapidly.

Liverpool's relative remoteness from privateering in the war which began in 1739 gave it an advantage over Bristol and London.[49] However, Liverpool's immunity to war and privateering was far from total and, between 1739 and 1748, at least 100 Liverpool ships were taken.[50] Ways were found to replace such losses: shipbuilding in the town was stimulated, and many more ships were purchased from yards along the American coast because Plantation-built shipping was cheaper except during the 1730s.[51] Liverpool masters also took out letters of marque to prey on French shipping. In 1744, the *Old Noll*, the *Terrible*, the *Thurloe* and *Admiral Blake* began operating as privateers, and a number of French ships were captured and pressed into service as English merchantmen: for example, the *Ville de Nantes* became the *Virginia Merchant* in 1745.[52] Bristol at this time turned, of necessity, to privateering, because the activity of French and Spanish privateers in the English Channel so inhibited her trade. Contemporaries blamed excessive privateering for Bristol's displacement by Liverpool because the concentration on privateering during this period and the Seven Years War was made at the expense of trading investment.[53] In contrast, Liverpool made progress during peace and war and by mid-century its trade had developed in scale and complexity. The port had become a major, and in some respects, a dominant player in transatlantic commerce.

Comparative Advantage

The demographic and commercial growth of Liverpool in the period is clear enough and a variety of approaches can explain it. An economic analysis might emphasise the growth of Atlantic trade and growth of consumer demand for colonial products in the eighteenth century; a geographical approach could focus on the growing importance of the town's location both seaward and landward; an urban growth analysis could use occupation structure to explain the economic potential of the town; a study of commercial success might highlight Liverpool entrepreneurship. Such approaches are all helpful in understanding the particular advantages the town enjoyed.

Atlantic trade benefited most European west-coast ports in the late seventeenth and eighteenth centuries. De Vries identifies them as a group, along with government capitals and towns in north-west Europe, which continued to grow despite a century of European urban stagnation.[54] West-coast British ports, Bristol, Liverpool and Glasgow in particular, were boosted by the increase in consumer demand for colonial staples such as sugar, tobacco and rum, which made regional marketing worthwhile and enabled them collectively to rival London. Clemens argues that Liverpool was particularly helped by a symbiotic trade with the colonies. Like Bristol merchants before the development of the African slave trade, Liverpudlians exported indentured labour, from Lancashire and from Ireland. Liverpool merchants offered, in addition, two other crucial exports: food from Ireland, increasingly important to sustain the population of monocultural sugar economies in Barbados and other West Indian islands; and salt, available in increased quantities with the development of the refining of rock salt in Liverpool and upriver.[55] Not only did these help balance trade but they also made possible the development of agricultural economies in the New World.

Such exports enabled Liverpool merchants to purchase colonial staples outright rather than taking them on consignment and thus to achieve more flexibility in their import and sale. For example, it allowed duty on imported tobacco to be evaded since it could be brought in damaged or underweight hogsheads which escaped duty, or re-exported in heavier hogsheads which earned a customs rebate. This proved an important commercial advantage to Liverpool merchants who became notorious for customs evasion: as much as 20 per cent of tobacco handled in the port escaped duty, a situation which led to a major customs review in 1702.[56] Another strategy was to unload colonial produce on the Isle of Man, which lay outside the English Customs system, and to quietly transport it to creeks on the mainland, to escape duty entirely.[57]

Liverpool's location was a major advantage in that its proximity to Ireland helped colonial as well as Irish trade and sailing to Dublin, Belfast or Cork, en route to the colonies, became a common practice, with three-quarters of West Indian shipping from the outports making such calls by the end of the seventeenth century. Moreover, Liverpool captains could choose a northern or southern route to the Atlantic depending on weather and privateers. Samuel Derrick, visiting from Bath in 1760, remarked:

> This port is admirably situated for trade, being almost central in the channel, so that, in war time, by coming north about, their ships have a good chance of escaping the many privateers belonging to the enemy ... Thus, their insurance being less, they are able to undersell their neighbours.[58]

Liverpool ships were not, as already noted, immune from French privateers, particularly in the wars during William and Anne's reigns and in the 1740s as well as in the Seven Years' war which Derrick had in mind, but they were not as frequently threatened in home waters as ships of Bristol or the south or south-eastern ports. It is significant that Liverpool shipping increased rather than decreased in the wars against Louis XIV's France.[59]

Proximity to Ireland brought the major benefit of Irish trade, arguably more important to Liverpool than transatlantic trade in this period. Dublin was the fastest growing city in eighteenth-century Europe with a population increase from 17,000 in 1650 to 168,000 in 1800.[60] Liverpool was its most convenient port connection with England, and trade was stimulated by Irish demand for Cheshire salt and Lancashire coal, staple raw materials extracted near to Liverpool. Though Dublin was the principal partner, substantial trade was also conducted with Drogheda, Belfast, Newry and Londonderry: in 1709 there were 484 consignments transferred to and from Dublin, and comparable figures were Drogheda 278, Belfast 158, Newry 62 and Londonderry 30.[61] The traditional trade with Ireland involved a large number of ships, some shuttling across the Irish Sea, some integrated into transatlantic commerce.

Liverpool was well located for access to the sea but not for connections with its hinterland. Langton has argued that inland communications were very poor in the early eighteenth century.[62] The principal road out of the town, to Prescot and Warrington, was inadequate and river links, although serviceable, did not extend far inland. The Mersey connected Liverpool with Manchester but was navigable only to Warrington, and even that was not possible until improvements in 1698. The Weaver, a tributary of the Mersey, provided a connection with the Cheshire salt towns of Northwich and Nantwich, but was navigable only as far as Frodsham Bridge, a mere couple of miles upstream from its junction with the Mersey. The staple exports of Liverpool, rock salt and coal, still had to be carried, for the most part, by road.[63]

The first initiative to improve road links came in 1726 when the council of Liverpool applied for an act to turnpike the road to Prescot to enable coal from Prescot Hall mine to be carried to Liverpool more easily. In 1746 the turnpike was extended to St Helens and in 1753 to Warrington.[64] The revolution in improving inland waterways also began in the early eighteenth century. An Act to make the Mersey and Irwell navigable to Manchester was obtained in 1720, followed, in 1721, by an Act to improve waterway links with Cheshire by making the Weaver navigable to Winsford. The Weaver Navigation opened in 1732, and in 1734 a further Act allowed it to be extended to Nantwich. Cheshire salt could be shipped to Liverpool cheaply and easily for the first time. Water links with Lancashire to the north were planned with an Act for the River Douglas navigation in 1720. This was completed in 1742 and enabled Wigan coal to be shipped via the rivers Douglas and Ribble and thence coastwise to Liverpool.[65] These were significant improvements but still left Liverpool less well connected with its hinterland than other provincial ports. Hull was much better served by rivers, the Aire and Calder, the Don and the Trent. Bristol enjoyed access via the Avon to the Bristol Channel ports and, via the Severn and minor rivers, to Gloucestershire, Worcestershire, Hereford and Monmouth, Warwickshire, and up to Shrewsbury.

It was not until after the period covered in this book that the most significant waterway improvements were made: the Sankey Brook Navigation, completed in 1761, allowed St Helen's coal from the Haydock and Parr collieries to be shipped to Liverpool; the Bridgewater Canal, opened in 1773, connected the town to Worsley mines; the Leeds–Liverpool Canal, opened in the late 1770s to Wigan (and later to Yorkshire), allowed coal from a major Lancashire coalfield to be directly shipped to Liverpool; the Trent and Mersey Canal, completed in 1777 to Staffordshire (and later, via linking canals, with the Midlands and South, the east coast, and the Severn), allowed heavy traffic from the Potteries.[66] The consequential increase in internal trade was dramatic, with 465,000 tons of materials and manufactures carried by the canals to and from Liverpool in 1788, almost as much as the 479,001 tons of Liverpool overseas trade at that time.[67] The unlocking of the industrial products of Lancashire, Yorkshire, Staffordshire and the Midlands and their impact on the port of Liverpool was, thus, a later development. As William Moss put it in the first 'guide' of 1796 redolent with civic pride:

> Its near connexion and ready communication by internal rivers and canals, with the extensive manufacturing town and neighbourhoods of Manchester; the coal county of Wigan, the unrivalled potteries of Staffordshire; the exclusive export of salt; its central situation on the western coast of the kingdom, thereby communicating readily with Dublin and the northern parts of Ireland; and finally, the goodness of the harbour and the very superior accommodation for shipping; have all conspired to form it into a vortex that has nearly swallowed up the foreign trade of Bristol, Lancaster and Whitehaven.[68]

During the earlier period relatively modest improvements in the shipping of coal, salt and Manchester goods constituted the more limited achievements.

The rapid urban growth of Liverpool, both before and after 1750, was partly due to the development of trade, but to dwell only on that function is to miss another basic cause of expansion. The town was an important processing and manufacturing centre as well, encouraged by the poor early eighteenth-century communication links with its hinterland which imposed costs on bringing in industrial goods. Some Liverpool industries were established in the late seventeenth century to process staple goods as in other port towns: for example, brewing and salt and sugar refining. Manufactures included many metal, leather, porcelain and glass products.[69] Liverpool was, at this date, a growing industrial town in a developing industrial region: Warrington had its specialised sailmakers and filemakers, St Helens its glassmakers, and Prescot its clock and watchmakers.[70] Langton and Laxton, in a study of the town in the 1760s, make the point that the craft sector seemed to be intensifying rather than diminishing.[71] The town was clearly more than simply a trade entrepôt.

Many of the industries were driven by Liverpool's port function, including the building and repair of ships and the processing of colonial staple products. Trade was also crucial in generating employment. There was a very high proportion of mariners, about a quarter of the working population in the mid-1760s, a striking statistic. The proportion during the period between 1660 and 1760 was similar, if not higher.

London mariners, by comparison, made up less than 5 per cent of its working population.[72] The wide range of employment opportunities in Liverpool, for mariners, for craftsmen and processors, for service trades and carriers, was a major factor in attracting immigrants.

Initiatives

This analysis has so far concentrated on trade, population and commercial advantage in impersonal terms. Liverpool's trade and population grew because of its access to booming Atlantic trade, its proximity to Ireland, its increasingly productive hinterland and a complex economy in which industry as well as trade played an important role. It was Liverpool's good fortune to be in the right place at the right time, but initiative and effort were needed to exploit opportunity. The Irish and Atlantic trades were developed by merchants and seamen who invested money and took risks. The hinterland was opened up by deliberate investment in roads and waterways. Docks were built, despite uncertainty about their engineering and finance, in order to improve port infrastructure. Liverpudlians were active in creating their own opportunities: promoting a port independent of Chester in the 1660s; beginning to engage in colonial trade from the 1660s; creating a parish in 1699; instigating the building of a dock in 1709; seeking a Prescot turnpike and promoting Acts for river improvements in the 1720s; and taking a dominant role in the slave trade by the 1740s. From this perspective, residents of the town appear a particularly enterprising species. Two of these initiatives, the building of port infrastructure and the successful incursion into the slave trade, are particularly revealing.

As noted above, ships were forced, before the eighteenth century, to anchor in the Mersey, a river with a fast and wide-ranging tidal flow, or in the Liver Pool, a shallow inlet just south of the castle, or even to lighten ship off the coast of Wirral in the Hoyle Lake, a sight noted by Celia Fiennes.[73] A quay or pier was built into the Mersey to improve access to the shore by ships anchored in the river but there were no other docking facilities. It is no surprise that, on 3 November 1708, the council ordered the town's MPs to treat with a suitable person to come to Liverpool and draw up plans for a dock to provide a solution to such problems.[74] The proposal was a major gamble as the only models for dock construction were the Howland wet dock for ship repair at Rotherhithe in London, and the Royal Navy dockyard at Portsmouth. Building dock walls on land partly reclaimed from the Liver Pool posed a major engineering challenge and there was no reliable way of estimating the cost of the enterprise. Thomas Steers, an engineer who had knowledge of the Howland wet dock in London, designed and oversaw the construction of the Liverpool dock to which a dry dock was added in 1718.[75] Defoe was emphatic about the first dock's significance:

> Here there was no mole or haven to bring in their ships and lay them up … for the winter, nor any key for the delivering their goods, as at Bristol, Bideford, Newcastle, Hull and other sea ports … Upon this the inhabitants and merchants have of late years, and since the visible increase of their trade, made a large basin or wet dock … As this is so great a benefit to the town, and that the like is not to be seen in any place in England … London excepted, it is well worth the observation and imitation of many other trading places in Britain.[76]

The cost of the development, £30,000, was substantial and led to acrimony over how the debt was to be paid. Yet within a decade of its opening there were few doubts of its value and its success led to the building of five other Liverpool docks during the eighteenth century. The council of Liverpool built a facility which attracted trade to the port and provided an ever-increasing income for the town: dock revenue brought in £810 in 1724; £1,776 in 1752 [77]

One reason for the council in Liverpool to undertake this pioneering enterprise was the inadequate natural berthing facilities in the Mersey. The advantages of purpose-built wet docks were only slowly realised elsewhere and the Liverpool dock was not matched by its competitors for sixty years. Hull had quaysides along the river Hull, a natural anchorage which perhaps delayed the building of its first dock until 1778, long after the need for it had become evident. Bristol had the advantage of city-centre quaysides beside the rivers Avon and Frome. Although access to these quaysides proved difficult for ships above 150 tons, it took almost a century for docks downstream to be built to accommodate larger vessels, a delay which inhibited trade. Glasgow solved its quayside problem by depending on harbours downstream at Port Glasgow (initiated in 1668 and completed in 1688), and Greenock (developed in 1636 and equipped with a new harbour in 1710), but both had the disadvantage of being some distance from the town.[78]

The dock was the most important but not the only project for improving the port. A second advance was the surveying of channels leading into the River Mersey. The first detailed charts of approaches to the Mersey, by Greenville Collins in 1693, facilitated a safer approach to Liverpool.[79] These were followed by the work of Samuel Fearon and John Eyes in 1736–37, and the buoying of channels into the Mersey via the Rock Channel from the Hoyle Lake.[80] A third enterprise was the provision of a new Customs House. The legal quays of Liverpool had consisted of 500 yards of shoreline close by the old Customs House at the bottom of Water Street, where commodities could be legitimately loaded and unloaded under the Customer's inspection. By 1722 a new Customs House had been built at the head of the new dock.[81]

A second example of Liverpool enterprise is its success in infiltrating the slave trade. In the first three decades of the century London and Bristol dominated the trade. As late as 1728–32 London and Bristol ships delivered over 10,000 slaves each every year, Liverpool less than 3,000. Little more than a decade later Liverpool carried over 7,000 slaves annually, Bristol about 5,000, London less than 2,000 and for the rest of the century Liverpool remained the dominant slave port.[82] Liverpool's organisation of the slave trade, with management companies by mid-century, marked a significant advance on its earlier colonial trade. Liverpool merchants seem to have reorganised the Chesapeake trade in the 1720s by sending factors to Maryland and Virginia to sell English manufactured goods, collect cargoes of tobacco ready for Liverpool ships, and sell slaves, all of which balanced the purchase of tobacco. In the Caribbean the scale of operation also increased, though here the sale of slaves outstripped the purchase of sugar and merchants accepted bills of exchange in return.[83]

The takeover of the slave trade is usually explained in terms of the cost and price advantage of Liverpool traders, shared to an extent by Bristolians. A contemporary assertion claimed that Bristol and Liverpool merchants carried slaves 15 per cent more cheaply than Londoners and that the risks of the trade suited individual provincial adventurers more than the corporate traders of London.[84] Liverpool had advantages over Bristol, too: Liverpool merchants were allowed longer credit on commodities, such as Lancashire textiles carried for sale to Africa, than Bristol merchants were on their wares.[85] Liverpool seamen's and captains' wages were lower than their Bristol counterparts, and port allowances given to Bristol masters were not given to Liverpudlians. Slaves were sold more cheaply by Liverpudlians in the West Indies and North America, partly because Liverpool factors had an incentive to increase sales to boost their income as they were paid on a percentage of sales, rather than by the set wage paid to the Bristol factors.[86] It is also argued that Liverpool captains were more adventurous in where they bought and sold slaves, buying in Sierra Leone and Cameroon, and selling in Jamaica, Grenada, Dominica, St Vincent, and even to Spanish islands such as Cuba, as well as to South Carolina, in contrast to Bristolians who limited buying to traditional markets on the Gold Coast and in Angola, and sold primarily to Virginia.[87] Morgan draws a general contrast between Liverpudlians and Bristolians to explain the relative decline of Bristol trade in the century. Bristolians were too specialised and traditional in their trade, repeating tried and safe trades such as transatlantic shuttle voyages for sugar. They became complacent. Liverpool merchants, often ex-seamen, captains and agents, took risks in trying new places and a wider range of commodities.[88] They were relative newcomers to trade and 'hungry' for success.

This survey of Liverpool's physical and economic growth provides a context for the more detailed analysis of social and political structures to be found in the chapters that follow. While maritime trade was not the only source of growth and prosperity in early modern Liverpool, it was nonetheless central, directly or indirectly, to the assumptions and strategies of a broad spectrum of the population. Maritime influence was evident in the demography of the growing town and its migratory 'pull' and 'push' operated at all social levels. It permeated the town's occupational profile and was both the source of much wealth and the cause of its premature distribution, when ships were lost or businesses failed. This 'engine of trade' encouraged co-operation in governance while provoking early indications of social disharmony. It stimulated the social and political changes under review; they, in turn, were instrumental in making the economic growth of the town possible.

Notes

1. R. A. Philpott, *Historic Towns of the Merseyside Area*, Liverpool, 1988, pp. 34–41.

2. R. Stewart-Brown, *Liverpool Ships in the Eighteenth Century*, London, 1932.

3. F. A. Bailey, 'The minutes of the trustees of the turnpike roads from Liverpool to Prescot, St. Helens, Warrington and Ashton-in-Makerfield, 1726–89', *THSLC*, 88, 1936, pp. 159–200.

4. J. E. Hollinshead, 'The people of South-West Lancashire during the second half of the sixteenth century', unpublished PhD thesis, University of Liverpool, 1986, vol. I, pp. 363–73.

5. E. M. Platt, 'Liverpool during the Civil War', *THSLC*, 61, 1910, pp. 183–202.

6. T. H. Hodson, *Cheshire, 1660–1780*, Chester, 1978, pp. 117–36.

7. R. C. Jarvis, 'The Head Port of Chester and Liverpool, its creek and member', *THSLC*, 102, 1950, pp. 75–80.

8. D. E. Ascott, 'Wealth and Community: Liverpool, 1660–1760', unpublished PhD thesis, University of Liverpool, 1996, Table 1.2.

9. See town size and hierarchy table in E. A. Wrigley, 'Urban growth and agricultural change: England and the Continent in the early modern period', in *The Eighteenth-century Town*, ed. P. Borsay, Harlow, 1990, p. 42; for Glasgow see T. M. Devine and G. Jackson, eds, *Glasgow Volume I*, Manchester, 1995, pp. 6, 10.

10. J. M. Ellis, *The Georgian Town 1680–1840*, Basingstoke, 2001, p. 35.

11. K. J. Allison, ed., *Victoria County History, York: East Riding*, vol. I, London, 1969; D. H. Sacks, *The Widening Gate: Bristol and the Atlantic Economy 1450–1700*, Berkeley, 1991, chapters 6, 8, and pp. 108–13; Devine and Jackson, *Glasgow I*, introduction; S. Middlebrook, *Newcastle upon Tyne*, Newcastle upon Tyne, 1950, pp. 86–90.

12. J. de Vries, *European Urbanisation 1500–1800*, London, 1984, appendix I, p. 270.

13. J. Langton and P. Laxton, 'Parish registers and urban structure: late-eighteenth century Liverpool', *Urban History Yearbook*, 1978, p. 76.

14. A. Rawling, 'The rise of Liverpool and demographic change in part of south-west Lancashire 1661–1760', unpublished PhD thesis, University of Liverpool, 1986; F. Lewis, 'The demographic and occupational structure of Liverpool: a study of the parish registers 1660–1750', unpublished PhD thesis, University of Liverpool, 1993; see also D. E. Ascott and F. Lewis, 'Motives to move: reconstructing individual migration histories in early eighteenth-century Liverpool', in *Migration, Mobility and Modernization*, ed. D. Siddle, Liverpool, 2000, pp. 90–118.

15. T. Baines, *History of the Commerce and Town of Liverpool, and of the Rise of Manufacturing Industry in the Adjoining Counties*, London, 1852, p. 416.

16. For useful reconstructed maps and descriptions of the town in the period 1660–1714 and 1714–1727 see S. M. Nicholson, *The Changing Face of Liverpool 1207–1727*, Liverpool, 1981, pp. 20–41.

17. N. Ritchie-Noakes, *Liverpool's Historic Waterfront*, London, 1984; A. Jarvis, *Liverpool Central Docks 1799–1905*, Gloucester, 1991; for proposed emulation in Hull see G. Jackson, *Hull in the Eighteenth Century*, London, 1972, p. 238.

18. Public buildings are listed in W. Enfield, *An Essay Towards the History of Liverpool*, Warrington, 1773, pp. 41–47; commercial premises are listed in F. E. Hyde, *Liverpool and the Mersey: The Development of a Port 1700–1970*, Newton Abbot, 1971, p. 22; for a comprehensive account of Liverpool's topography and urban environment, see Lewis, 'Demographic and occupational structure', pp. 25–36.

19. Baines, *History of the Commerce*, p. 417; J. R. Hughes, 'A sketch of the origin and early history of the Liverpool Bluecoat Hospital', *THSLC*, 2, 1859, pp. 163–86; T. H. Bickerton, *A Medical History of Liverpool from the Earliest Days to the Year 1920*, London, 1936; R. Davis, 'Seamen's sixpences: an index of commercial activity 1697–1828', *Economica*, 23, 1956, p. 329.

20. C. W. Chalklin, 'The greater urban estates: Bath, Birmingham, Manchester and Liverpool', in *The Provincial Towns of Georgian England*, ed. C. W. Chalklin, London, 1974, p. 100.

21. I. C. Taylor, 'The court and cellar dwelling: the eighteenth-century origin of the Liverpool slum', *THSLC*, 122, 1971, pp. 68–90; Ascott, 'Wealth and community', pp. 15–17; maps in *The Changing Face of Liverpool* reveal the spread of streets, work premises and institutions.

22. R. Blome, *Britannia*, 1673, pp. 233–34.

23. C. Morris, ed., *The Journeys of Celia Fiennes 1685–c1712*, London, 1947, pp. 183–84.

24. D. Defoe, *A Tour through the Whole Island of Great Britain*, ed. G. D. H. Cole, London, 1927, Vol. 2, letter X, pp. 664–65.

25. Defoe, *A Tour*, p. 665.

26. *The Liverpool Memorandum-Book or Gentleman's Merchant's and Tradesman's Daily Pocket-Journal for the year MDCCLIII*, printed for R. Williamson, p. 6.

27. P. Clemens, 'The rise of Liverpool 1665–1750', *EcHR*, 29, 1976, p. 212.

28. Liverpool Port books: PRO E190/1337/16; E190/1357/8.

29. Jackson, *Hull*, p. 67.

30. Clemens, 'The rise of Liverpool', p. 211.

31. PRO: E190/1337/16; M. Power, 'Councillors and commerce in Liverpool 1650–1750', *Urban History*, 24, 1997, pp. 314–15.

32. M. Blundell, *Cavalier: Letters of William Blundell to his Friends, 1620–98*, London, 1933, p. 119.

33. C. N. Parkinson, *The Rise of the Port of Liverpool*, Liverpool, 1952, p. 54.

34. H. Peet, ed., *Liverpool Vestry Books, I, 1681–1799*, Liverpool, 1912, appendix B, pp. 409–10.

35. *Calendar of State Papers Domestic 1689–90*, pp. 48, 81.

36. B. Poole, 'Liverpool's trade in the reign of Queen Anne', unpublished MA dissertation, University of Liverpool, 1961, pp. 64, 273.

37. PRO: E190/1375/8; Power, 'Councillors and commerce', p. 315.

38. Poole, 'Liverpool's trade', pp. 77–94.

39. PRO: CO 390/8 ff. 47-51: Customs House Accounts AE 1698–1720.

40. T. S. Willan, *The English Coasting Trade, 1660–1750*, Manchester, 1938, pp. 185–86.

41. M. Power, 'Creating a port: Liverpool 1695–1715', *THSLC*, 149, 2000, pp. 51–71.

42. Hyde, *Liverpool and the Mersey*, p. 23.

43. Parkinson, *Rise of the Port of Liverpool*, p. 109; Poole, 'Liverpool's trade', p. 64.

44. M. M. Schofield and D. J. Pope, *The Liverpool Plantation Registers 1744–73 and 1779–84*, Wakefield, EP Microform, 1978. The original registers are in the Maritime Archives and Library, Merseyside Maritime Museum: D/514/2/1.

45. K. Morgan, *Bristol and the Atlantic Trade in the Eighteenth Century*, Cambridge, 1993, p. 190; T. M. Devine, 'The golden age of tobacco', in Devine and Jackson, eds, *Glasgow I*.

46. PRO: CO 390/12, p. 218.

47. Parkinson, *Rise of the Port of Liverpool*, pp. 86–88; for 1749 see PRO: EXT 1/299, p. 9.

48. Clemens, 'The rise of Liverpool', pp. 217–18.

49. Clemens, 'The rise of Liverpool', pp. 218–19.

50. Gomer Williams, *History of the Liverpool Privateers and Letters of Marque, with an account of the Liverpool slave trade*, London, 1897 (repr. Liverpool, 2004), appendix 1, p. 659, (noted as 'necessarily incomplete owing to the circumstances of the times').

51. Stewart-Brown, *Liverpool Ships*; R. Davis, *The Rise of the English Shipping Industry in the Seventeenth and Eighteenth Centuries*, London, 1962, pp. 66–68.

52. Williams, *Liverpool Privateers*, p. 39; A. C. Wardle, 'The early Liverpool Privateers', *THSLC*, 93, 1941, p. 73, mentions the captured *Ville de Nantes*. See also Schofield and Pope, Liverpool Plantation Registers 1745.

53. Morgan, *Bristol and the Atlantic Trade*, pp. 19–22.

54. De Vries, *European Urbanisation*, pp. 136–42.

55. Clemens, 'The rise of Liverpool', pp. 213–14; Hyde, *Liverpool and the Mersey*, pp. 27–28.

56. Clemens, 'The rise of Liverpool', pp. 214–15; Power, 'Creating a port', pp. 69–70.

57. Poole, 'Liverpool's trade', p.125; R. C. Jarvis, 'Illicit trade with the Isle of Man, 1671–1765', *TLCAS*, 58, 1945–6, pp. 250–51.

58. S. Derrick, *Letters Written from Leverpoole, Chester, Corke, the Lake of Killarney, Dublin, Tunbridge-Wells, Bath*, London, 1767, p. 24.

59. Clemens, 'The rise of Liverpool', p. 216.

60. De Vries, *European Urbanisation*, appendix 1, p. 271.

61. PRO: E179/1375/8.

62. J. Langton, 'Liverpool and its hinterland in the late-eighteenth century', in *Commerce, Industry and Transport*, ed B. Anderson and P. Stoney, Liverpool, 1983, p. 2.

63. T. C. Barker, 'Lancashire coal, Cheshire salt and the rise of Liverpool', *THSLC*, 103, 1951, pp. 86, 90–92.

64. Bailey, 'Minutes of the trustees of the turnpike roads', pp. 159–200; S. Marriner, *The Economic and Social Development of Merseyside*, London, 1982, p. 16.

65. Marriner, *Economic and Social Development*, pp. 17–19.

66. Marriner, *Economic and Social Development*, pp. 19–21; Langton, 'Liverpool and its hinterland', pp. 3–7.

67. Langton, 'Liverpool and its hinterland', pp. 8–9.

68. William Moss, *The Liverpool Guide: Including a Sketch of the Environs*, Liverpool, 1796, pp. 1–2.

69. Hyde, *Liverpool and the Mersey*, p. 12.

70. Marriner, *Economic and Social Development*, pp. 46–57.

71. Langton and Laxton, 'Parish registers and urban structure', p. 82.

72. Langton and Laxton suggest about 24 per cent in the mid-1760s: 'Parish registers and urban structure', p. 80. This lies within the range of the estimates in Chapter 3, below. The London estimate has been reworked from the data presented by A. L. Beier, 'Engine of manufacture: the trades of London', in

London 1500–1700, ed. A. L. Beier and R. Finlay, London, 1986, p. 148.

73. Morris, *Journeys of Celia Fiennes*, p. 180.

74. J. Longmore, 'Liverpool Corporation as landowners and dock builders, 1709–1835', in *Town and Countryside*, ed. C. W. Chalklin and J. R. Wordie, London, 1989, pp. 117–22.

75. H. Peet, 'Thomas Steers: the engineer of Liverpool's first dock: a memoir', *THSLC*, 82, 1930, pp. 163–242.

76. Defoe, *A Tour*, Vol. 2, p. 667.

77. Hyde, *Liverpool and the Mersey*, pp. 13–14, 240, 247; Power, 'Creating a port', pp. 59–61.

78. Jackson, *Hull*, pp. 243–61; a floating harbour was built in 1804–09, see Morgan, *Bristol and the Atlantic*, pp. 9, 29–32, 220; G. Jackson, 'Glasgow in transition, c.1660–c.1740', in Devine and Jackson, eds, *Glasgow I*, pp. 69–70.

79. Greenville Collins, *Great Britain's Coasting-Pilot. The first part. Being a new and exact survey of the sea-coast of England, from the … Thames to the westward, with the islands of Scilly, and thence to Carlile*, London, 1693.

80. S. Fearon and J. Eyes, *A description of the sea coast of England and Wales, from Black-Comb in Cumberland to the point of Linus in Anglesea … with proper directions to avoid all dangers, and sail into any harbour … as also many prospects of the same … according to an actual survey, etc.*, Liverpool, 1738.

81. E. H. Rideout, *The Custom House, Liverpool*, Liverpool, 1928, pp. 3–12.

82. Morgan, *Bristol and the Atlantic*, p. 133.

83. Clemens, 'The rise of Liverpool', pp. 220–22.

84. *A Short View of the dispute between the Merchants of London, Bristol and Liverpool and the advocates of a new joint-stock Company concerning the regulation of the African Trade*, 1750, p. 6.

85. Morgan, *Bristol and the Atlantic*, p. 143.

86. J. Wallace, *A General and Descriptive History of the Ancient and Present State of the town of Liverpool … Together with a circumstantial account of the true causes of its extensive African trade, etc.*, Liverpool, 1795, p. 216.

87. Morgan, *Bristol and the Atlantic*, pp. 140–45; Wallace, *General and Descriptive History*, pp. 215–17.

88. Wallace, *General and Descriptive History*, pp. 215–18; Morgan, *Bristol and the Atlantic*, pp. 199, 221–24.

2

Population and Demography

In the period from 1660 to 1760 Liverpool emerged from almost total obscurity in the population hierarchy of English towns to rank sixth by the mid-eighteenth century. This chapter looks at the character of this growth, estimates of population size from rate and tax assessments, aspects of mortality and fertility derived from parish register vital event records, the role and nature of migration and household mobility within the town.

The Population

Before the advent of civil registration in the early decades of the nineteenth century, reliable and accurate enumerations of total population are few. However, enlightened estimates can be made based upon certain indirect sources, for example, hearth tax or rate assessment documents. In the case of Liverpool, four hearth taxes survive for the years 1663, 1664, 1666 and 1673, and the content of these is summarised in Table 2.1.[1] It is perhaps surprising that the number of hearth tax entries is virtually the same in 1663 as in 1673, particularly so when parish register entry totals in the 1660s and 1670s suggest an almost uninterrupted surplus of baptisms over burials and hence population growth potential. With the exception of the 1664 tax, the only Lancashire return to record exemptions, the apparent stagnation and even depletion in hearth tax numbers may be a direct reflection of documentary incompleteness, a common complaint of many taxation returns of the period. In addition, writers have increasingly attributed difficulties of hearth tax interpretation to the actual method of collection of the tax and discrepancies both between and within administrative regions.[2] As perhaps the only set of sources from which estimates of population size in this period can be made, the significance of possible omission or shortfall is important. Various multiplier figures for mean household size have been suggested for the calculation of total popula-

Table 2.1 *Liverpool Hearth Taxes 1663, 1664, 1666 and 1673*

Year	Numbers liable for taxation			Numbers exempt from taxation			Total Hearth Tax entries
	male	*female*	*Total*	*male*	*female*	*Total*	
1663	207	47	254				254
1664	203	37	240	24	19	43	283
1666	199	29	228				228
1673	219	33	252				252

tion from hearth tax returns. Although debate continues on the size of the pre-industrial household, using Laslett's mean household size of between 4.5 and 4.7, population from the more complete 1664 tax can be estimated at between 1274 and 1330.[3] Similar calculations based upon the remaining taxes must make some allowance for the unrecorded poor. From the 1664 tax, 43 persons were exempt and 240 liable for taxation, a ratio of approximately 1:6. Though the proportion of poor within the community no doubt varied through time, revision of remaining hearth tax totals by this factor produces the estimates in Table 2.2.

Estimation of population in this way, though nearer the statistical truth, must inevitably fall short of total coverage. Even from the 1664 tax, the extreme poor may have been omitted, although evidence from the town books suggests that the truly destitute were not such a wide-spread group until the 1680s. From about 20 adults in 1681 in regular receipt of relief, the size of the pauper community became a major and growing problem by the mid-eighteenth century, and an increasing burden to the parish authorities.

In terms of the geographical extent of the town in this period, the hearth taxes indicate that the inhabited area of seven streets had undergone little expansion since the town's beginnings in the thirteenth century (see Figure 1.1).[4] The Moore Rental, a document listing the value and location of Sir Edward Moore's numerous properties within the borough, provides a useful guide to the physical extent and character of the town in 1667, by which time there were 11 streets, three of which were created by Moore himself: Fenwick Street and Alley, Bridge Alley and Moor Street.[5] Municipal records some ten years later in 1677 point to considerable building activity, with the number of thoroughfares extended to eighteen.[6]

Similar problems to those encountered with the hearth tax are found when using rate assessment documents in the estimation of population size and location. For the early eighteenth century, two rate assessment documents survive: the 1705, levied as an 'Act for granting an Aid to

Table 2.2 *Population estimates from Hearth Tax totals*

Year	Total Hearth Tax entries	Population estimate (mean household size 4.5–4.7)	Revision of Total Hearth Tax entries by ratio 1:6	Revised population estimate (mean household size 4.5–4.7)
1663	254	1,149–1,194	296	1,332–1,392
1664	283	1,274–1,330		
1666	228	1,026–1,072	266	1,197–1,250
1673	252	1,134–1,185	294	1,323–1,382

Her Majesty by a Land Tax' and the 1708 rate, for the purposes of raising relief for the poor.[7] Unfortunately, the 1705 rate extends to the southern side of the town only, that is the area from an imaginary line drawn along Dale Street from the east and extended down Water Street as far as the river, and is therefore of limited use. By contrast, the 1708 assessment is geographically complete and covers the whole town and borough of Liverpool. Although the poor and those exempt from payment were not liable for assessment, many such individuals may have been listed in the rate as tenants of properties owned by named rate-payers. Although the structure of the rate complicates the calculation, an estimate of population size can be made based on the listing of 1,287 inhabited houses. Using a mean household size of 5, and making some additional allowance for the poor, those exempt and absentees, an estimate of population size produces a figure of slightly less than 6,500 inhabitants.

In terms of the geographical extent of the town in this period, the 1708 rate lists 34 streets, 21 on the south side of the town with 636 inhabited houses on which rates were paid, and 13 on the north side, with similarly 490 inhabited houses (see Figure 1.2).[8] Perhaps most noticeable from the rate is the relatively small number of inhabited houses to the southeast and about the area of what would eventually be St Peter's church, and the particularly dense areas of habitation about the axis of the Dale Street, Water Street, Castle Street intercept. From other accounts, there is also evidence to suggest that a considerable proportion of the less well-documented population lived in the medieval alleys and courts behind the principal thoroughfares, especially in the old town area between Dale Street and Tithebarn Street.[9] With little regulation of urban growth in the early eighteenth century the expansion of the town was somewhat haphazard, particularly around the waterside area.

With an additional 16 streets added to those of the original medieval pattern, James Chadwick's map of 1725 (Figure 1.3), compiled from actual survey and measurement, reveals that traces of an older Liverpool were rapidly disappearing as local industry, trade and commerce diversified and the population grew. Population expansion necessitated physical expansion of the town and by 1753 the number of recognised thoroughfares was a staggering 222 (see Figure 1.4).[10]

Sources from which to calculate population size for later decades of the eighteenth century are few. An assessment of 1743, possibly for poor relief, survives which lists owners, tenants and amounts paid by both, arranged by street. Although 2,676 individuals are named, mainly from the middling and wealthier sections of the community, clearly many others were omitted, making the assessment of limited value in approximating population size.

Estimates vary but it is generally agreed that the population had reached approximately 20–22,000 by the mid-eighteenth century.[11] By 1773, William Enfield estimated the population of Liverpool at 34,407 inclusive of those in institutions such as the Workhouse and Infirmary, but exclusive of those at sea. Concerning this latter group he speculated that of the 5,967 total seafarers employed in Liverpool, two thirds would be absent from the port at any one time, thus leaving approximately 2,000 men accountable in the resident population.[12] In terms of household size, he also offered the only contemporary estimation, calculating that with the omission of the Poorhouses and the Infirmary, the average number of persons in each house was 5.7, and the number in each family 4.2.[13] Based on estimates of household size elsewhere, Liverpool was not exceptional in experiencing high numbers of persons per house by the mid- to late eighteenth century.[14] However, population density rather than household or family size may have been more influential on the quality of urban life for eighteenth-century Liverpool residents. Using Charles Eyes' map of 1785 to calculate township area, population density can be estimated at roughly 820 persons per square kilometre in 1708, 2,940 persons in 1750 and 4,350 persons in 1773.[15] Although a rather crude estimate, and complicated by the irregular shape of the township boundary, figures may actually be under- rather than overstated, since the area includes some considerable tracts of open, uninhabited land. The town's population lived in a relatively confined area therefore, bordered to the southwest by the Mersey channel, and rarely above the 50-foot contour that circled much of the built-up area. Population pressure may not have significantly eased until the late eighteenth century when outward migration prompted urban expansion along township boundaries. Cartographic evidence from the late eighteenth century indicates that much of the Townfield close to the centre of the town had virtually disappeared by this time. Indeed, by the early nineteenth century the population was beginning to overflow the township boundaries, although nearly a century earlier there had been little evidence of population pressure.[16]

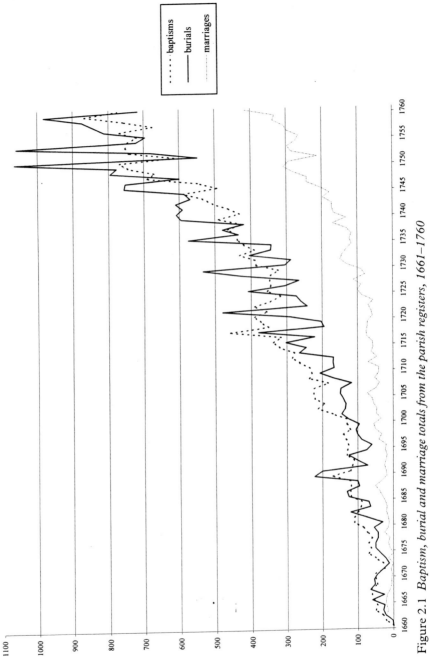

Figure 2.1 *Baptism, burial and marriage totals from the parish registers, 1661–1760*

Placing Liverpool's population growth in a regional and national context, estimates based on birth and death totals show that population within the surrounding area of southwest Lancashire trebled between the 1660s and 1750s, and in the early years of the period approximately 6.5 per cent of the southwest Lancashire total lived in Liverpool. By 1717 the proportion was 37.5 per cent and had risen to 51.5 per cent by 1755.[17] National estimates suggests that the population of England grew by just 16 per cent between 1664 and 1755, with the number of births and deaths in the country 17 per cent greater in the 1750s than in the 1660s. This increase is in sharp contrast to the 284 per cent increase estimated for part of southwest Lancashire.[18] Within this region, Liverpool would seem to have experienced population expansion of a magnitude far greater than that of the country as a whole.

To gauge the nature of this growth, aggregate analysis or assessment of yearly vital event totals can give some indication of the relative balance between births and deaths, or in more crude terms, baptisms and burials. For the period 1660 to 1699 event totals are drawn from the Chapel of Our Lady and St Nicholas, the only Anglican place of worship in the town. The event totals from St Peter's church can be added in 1704, with St George's following in 1734 and St Thomas's in 1750. These totals, as well as marriages, are shown in Figure 2.1.

From Figure 2.1 we can see that the excess of baptisms over burials was small in most years and almost negligible between the mid-1720s and the mid-1740s, indicating that little of Liverpool's growth was attributable to natural increase. The cumulative surplus of baptisms over burials generated in the century between 1660 and 1760 amounted to just under 5,500, with gross population expansion over the same period approximately 24,500, suggesting that barely 22 per cent of Liverpool's growth was by natural increase. The remainder, almost 80 per cent, was supplied from elsewhere. Indeed, net migration into the town accounted for well above 70 per cent of population increase until the final decade of the eighteenth century.[19]

Although aggregate analysis can reveal much about general shifts in vital event totals, outside the contextual boundary of total population it can only provide an impression of population course and cannot tell us of the dominance or imbalance of fertility, mortality or migration through time. In the following section, based partly on evidence from a family reconstitution study of the Liverpool parish registers and a number of additional sources, these aspects will be investigated in greater depth.

Family Reconstitution

Family reconstitution involves the linking of parish register baptism, burial and marriage records to chart the life history of individuals, and when grouped, family units.[20] The nature of the technique gives the potential for very detailed and precise calculation of demographic measures. However, the process of linking records is extremely labour-intensive and until recently, with the introduction of computerised methodologies, studies have tended to concentrate on small towns, parishes, or groups of communities usually with minimal influence from migration. Although growing in number, relatively few large towns and, in particular, maritime locations have been reconstituted thus making direct comparison with Liverpool's experience difficult.[21] In addition, doubts have been cast upon the validity of the technique, and more importantly, the accuracy and typicality of the family histories derived.[22] Much criticism stems from the fact that demographic analysis from family reconstitution relies upon the use of complete family histories; by definition, those families that remained in a parish over a considerable period of time. Parishes where inward and outward migration were common often result in fragmented family histories, thus limiting the number of families that can be counted in the calculation of certain demographic parameters. Family reconstitution also tends to ignore the proportion of the population that remained permanently celibate and those who never married. The loss of the latter group is especially unfortunate considering their considerable influence on the mechanisms of population structure and change.

Using the Anglican parish registers as a source, family reconstitution also overlooks or gives only a partial picture of those who did not record vital events in the Anglican registers, or used them selectively. This influence may have been relatively strong in Liverpool, since it has been calculated that the national coverage of births recorded in the Anglican parish registers was higher than that for the southwest Lancashire region containing Liverpool. Proportions stood at 90.7 per cent for southwest Lancashire between 1660 and 1759 and 81.3 per cent for Liverpool between 1661 and 1760. The main cause of shortfall was the strong nonconformist body in the region and this was particularly influential from the early to mid decades of the eighteenth century onwards. From population modelling, including minor corrections for gaps in the registers, it has been estimated that slightly less than 84 per cent of births and exactly 97 per cent of deaths were recorded in the Anglican registers for the period 1660–1760.[23]

Despite problems, family reconstitution remains a powerful tool for investigating the demography of populations. For the purposes of this study, information is drawn from a combined total of over 50,000

Anglican parish register events of baptism or birth, burial and marriage, as well as a number of additional sources. As a base for demographic analysis, a selection of 3,212 family reconstitution units has been used derived from total parish register events, 1660–1750, although the number of family units or individuals involved in the calculation of a particular demographic characteristic will vary according to the nature of that characteristic.[24]

Mortality

As a prelude to family reconstitution, aggregate analysis or the counting of vital event numbers is often undertaken. As a measure of mortality experience by gender, it is worth considering the sex ratio at burial for both adults and children within the population (Table 2.3). For children, the sex ratio at burial indicates a consistent surplus of male over female deaths. Similarly, considering adult deaths only, and with the exception of the period 1731–40, at no point did the balance of deaths suggest a surplus of women in the population, a characteristic commonly believed to typify the pre-industrial town. This imbalance may be rooted in the character of migrants entering the town. Though women encountered a growing range of employment opportunities in the developing economy, particularly in the domestic and service sectors, a considerably greater number of males may have been drawn to Liverpool, attracted by the abundant and varied employment opportunities, particularly within the maritime sector.

Interesting differences also emerge when crude totals of adult and female burials are compared. Liverpool's male mortality experience may have been prone to peculiar forces, most obviously an employment

Table 2.3 *Sex ratio at burial (males per 100 females)*

	Overall population	*Adults*	*Children*
1661–1670	114	117	111
1671–1670	164	173	152
1681–1680	124	159	101
1691–1700	106	105	107
1701–1710	120	114	126
1711–1720	119	125	115
1721–1730	106	101	110
1731–1740	100	97	102
1741–1750	105	106	105

Source: Liverpool parish registers, 1661–1750

structure in which seafarers formed the largest single employment group. One shipwreck, from which bodies could be recovered for burial registration in the port, could inflate adult male burial totals considerably. The early 1740s saw a number of such peaks in adult male burial totals, during which time the parish registers record a considerable number of sailor deaths by drowning, often accompanied by the name of a ship or Man-of-War. Indeed, it is perhaps appropriate to the town that the only cause of death recorded in the parish registers for the period 1660 to 1750 is 'drowning'. By contrast, such perils rarely affected women. More severe for them were the hazards of childbearing and motherhood, aspects of which will be discussed later in this chapter.[25]

Mortality from Family Reconstitution

Although the parish registers do not record age at death, by linking a burial to a baptism, or more precisely birth record, age at death can be calculated and thus, in theory, mortality rates calculated for any defined age group. However, with high rates of both inward and outward adult migration, and the truncating effect imposed by the time span 1660 to 1750, the accurate calculation of adult age-specific mortality rates has proved impossible for the Liverpool population.

Infant and child mortality rates are more easily produced although a number of ways exist in which infants could be omitted from the recording procedure. Where infants died very shortly after birth, date of baptism and/or birth might not have been recorded. For mortality calculation purposes, this necessitates the manufacture of a 'dummy' or assumed date of birth. This requirement is only necessary up to 1697 when date of birth as well as date of baptism were consistently recorded in the Liverpool parish register. Thereafter, 90 per cent of records record both date of birth and date of baptism.

In terms of burial, an infant might go unrecorded in cases where the mother died in childbirth or very shortly afterwards, and the infant was included for interment without individual documentation. Stillbirths were not recorded in the parish registers in the period to 1750, although from the 1772 Liverpool Bill of Mortality, 25 such births were recorded out of an approximate baptism total of 1,375 for that year, suggesting that barely 2 per cent of baptisms were identified in this way.[26] Harder to detect are losses by abortion or miscarriage, although through family reconstitution the latter can sometimes be gauged from the disruption to expected birth patterns within a family. Finally, abandonment of infants and children and even infanticide may have played a minor part in burial shortfall.

Bearing in mind these possible causes of omission, mortality rates have been calculated using legitimate infant births drawn from families with known date of marriage. Infant deaths can be divided into two components: endogenous mortality comprising those cases of death attributable to causes preceding or associated with birth, including malformation, debility and obstetrical trauma; and exogenous mortality, concerning those deaths attributable to environmental factors after birth, such as lack of hygiene, poor nutrition, infection or accident.

For the period 1661 to 1700 difficulties within the data make the calculation of an exact rate unreliable. From the more complete marriage-based reconstitution histories, the rate was 147 per 1,000, with 60 per cent of deaths within the endogenous category and 40 per cent in the exogenous. The rate for non-marriage-based families, while maintaining the same distribution between endogenous and exogenous components, was at a higher level of 230 per 1,000.

Results for the period 1701–1750 are more robust. Based upon 1,112 births and 281 deaths, an infant mortality rate of 253 per 1,000 is calculated. The components of this rate are almost exactly balanced between endogenous and exogenous elements: 49 per cent attributable to endogenous mortality with a rate of 124 per 1,000 and 51 per cent attributable to exogenous with a rate of 129 per 1,000.

Although relatively few detailed family reconstitution studies of infant mortality, particularly those that indicate the balance between exogenous and endogenous components, have been carried out for larger towns and ports in pre-industrial England, some comparisons with Liverpool can be made. Findings from a broad selection of family reconstitution studies, summarised in Table 2.4, suggest that considerable geographical variation was present in the level of infant mortality within England.

Values calculated from a selection of 26 'national' locations suggest a mean infant mortality rate of just over 190 deaths per 1,000 live births.[27] However, in both select London urban parishes and other rural contemporary parishes infant mortality rates substantially over 200 per 1,000 were not unknown. This suggests that the infant mortality rate of 253 per 1,000 calculated for early to mid-eighteenth-century Liverpool, though relatively high, was not dramatically dissimilar to rates found in some contemporary urban and rural locations.

To what extent mortality of this order can be identified as part of a long-term trend in Liverpool is made difficult to judge because of the limited number of families from which reliable mortality rates can be calculated before the eighteenth century. Estimates of Liverpool's infant mortality rate in the period 1661–1700 of between 147 and 230 per 1,000 appear relatively high when compared to other locations, again with the exception of London parishes. It may have been the case, therefore, that relatively high infant mortality was an established feature of Liverpool's demography well before the beginning of the eighteenth century, with considerable emphasis upon infant deaths within the first month of life.

Table 2.4 *Infant mortality rates per 1,000 live births – some comparisons*

	Date	Births	Total	Endogenous rate	Exogenous rate
Liverpool	1701–1750	1,112	253	124	129
26 'national' parish parish sample	1650–1674		166.7	87.3	79.4
	1675–1699		185.4	88.3	97.1
	1700–1724		190.7	84.0	106.7
	1725–1749		190.8	80.5	110.3
	1750–1774		162.8	61.3	101.5
	1775–1799		156.7	52.6	104.1
Colyton, Devon	1650–1699	1,467	109	44	65
	1700–1749	1,133	109	30	79
	1750–1799	1,469	94	38	56
Alcester, Warwick	1650–1699	1,685	188	85	103
	1700–1749	1,207	220	105	115
	1750–1799	113	97	29	68
Banbury, Oxford.	1650–1699	2,987	167	96	71
	1700–1749	3,365	240	118	122
	1750–1799	4,047	199	93	10
Aldenham, Herts,	1650–1699	1,093	118	57	61
	1700–1749	1,204	147	62	85
	1750–1799	1,208	143	34	109
Whiston and Halsall, Lancs.	1650–1699		144	70	74
	1700–1749		179	81	98
Shepshed, Leic.	1600–1699	1,531	126	76	50
	1700–1749	1,254	155	71	84
	1750–1799	2,498	156	88	68
London parishes					
St Peter, Cornhill	1691–1700	284	215	154	61
St Michael, Cornhill	1691–1700	195	169	78	91
St Mary, Somerset	1691–1700	292	182	85	97
St Botolph, Bishopsgate	1690	364	176	62	114

Sources: Liverpool: Family reconstitution sample.
Twenty-six 'national' parish sample, see E. A. Wrigley, R. S. Davies, J. E. Oeppen and R. S. Schofield, *English Population History from Family Reconstitution 1580–1837*, Cambridge, 1997, pp. 217–42.
Four English parishes, E. A. Wrigley, 'Births and Baptisms: the use of Anglican baptism registers as a source of information about the numbers of births in England before the beginning of civil registration', *Population Studies*, Vol. 31, 1977, Table 3, p. 286.
Two southwest Lancashire parishes (Whiston and Halsall/Downholland): A. J. Rawling, 'The Rise of Liverpool and Demographic Change in part of South West Lancashire, 1661–1750', unpublished PhD thesis, University of Liverpool, 1986, Table 3.6, p. 62.
Shepshed: D. Levine, *Family Formation in an Age of Nascent Capitalism*, New York, 1977; calculated from Tables 5.7 and 5.8, pp. 68–69.
London parishes: R. A. P. Finlay, *Population and Metropolis: The Demography of London 1580–1650* Cambridge, 1981, Table 2.8, p. 35.

To better gauge the mortality experience of infants within the population as a whole, life tables have been constructed, according to the method outlined by Henry and, later, for English data, by Wrigley.[28] Rates have been calculated for the age groups 0–1 years, 1–4, 5–9, 10–14 and 1–14 years. Figures are presented with sexes combined for all occupations and by occupational group, non-seafarers, and sailors and mariners. While this approach produces reasonably reliable results for the lower age groups, individuals above 10 years of age may be less reliably traced, having perhaps left home to take up apprenticeship or go into service. It should also be remembered that these rates represent only those individuals encountered through reconstitution, and according to the conventions of this technique, though a family need only have been present in the parish for one year to be included in the calculation, substantial numbers of migrant families may not have satisfied even this most basic requirement.

In addition to child life tables, successful reconstitution should enable the construction of adult life tables based upon the married population, where age at marriage is known and some adjustment is made for cases where date of burial is unavailable. In a population such as Liverpool's, where the majority of marriage partners originated from outside the parish, age at marriage is rarely known and thus some method must be found to bridge the gap between required and available information. One approach entails fitting model life tables to infant and child mortality rates. In many ways this is not an ideal solution, since it has been found that in certain of those studies where adult life tables could be constructed, mortality rates for adults and children were often quite distinct, and thus overall expectation of life seriously under- or over-estimated when projected from model life table child mortality rates.[29] Indeed, this method becomes increasingly unsatisfactory if it is considered that adult mortality levels in pre-industrial England may have been higher than those of children.[30] Despite this difficulty, expectation of life at birth has been estimated based upon child mortality rates fitted to model life tables originally proposed by Coale and Demeny.[31] Where values fall between levels, averages have been calculated and levels are shown for male and female rates combined according to the North set of tables. Expectation of life at birth (e_0) is therefore shown in Table 2.5 for all occupations and further shown by occupational group.

Several issues arise from Table 2.5. First, expectation of life at birth when calculated from infant and child mortality rates appears low. Whereas expectation of life at birth may have been 30 years or less in the Liverpool population, an overall mean estimate from 26 English locations for the period 1700–1749 suggests a value of between 35.2 and 37.3 years.[32] Secondly, the mortality rate in age group 1–4 years, across all occupational groups, appears slightly higher than that for 0–1 year-olds.

Table 2.5 *Infant and child mortality rates and expectation of life at birth from model life tables, sexes combined, by occupational group*

Age	All occupations total births 1112			Non-seafaring occupations total births 839			Sailors and mariners total births 273		
	Mortality rate $1000q_x$	Survivors $1000l_x$	Expectn. of life at birth e_0 (level)	Mortality rate $1000l_x$	Survivors $1000l_x$	Expectn. life at birth e_0 (level)	Mortality rate $1000l_x$	Survivors $1000l_x$	Expectn. life at birth e_0 (level)
0	253	1000	27 (4.5)	244	1000	30 (5)	278	1000	25 (3.5)
1–4	288	747	22 (2.5)	287	756	20 (1.5)	285	722	20 (1.5)
5–9	115	532	21 (2)	87	539	29 (5)	210	516	–
10–14	50	471	26 (4)	34	492	30 (6)	120	408	–
1–14	401	447		371	475		504	359	

Source: Family reconstitution sample, 1701–1750

Thirdly, distinct differences in the magnitude and character of mortality can be seen when mariner and non-mariner families are compared. In a national context, infant and child mortality rates found in Liverpool appear relatively high when compared with mean rates calculated for a broad selection of English locations.[33] However, rates in Liverpool should not be regarded as unusual. Similarly high mortality rates can be seen in certain poorer individual London parishes of the late seventeenth and early eighteenth centuries, as well as in select locations elsewhere.[34]

Regarding differences in mortality rates in Liverpool between age groups 0–1 years and 1–4 years, possible explanations may lie in the nature of child care and feeding habits, in particular wet nursing and breastfeeding practices. From local records it is difficult to establish whether the practice of wet nursing was widespread, particularly among the lower classes. It is probable that a proportion of infants may have died away at nurse, thus depleting the infant mortality rate, but losses were not substantial. Similarly, direct evidence of breastfeeding within families in Liverpool in this period is scarce. As an alternative, it may be possible to identify aspects of child-feeding practice through graphical representation and analysis of cumulative infant mortality rates. It has been found that a convex line shape is often associated with heightened mortality risk in the first months of life related to artificial feeding. By contrast, a concave shape is often taken as indicative of breastfeeding practice, with a slight upturn in the later months, reflective of increased mortality risk associated with weaning and increased risk from contamination in the transition to solid food.[35] When expressed in this form, evidence for Liverpool suggests that breastfeeding was probably widespread, but may have been abandoned in the later months of infant life, with the result that infant deaths in the last quarter of the first year show a marked upturn.[36] Continuation of this trend beyond the first year may have contributed to the higher mortality rates found in the 1–4 year age category, the period when the transition to solid food would occur.

Regarding the third main characteristic from Table 2.5, with the exception of the age category 1–4 years, infant mortality rates and child mortality rates for mariner families appear both considerably higher than those found in many other contemporary English towns, and also higher than those for non-mariner families in Liverpool itself. Moreover, the high level of mortality in infancy and early childhood encountered in mariner families appears to be continued into the older age groups, whereas the mortality level in corresponding age categories in non-mariner families falls rapidly away. It should be borne in mind, however, that the limited sample size for this occupational category inevitably introduces some element of unreliability into aspects of mortality calculation. Many factors, both socio-economic and environmental, may have been instrumental in influencing such distinctions. For example, it is well recognised that mariners were very poorly paid and treated, and relied upon a labour market seasonally influenced by the growing season of crops such as sugar and tobacco, and by climate and weather conditions in the oceans of the world.[37] Year-round employment was not assured, generating a sense of seasonal insecurity not dissimilar to that experienced among the agricultural community. Other employment forms may have been equally precarious, but with Liverpool's expansion, building trades had ample opportunity to flourish, the service sector was expanding and diversifying, and even the unskilled, casual labourer may have found considerable opportunity.

In terms of family life, considerable time spent at sea would in effect have left the wife as the single upholder of child maintenance and welfare for relatively long periods of time. We know relatively little of working conditions for women in seventeenth- and eighteenth-century Liverpool, but participation in the workforce may have been sufficient to have considerably influenced mortality levels among infants and children. For example, the protection afforded by breastfeeding may have been disrupted because of wives working in the absence of sailor and mariner husbands. The net result may have been earlier weaning, and with the potential for the introduction of contaminants in both food and water, higher levels of mortality among children, particularly in the later months of infancy and within the age group 1–4 years. Finally, with Liverpool's maritime workforce engaged in both national and global trading patterns, new strains and outbreaks of disease picked up elsewhere may have returned home with mariners and unknowingly been introduced into their homes and to their children, and then on into the very heart of the community.

Regarding environmental influences, like many pre-industrial workers, Liverpool's mariners tended to live in close proximity to their place of work. Although occupational zoning was not pronounced before 1700, apart from the butchers' Shambles, by the mid-eighteenth century a certain amount had become evident. Most new building activity was on the periphery of the dock area and, with the exception of the quayside and warehousing developments, some distance from the immediate shore-line. Mariners were therefore increasingly concentrated into the area close to the dock and waterfront, a cramped and unhealthy environment.

From a study of seventeenth-century London, marked differences in the expectation of life have been noted for those living in riverside and inland parishes, possibly produced by contrasts in the nature of water supply. Riverside parishes tended to draw water directly from the Thames, while the remainder of the city obtained water from wells, pipes and conduits from the wells, from other rivers or from the Thames itself, that is, by a variety of means.[38] While it would be unwise to assume that simply because Liverpool's sailors and mariners tended to live nearer the water's edge, they drew their supply direct from the Mersey, if proximity to source was a deciding factor then many may have opted for this source in preference to the official town supply, Fall Well, situated on the south side of the Pool. Though contemporary accounts suggest that the well supply was often of poor quality, left salty and brackish by the infiltration of sea-water, even where sporadic contamination occurred, those receiving well water were perhaps less at risk than those who relied upon the riverside water supply. Any conclusion on the influence of environmental factors can be but speculative, but perhaps the sailor and mariner community was prone to the worst of negative extremes encountered in the town.

In sum, infant and child mortality rates calculated for mariner families clearly indicate that this sector of the community, one of potentially low status and social standing, fared least favourably in terms of mortality experience within the Liverpool population. Prone to peculiar forces, the children of Liverpool's maritime workforce could not expect to survive their 'landed' contemporaries in equal numbers, nor be so certain of reaching adulthood. However, their situation appears all the more acute given that the overall level of both infant and child mortality in Liverpool was relatively high when compared to other locations of the period, and estimated life expectancy correspondingly low. Again, it would appear that this sector of the workforce, through occupational association and exposure to the worst vices of the early urban environment, displayed mortality characteristics quite distinct from the population in general.

Adult Mortality

In aggregate terms, some consideration has already been given to differences encountered between male and female burial totals, but with limited knowledge of date of birth or baptism and thus age at death for those within the reconstitution sample, age-specific mortality levels for the adult population cannot be calculated. In terms of occupational mortality influence, some insight into the peculiar contribution of sailors and mariners has been provided, but perhaps equally as severe as the mortality risk associated with certain occupations or trades was that posed by the hazard of childbearing and motherhood. Not only was death in childbirth common, but complications after the birth, in the form of sepsis or puerperal fever, could also be fatal. Defining and identifying such deaths, however, is not without its problems.[39] Before the establishment of civil registration in 1837, the only English source to consistently record cause of death was the London Bills of Mortality. Deaths in 'childbed' per 1,000 baptisms calculated from this source indicate a rate of 14.5 for the period 1700–49.[40] For Liverpool, a very crude indication of death in childbirth can be gained for the year 1772. Of the 1,085 deaths recorded in the Bill of Mortality, 11 cases of death from 'lying-in' can be identified, constituting 1 per cent of all deaths recorded that year.

For locations lacking cause-specific listings of death, an alternative means of assessing maternal mortality must be used. One method involves an assessment of all deaths occurring within a specified number of days after the termination of the pregnancy. Though definition varies, maternal death is defined by some as death of the mother within 42 days of termination of pregnancy.[41] Family reconstitution offers the potential to reliably chart this interval between last recorded child birth and the death of the mother. However, maternal mortality may still be under-estimated since deaths associated with such events as stillbirths, aborted pregnancies, miscarriages and death of the child in the womb rarely rate a comment in the majority of parish registers, and certainly not in Liverpool. It must also be remembered that in the process of family reconstitution, only legitimate births and births recorded after marriage are considered, thus creating the potential for shortfall in the calculation of mortality rates. In order to overcome this possible shortfall, some method is required to discover the proportion of maternal deaths associated with stillbirths and undelivered pregnancies. By identifying trends found in more informative but comparable Swedish data, Schofield is able to suggest a means by which the total maternal mortality rate can be predicted based upon the live-birth maternal rate, with allowance made for such events. Revised maternal mortality rates for an English 13-parish sample suggest a figure of 11.3 per 1,000 births for the period 1700–1749.[42] Using a similar revision process, maternal mortality in Liverpool for the period 1701–1750 can be estimated at 13.2 deaths per 1,000 births. Although higher than the 13-parish sample for the comparable period, the Liverpool rate falls well below the uncorrected rate derived from the London data. As studies suggest, a clear tendency existed for parishes with low infant mortality to experience few maternal deaths and, conversely, parishes with high infant mortality to suffer a greater number of maternal deaths.[43] Though factors associated with and contributing to maternal death in Liverpool may have been slightly more severe than in many contemporary locations, evidence suggests that both mothers and their children were far less at risk than their urban contemporaries in the capital.

Fertility and Nuptiality

Intimately linked to the act of marriage is that of reproduction, and from a number of studies of marital fertility in pre-industrial England, certain

general conclusions have been drawn. First, marked regional variation
was not apparent, unlike many other European countries. Secondly,
marital fertility in England varied little through time. And finally, a
regime of natural fertility was in place, that is, reproduction within
marriage was not deliberately limited.

Besides the powerful influence of age at marriage and deliberate
limitation of births, a variety of further factors can influence reproductive behaviour. Some are considered background influences, for
example, socio-economic or cultural variables, whereas other have more
direct bearing, namely sterility, foetal mortality, the duration of the non-
susceptible period (the period following a birth during which the mother
cannot conceive again) and fecundability (the probability of conception
in each month at risk).[44] These four factors have direct influence on
fertility, and only through these factors can the background influences
have effect. In this study, of the four, two have not been addressed:
foetal mortality, since no information on stillbirths, miscarriages or
other forms of pregnancy wastage is recorded in the parish registers; and
sterility, referring to those who have never borne children and those who
become sterile as a consequence of birth or pregnancy. The calculation
of age-specific fertility rates has also not been attempted since the age of
the mother is rarely known. However, family reconstitution of the
Liverpool population is well suited to the study of birth intervals and
figures are presented for the period 1701–1750 for all occupations and
by occupational group in Table 2.6.

Figures from Table 2.6 suggest a mean birth interval from marriage to
sixth birth of 24.1 months, and considering only those births from first
birth onwards, that is excluding any potential influence from pre-nuptial
pregnancy, the mean interval can be calculated at 23.7 months. When
dis-aggregated according to occupational group, sailors and mariners
and non-seafaring occupations, a number of striking features emerge.

Table 2.6 *Mean birth intervals in months (number of cases) 1701–1750*

	0–1st	1st–2nd	2nd–3rd	3rd–4th	4th–5th	5th–6th	0–6th	1st–6th
All occupations	18.5 (455)	26.4 (272)	28.8 (204)	27.5 (140)	27.8 (91)	25.1 (65)	24.1 (1227)	27.3 (772)
Non-seafarers	17.1 (328)	25.2 (192)	28.3 (158)	27.0 (112)	27.6 (75)	24.9 (56)	23.3 (921)	26.7 (593)
Sailors and mariners	22.4 (129)	29.3 (80)	30.4 (46)	29.3 (28)	28.8 (16)	26.4 (9)	26.5 (306)	29.4 (179)

Source: Family reconstitution sample, 1701–1750

Table 2.7 *Pre-nuptial pregnancy (percentage of all marriages with children) Liverpool 1701–1750*

	Intervals less than 9 months	Total birth intervals 0–1	Percentage pregnant at marriage
All occupations	91	455	20.0
Non-mariners	77	328	23.5
Mariners	14	127	11.0

Source: Family reconstitution sample, 1701–1750

First, the initial period between marriage and first birth is considerably longer for mariners than non-mariners: 22 months compared to 17 months. Secondly, whether the mean birth interval after the first birth event (1–6) or the mean of all intervals (0–6) is considered, non-mariner families experienced markedly shorter periods between births. Indeed, the mean birth interval of 23.3 months approximates to a marital fertility rate of at least 500 live births per 1,000 woman-years lived, suggesting particularly high fertility.

Considering the first of these characteristics, that is the difference in interval between marriage and first birth, from Table 2.7 it can be seen that at least 20 per cent of all Liverpool women were pregnant at time of marriage, a proportion in keeping with national estimates.[45] However, when assessed by occupational group, striking differences emerge, with only 11 per cent of mariners' brides pregnant before marriage. Clearly, considerable pre-marital sexual activity was present in the community, but curiously to a lesser extent among mariners and their future brides. As one writer suggests, many mariners may have purposely avoided a lengthy courtship period, and thus the possibility of pre-marital conception, by choosing the quickest and most direct route to marriage whether by the choice of marriage by licence instead of banns, or by clandestine marriage.[46]

When using birth intervals, and particularly first birth intervals, as a measure of fertility it is important to acknowledge that a number of such intervals may have gone unrecorded for a variety of reasons. Local, short-distance migration was a common feature of the period and, as a consequence, registration of birth events may not have taken place in the same parish as marriage of the parents. In addition, a common custom was to baptise the first child in the mother's parish of origin. If such a tradition was widely practised in Liverpool, given the extent of migration into the town it is conceivable that over 80 per cent of married women would have recorded the first birth outside the parish. For these reasons, conclusions drawn from statistical analysis of first birth timing in Liverpool and its influence on overall fertility must be viewed with caution.

Taking a broader approach to factors affecting fertility, age at marriage has considerable bearing upon reproductive rates. The calculation of age at marriage requires that an adult baptism or birth record be linked to a marriage record, and again, because of the influence of migration, the success of this exercise is relatively poor. However, limited evidence suggests that in the first half of the eighteenth century, female age at marriage in Liverpool was 23.1 years (71 cases) and male age at marriage 25 years (53 cases). Although undergoing fluctuation, mean estimates of age at marriage from a countrywide sample indicate values of between 24.8 and 26.3 years for women, and between 26.5 and 27.4 years for men for the period 1700–1749.[47] Early marriage may therefore have contributed to Liverpool's relatively high marital fertility rate, but again conclusions cannot be based upon firm statistical evidence. There is also some suggestion that mariners may have married earlier than non-mariners, but again data are too limited to be conclusive. Mean age at marriage for Liverpool sailors and mariners was 23.5 years, based on 29 cases, and for other occupations 25.6 years based on 61 cases.

In the study of birth spacing, it is also necessary to consider those factors that may have influenced the potential for further conception following a birth. Sending an infant away to a wet nurse would have increased the likelihood of conception, since the security afforded by breastfeeding would not have been present. Similarly, if an infant died shortly after birth, breastfeeding would be interrupted and the potential for further conception increased. Evidence of wet-nursing is difficult to find in contemporary Liverpool records, but by contrast statistical analysis of infant mortality rates suggests that breastfeeding was probably widespread.[48] In such circumstances, relatively high infant mortality in Liverpool may have gone hand in hand with relatively high fertility, a feature common to many pre-industrial populations. However, this does not explain the relatively longer intervals experienced by mariner families. One possible contributing factor may have been the periodic absence of mariner fathers from the port and thus the reduced opportunity and likelihood of conception within this group. Though a substantial proportion of maritime trade in the early to mid-eighteenth century was relatively short-distance coastal traffic and may not have resulted in long absences, the period also saw the emergence and successful establishment of long-haul transatlantic voyages, often necessitating long periods of separation of man and wife. It is also possible, however, that a number of very long, and possibly biasing intervals found in the sample may have been the result of incomplete or disrupted registration of events, or incorrect record linkage due to variable quality of the parish registers.

Migration and Population Mobility

Research has shown that the population of England in the pre-industrial period was highly mobile, often over short distances. Inward migration to large and small towns alike was fundamental in sustaining population growth and the supply of labour necessary for many early urbanising economies. Several studies of aggregate population dynamics have confirmed that the major part of population growth in Liverpool from the late seventeenth century onwards was produced by inward migration.[49] However, with the exception of a study of individual Liverpool migration case histories, relatively little is known of the origin of these migrants, the distances they travelled and less still of their character in terms of age, life-cycle stage or occupation.[50] The following section investigates these characteristics based upon parish register entries, family reconstitution evidence and rate and tax assessments.

With a large proportion of population movement known to have occurred over relatively small distances, it is likely that substantial flows of migrants emanated from the immediate hinterland. This migrant supply would have been dependent upon not only the surplus of births over deaths generated by each of these areas, but also the extent to which each region absorbed surplus labour within its own economy. For Cheshire and North Wales, knowledge is limited. However, analysis of surrounding southwest Lancashire parishes based on parish register totals of births and deaths and estimated population size derived from the Hearth Tax of 1664 and the Notitia Cestriensis of 1717 is enlightening. Prior to 1717 population surplus from neighbouring townships made a significant contribution to Liverpool's population growth. After 1717, natural increase was absorbed in these areas, leaving little surplus migrant potential, with the result that Liverpool's growing population was most probably supplied from beyond the immediate southwest Lancashire hinterland.[51]

Although somewhat criticised as a source of information on migration, some broad insights into the origin of these migrants may be gained from parish register marriage entries where place of residence of both bride and groom is stated. The problem lies in the fact that stated place of residence may not have been actual place of residence, especially among male partners. A groom would often travel to the bride's parish for the ceremony, stating this as his residence *at time of marriage*, although in reality he was resident elsewhere and may have returned to that parish with his wife after marriage. In addition, to what extent place of residence can be taken as synonymous with place of origin is debatable. For Liverpool at least, population modelling suggests that the level of natural increase within the indigenous population was so low that a substantial proportion of those marrying in the town could not have been born there. Other problems peculiar to assessing marriage partners in this particular context also apply. Marriage registration in Liverpool was complicated by the influence of the mother church at Walton. Evidence from the family reconstitution sample suggests that approximately 20 per cent of those marrying in Walton went on to record further events in Liverpool. This may be a somewhat biased conclusion though, since flows in the opposite direction, that is, marriage in Liverpool and registration of further events in Walton has not been analysed. In addition, the number of male and female partners both resident in the Liverpool parish may be seriously under-estimated from time to time. Ambiguity of expression arises in the marriage register where a single residence reference is placed at the end of an entry, making it unclear whether the location refers to the male, female, or both partners. To compound this problem, the parish clerks often made a point of noting marriage partners non-resident or exogamous to the parish to the neglect of recording Liverpool residents, with the result that the number of marriage entries with both male and female place of residence stated is limited. Fluctuation in register quality is also a hurdle.[52] This aside, the origin of marriage partners, whether registered as resident (endogamous), or non-resident (exogamous) to Liverpool at time of marriage registration, is presented in Table 2.8, for all Anglican parish register entries where both male and female place of origin is stated.

In many English regions it was customary to marry in the bride's home parish, and evidence from Table 2.8 confirms that Liverpool marriage partners behaved accordingly, with native brides almost consistently

Table 2.8 *Residence of marriage partners, where origin of both partners known, expressed in percentage terms*

	1661–1670	1671–1680	1681–1690	1691–1700	1701–1710	1711–1720	1721–1730	1731–1740	1741–1750
Male endogamous Female exogamous	0	2	5	5	4	17	9	11	14
Female endogamous Male exogamous	12	12	6	8	13	13	12	15	19
Male endogamous Female endogamous	50	33	42	45	37	5	7	0	0
Male exogamous Female exogamous	38	53	47	42	46	65	72	74	67
Number of cases	43	51	125	87	142	96	215	208	196

Source: Liverpool parish registers, 1661–1750

outnumbering native grooms in the period. Until the early eighteenth century, the proportion of partners both endogamous to Liverpool underwent fluctuation, although constituting at least a third of all marriages. Consistent with the general perception that Liverpool was unable to supply much of its own population growth by the early to mid-eighteenth century, the proportion of endogamous marriages dwindled from 1711 onwards, although some shortfall in recording standards may have exaggerated this trend.

By far the dominant characteristic of Table 2.8 is the high proportion and general increase in exogamous partners throughout the 90-year period, with the majority of marriage partners originating outside the town from the 1720s and 1730s onwards. Liverpool was certainly a popular venue for the celebration of marriage, but to what extent marriage provoked short-term mobility, convergence for the ceremony and then return to a distant parish, and to what extent long-term migration, the starting point for life in the early urban environment, remains unknown. Gross parish register marriage entries offer no answer, while evidence from more detailed family reconstitution histories is surprisingly scarce. Based on 70 family histories with male and female place of residence stated at time of marriage, and at least one subsequent vital event registration (in this case a child baptism or burial) three aspects emerge. Before 1700, couples with each partner from Liverpool tended to remain in the town to rear children while couples of mixed origin (particularly those with non-Liverpool brides) recorded almost no further events in the parish. Post-1700, in line with general population dynamics, the number of families with parents of distant origin was in the majority as the number of families with parents endogamous to Liverpool dwindled.

Although findings post-1700 are as expected, some useful insights into population movement of Liverpool townsfolk in the late seventeenth century have been gained from analysis of neighbouring parish registers. Over 100 printed volumes of the Lancashire Parish Register Society were examined for evidence of Liverpool individuals primarily recording marriage, but also other vital events. In addition, marriage licences published by the Record Society of Lancashire and Cheshire were examined for the period 1661–1700, and marriage bonds for the period 1700–1719.[53] Varying coverage and record quality prohibits statistical analysis of the data but several interesting features emerge. For example, a number of locations appear to have been chosen as a location for marriage by relatively large numbers of Liverpool marriage partners. Winwick and Garstang were popular throughout the period, as were Ormskirk and Croston in the late seventeenth and early eighteenth century. Lancaster was also popular in the 1680s but records are incomplete.

Clearly, no simple relationship existed between place of origin and place of marriage. Many marriage partners, supposedly 'of Liverpool', revealed previous ties by marrying in remote locations. Whether these people remained in the parishes outside Liverpool, or did in fact return to the town, remains unknown, although given the substantial influence of inward migration on Liverpool's population structure, it is likely that many were only temporarily absent from the town for marriage celebration.

Examination of marriage registers, licences and bonds for Liverpool and the surrounding parishes may provide a more rounded view of certain migration characteristics, but many individuals will still be overlooked, particularly given the influence of nonconformity in the town and surrounding area. In Liverpool a number of nonconformist chapels existed. For example, the Independent Chapel, commencing registration in 1709, kept no record of marriage or burial but documented baptism. Unfortunately, place of residence or origin was not stated. Baptism registration in St Mary's Catholic chapel commenced in 1741, with the name of the child and that of the mother and father, occupation of the latter and, from time to time, place of residence stated. With a striking predominance of Irish surnames, and several places of residence given as 'of' or 'formerly from' Ireland, the document gains significance as evidence of early migration, before the more well-documented flows of the nineteenth century. A Quaker Meeting House was erected in Liverpool itself in 1706, attached to which was a burial ground, but no records would seem to have survived. Liverpool Quakers were likely to have attended the Hardshaw West Monthly Meeting at St Helens, where a register of births and burials was kept from 1678 to 1786.[54] Marriages were not recorded although a strong Liverpool nonconformist presence can be noted in the other event registers. For example, a number of known Presbyterians and Independents married at Childwall.

Geographical Origin and Migration

Following analysis of basic patterns of marriage residence, three further key issues arise: distance, place and gender. In essence, how far did marriage partners travel? Which were the areas that fuelled these flows, and did men and women behave differently in their mobility habits? By mapping the horizons of those marrying in Liverpool, it is possible to quantify distances travelled by marriage partners foreign to the town. Some difficulties arise in pinpointing exact locations, particularly where place of residence is recorded either as a general area or parish. Estimation of distance travelled to Liverpool is also notoriously difficult, given the broad hinterland catchment straddling three distinct landmass areas. This aside, evidence from family reconstitution histories suggests that although the majority of partners originated from within twenty miles of Liverpool, almost a third of couples hailed from locations twenty to forty miles distant, and a handful from over fifty miles away. Within this pattern, male partners tended to have travelled further than their female counterparts, with marriages between male migrants from ten to forty miles away and Liverpool women particularly common.[55]

Addressing the second issue, place of origin and location, an impressionistic overview of marriage partner origin stated in the parish registers suggests a very broad catchment area comprising the immediate hinterland, as well as locations in Scotland and Ireland, and even the West Indies and America. Graphic representation of distance from Liverpool and location for individual marriage partners is problematical since assessment of each marital unit requires two distinct elements to be represented; male and female residence shown relative to Liverpool, and to each other. A more simplistic exercise is to break down migrant origin according to key areas, chosen here as Liverpool, Lancashire, Cheshire, North Wales, other locations within Britain, and abroad. For purposes of comparison, the period 1660 to 1750 was divided at the watershed year of 1717. The sample is based on family reconstitution histories with stated origin for both marriage partners, regardless of further parish event registration. In the period 1661–1717, evidence from 110 marriages suggests that over 40 per cent of couples originated from Liverpool, a third from the Lancashire area, and almost 3 per cent from Cheshire. By contrast, in the period 1718–1750, based on 148 marriages, only 4 per cent of partners were Liverpool residents, 60 per cent from Lancashire, 14 per cent from Cheshire, and a minor contribution from North Wales.

Considering those marriage partners who went on to register some further event in the Liverpool parish registers, such as a birth or burial, conclusions must inevitably be more speculative because of reduced sample size. For the period 1661–1717, based on 39 cases, the vast majority of partners, almost three-quarters, were Liverpool residents, with some contribution from Lancashire and to a lesser extent Cheshire. By the second period, and based on only 18 cases, the contribution of Liverpool partners had been reduced to just over a fifth, with almost a third of partners from Lancashire, and a handful from Cheshire. Again, for the period 1661–1717, patterns appear to accord with the basic notion that Liverpool did not require large numbers of migrants to maintain population growth. However, when considering the second period, 1717–1750, one of the major flaws of using parish register entries to chart migration characteristics in this fashion is revealed. Whereas population modelling suggests that the neighbouring townships of Lancashire were unable to supply migrants to Liverpool from the second decade of the eighteenth century onwards, parish register entries would suggest that the Lancashire region maintained and even increased its supply of migrants, that is marriage migrants, in the period. Clearly, the use of marriage registration as an indicator of migration activity has its limitations, particularly when it is considered that the majority of such migrants were probably young, single adults seeking economic opportunities in the town. Analysis of parish register marriage entries does at least add some weight to the assessment that migrants to Liverpool from 1717 onwards were mainly supplied from outside the region. Cheshire, in particular, may have been influential.

Our knowledge of migrant origin, from both population modelling and from patterns revealed by parish register marriage records, can be crudely placed against the economic and labour force developments in the town and surrounding area for the period. Before the early eighteenth century, Liverpool was able to supply a proportion of its own population growth and, presumably, the labour force necessary to maintain the small seafaring economy from within its own township. By the early decades of the eighteenth century, the town's migratory pull was significantly greater. With diversification of the economic base, especially the dock developments of the early eighteenth century, labour was increasingly required from elsewhere to maintain and satisfy Liverpool's demand. Sailors, in particular, from the many port communities of Cheshire, North Wales, Wirral and abroad found abundant employment in the world-wide trading economy of Liverpool. But the majority were, in a phrase, footloose single members of the workforce and for this reason their immediate presence is overlooked in the analysis of marriage records.

The development of the port also generated a huge demand for general labourers to be involved in the erection and building of dock buildings and related warehousing. Diverse manufacturers and those involved in skilled trades also established themselves. Growing in number and strength, they drew upon an increasingly wide catchment for young labour. Apprenticeship records for the period 1707–1757 indicate that although the majority of young, predominantly male migrants hailed mostly from within fifteen to twenty miles of Liverpool, a handful originated from further afield – London, Ireland and Scotland, America and the West Indies – mirroring the interest in Liverpool as a centre for financial trading and cargo handling by merchants and financiers originating from both sides of the Atlantic.[56]

Viewing migrants as a potential labour source highlights the third strand of analysis, differences in migration behaviour between males and females. About the employment opportunities available to women in the Liverpool economy we know surprisingly little.[57] As certain sectors diversified, women from outside the area may have found work in a number of developing manufacturing and production concerns. However, unlike the shipping fleet with its voracious thirst for male labour, the chief employment sector open to young, single, migrant women was probably domestic service. In terms of origin, it would seem reasonable to suggest that these women were likely to have originated from much the same catchment area as the majority of their male apprentice contemporaries, often a relatively small distance from Liverpool itself.

Personal Mobility and Family Reconstitution

Physical mobility, especially among the young, has been recognised as a characteristic feature of pre-industrial populations. However, while most studies have centred upon the analysis of movement in spatial terms, few have attempted to observe the characteristics of movement through time. One exception is found in the work of Souden, who charted migrant histories based upon the populations of select towns and villages over the period 1601–1780.[58] This was achieved by classifying males and females recorded in family reconstitution studies according to the number and type of records available for each, and was based on the assumption that in the series of records produced by family reconstitution, lack of registration of vital events was inferential evidence of residence elsewhere.[59] Hence four life-cycle stages, deduced from vital event type, can be recorded for husbands and wives from families where date of marriage is known and there is baptism evidence of two or more children, thus implying some degree of mid-point life-cycle residency within the parish. The four stages can be summarised thus:

[- / -]	without baptism; without burial
[- /bur]	without baptism; with burial
[bap/ -]	with baptism; without burial
[bap/bur]	with baptism; with burial

The first record combination indicates neither baptism nor burial in the parish by the couple, only registration of events in mid-life; the second implies a movement into the parish after baptism but before marriage, and then residence until burial; the third, a movement out of the parish after marriage and child-bearing; and the fourth, a long history of permanency within the parish. This method of analysis is not without problems, however. Not only will family histories be deficient where under-registration of ecclesiastical events occurs, but family reconstitution, by definition, catches only a particular subset of the population. Those who remained permanently celibate and non-married adults will be excluded. The latter category is of particular importance since it would probably contain a large number of single adults, some of the most mobile individuals within the population.[60] However, the technique provides a simple means by which to examine and compare population movement trends over time, both between individuals from different areas of the country and individuals at common points in life-cycle stage. Souden found that the distribution of events tended to differ according to the economic character of a particular settlement. Those with rural industry and, to some extent, larger market towns tended to provide sufficient employment to maintain residents in the early eighteenth century as well as attracting considerable flows of migrant labour, with high levels of implied residence in the mid-points of the life cycle and at burial. Other eighteenth-century villages experienced high levels of instability and transience, often related to land ownership and poverty. Movement was therefore considerable, both inward and outward, with undocumented points at the beginning and end of the residence histories.[61]

Whereas Souden was able to chart change in migration behaviour over a considerable time period, thus highlighting the opening up of many rural communities or the increasing effect of migration on a number of market towns and centres of rural industry, such analysis of temporal change in Liverpool is restricted by the choice of dates 1660–1750. However, characteristics for male and female adults from family reconstitution histories with marriage and the baptism of two or more children have been summarised in Table 2.9 and further presented for the period 1691–1720, thus making comparison with Souden's marriage cohort of the same period possible.

From Table 2.9, the influence of migrants on Liverpool's population can be readily identified, with the proportion of adults recording baptism in the parish particularly low in the period 1691 to 1720. It is also noticeable that less than half of marriage partners record burial in the Liverpool parish. With at least a third of the adult male workforce involved in seafaring, male burial registration may have been depressed by loss of sailors and mariners at sea, although a proportion of such individuals would have been single at time of death and therefore not

Table 2.9 *Percentage baptism and burial links based upon family reconstitution histories with baptism of two or more children*

	[– / –]		[– / bur]		[bap/ –]		[bap/bur]	
	male	female	male	female	male	female	male	female
Liverpool, 1661–1750	71	71	18	15	8	11	3	3
Liverpool, 1691–1720	48	60	44	27	5	12	3	1

Notes: Liverpool, 1661–1750, number of cases, 333
Liverpool, 1691–1720, number of cases, 89

included in the family reconstitution exercise. The possible causes behind the low number of women remaining in the parish from marriage to burial are more difficult to unravel. Death of a spouse may have prompted remarriage and consequently name change, thus making the reconstruction of life events more difficult. External forces, including removal from the parish under Poor Law settlement terms, may also have been an influence.[62]

Population movement out of the parish was also influenced by less authoritarian imperatives. Whether before burial or perhaps in illness before death, individuals may have chosen to return or been returned to their parish of origin or chosen location for interment.[63] Even though having spent the majority of their lives in the parish, such a 'traffic in corpses' would tend to give a false impression of residence characteristics if it occurred on a large scale. Gauging the extent of the import and export of burials in Liverpool is frustrated by the fragmentary nature of the evidence: brief notes from wills and occasional reference to the cost of burial, in particular pauper burial, in the Vestry Books.[64] However, the significant difference in male and female burial characteristics shown in Table 2.9 may in part be explained by the large number of women, particularly the old and widowed, in receipt of parish relief, and therefore increasingly the subject of parish responsibility and public burden. As the eighteenth century progressed, the cost of moving such individuals by removal order back to their parish of origin may have been outweighed by the cheaper alternative of a pauper burial. In the late seventeenth and early eighteenth centuries, however, the system may have operated more traditionally, and although removal orders tended to target males and their dependants, simply because of the greater relative proportion of women dependent on the authorities, more women than men may have been returned to their parish of origin, either in old age or for burial.

Under whatever circumstances, family reconstitution evidence implies that few individuals married in Liverpool between 1691 and 1720 spent their entire lives in the parish. The majority of women, almost two-thirds, raised families in the parish but were neither born nor buried there. Nearly half of all married men showed similar characteristics but exhibited a greater likelihood of being buried in the parish. Although this tends to contradict the pattern described above regarding the distribution of poor relief and the application of removal orders, the difference may in part be due to the difficulty of tracing burial of women after re-marriage because of name change. It should be borne in mind, however, that reconstituted family histories for Liverpool townsfolk are extremely fragmentary, with few individuals recording vital events at all stages in the life-cycle, that is, adult baptism, marriage, childbirth and burial and adult burial. Moreover, the limited study period inevitably leads to a shortfall in adult baptisms associated with marriages in the late seventeenth century, and missing burials associated with marriages towards the mid-eighteenth century. However, even for the middle 30-year marriage cohort, comparable to Souden's of 1691–1720, there is no significant improvement in the completeness of Liverpool reconstituted families.

Mobility within the Town

With some knowledge of population movement both to and from Liverpool in the late seventeenth to mid-eighteenth century, how did the so-called 'resident' population behave? In a similar fashion to Souden's record of implied residence within the parish, it is possible to plot movement and change of location from family reconstitution evidence. Consider the following stylized family reconstitution history.

	1660	1661	1662	1663	1664	1665
Marriage	X———————————————————X					
	Dale St					
1st child	(born)	X————X	(buried)			
	Dale St		Moor St			
2nd child		(born)	X————X	(buried)		
		Water St		Moor St		
Parental burial	X———————————————— X (buried)					
						Dale St

Marriage was celebrated in 1660, with place of residence given as Dale Street. The first birth was also registered with place of residence given as Dale Street, indicating persistence in that location for at least a year. With the birth of a second child, residence is given as Water Street, thus indicating a change of address. Continuing to chart place of residence in this manner, over the five-year period that the family was in observation, three distinct places of residence can be identified, indicating three separate moves, although the reconstitution history began and ended in Dale Street. Unfortunately, since the parish registers fundamentally provide a record of vital events and not residence, this approach suffers from one major flaw. If no vital event is recorded in a year when change of location takes place, no indication of movement will be apparent, although change of location may later become obvious. However, considering that the bulk of records relating to a family are usually those dealing with childbirth and burial and therefore often following in quick succession, where registration quality is maintained this approach provides a reasonably adequate indicator of movement habits.

By adopting this means of analysis, frequency of movement was assessed based on a selection of 100 reconstituted families with marriage record and at least two further events recorded. Allowing for the probability that with increasing time a family was more likely to contemplate a move, comparisons in family mobility habits can be compared by plotting the number of families completing a particular number of moves against years in observations. From the 100 reconstituted family histories, almost 40 per cent recorded no movement, although many were in observation for very few years. Nearly a third of families moved once, generally after four to ten years in observation. Movement two or more times was experienced by approximately 25 per cent of families, while 10 per cent of the total moved at least three or four times, usually with one move following relatively soon after the other.[65]

Though difficult to quantify, it is also possible to make some general comments upon the nature and direction of this movement. Throughout the 90-year period, distance moved by households was generally small, often only between neighbouring streets and mostly within the same area of the town, either the north or south end. It is only by the very late 1740s that a handful of families contemplated re-location to the periphery of the town, the areas centred around Derby Square and beyond St George's church. Such movement was intimately bound up with the changing working practices of certain economic sectors, and the beginnings of home and workplace separation, in this case by the relatively wealthier merchant classes.

Finally, this analysis of movement is necessarily based upon those families with large numbers of associated parish register records, by implication some of the most stable members of the community. Therefore, in common with Souden's approach, and family reconstitution itself, it does not accommodate those who did not marry and produce children, single adults, many of whom formed the bulk of the migrant population, and transients. Fortunately, from the parish registers, it is possible to glean additional information on the presence of such individuals within the community. Though in a town the size of Liverpool it is unlikely that the clerks and ministers of the churches had an intimate and encyclopaedic knowledge of their parishioners as may have been the case in smaller, closed communities, it is clear that some effort was at least made to identify individuals foreign to the town. By the beginning of the eighteenth century, 'strangers' and people of 'unknown' identity and origin became an increasingly common phenomenon in the parish registration volumes, particularly among burial entries. As already suggested, the need to regulate parish responsibility in terms of providing relief and burial for the poor and sometimes itinerant may have prompted a desire to monitor the extent of this group. However, those who were able to provide their own means of subsistence were equally under scrutiny. From the town books, the authorities appeared so wary of strangers trading in the Liverpool economy that notes were exchanged guaranteeing that the businessmen would leave after a fixed length of time, and bear no debt to the town or Council.[66] In addition, 'inmates' or poor lodgers, often taken in by sympathetic family or acquaintances, were to be found in increasing numbers by the beginning of the eighteenth century.[67] Harbouring such individuals was against the bye-laws of the town and those offering aid were liable to penalty, such was the town's imperative to keep away the economically inactive and possibly burdensome.

In conclusion, it would appear that mid-seventeenth- to mid-eighteenth-century Liverpool was a town with a distinctive demography. In the closing decades of the seventeenth century, the population was relatively small and self-sustaining. By the early decades of the eighteenth century, natural increase was limited, with the result that over three-quarters of population growth was attributable to migrant inflow. Thus, from a modest settlement, the town was to emerge from relative obscurity to rank as the fifth largest provincial centre in the century following the Restoration.

Analysis of mortality in eighteenth-century Liverpool by family reconstitution suggests that mortality rates among infants and children were high when compared to many contemporary non-urban locations. Within the population, the children of mariners fared least favourably, with high mortality rates in infancy continuing not only into the early but also the later childhood years. Though insufficient information is available from the parish registers to calculate adult mortality rates, from life-table estimates adult expectation of life was low, and particularly so among the mariner sector.

Concerning aspects of nuptiality and fertility, age at marriage in Liverpool, based upon a limited selection of family reconstitution histories, was low for both males and females by national standards. Mariners in particular married young, a response perhaps to the relative freedom from the necessity for land acquisition and capital accumulation before marriage associated with non-seagoing professions. Maritime employment may also have been influential upon the pattern of reproduction within marriage. Based upon birth interval analysis, though fertility within the non-maritime community was relatively high, sailors and mariners often experienced prolonged intervals between successive births, and thus maintained a relatively lower fertility regime. Periodic absence from the port may have reduced fecundability, and probably did little to raise marital fertility rates within such families. Even outside the bond of marriage, mariners were distinctive in their behaviour, recording relatively lower rates of pre-marital conception than their non-maritime contemporaries. Clearly, the mariners of Liverpool exerted a significant, even idiosyncratic influence upon the demography of the seventeenth- and eighteenth-century town.

Notes

1. 1663, PRO E179/250/8; 1664, PRO E179/250/11; 1666, PRO E179/250/9; 1673, PRO E179/132/355. See Appendix 1 Sources and Methods: Fiscal records.

2. T. Arkell, 'Printed instructions for administering the Hearth tax', in *Surveying the People*, ed. K. Schürer and T. Arkell, Oxford, 1992, p. 38.

3. P. Laslett, 'Mean Household size in England since the sixteenth century', in *Household and Family in Past Time*, ed. P. Laslett and R. Wall, Cambridge, 1972, pp. 125–58.

4. S. M. Nicholson, *The Changing Face of Liverpool, 1207–1727*, Liverpool, 1981, p. 7.

5. T. Heywood, ed., *The Moore Rental*, CS, 10, Manchester, 1847. H. Peet, ed., *Liverpool in the Reign of Queen Anne 1705 and 1708*, Liverpool, 1908, p. 18.

6. Peet, *Liverpool in the Reign of Queen Anne*, p. 19.

7. Peet, *Liverpool in the Reign of Queen Anne*, p. 3.

8. Peet, *Liverpool in the Reign of Queen Anne*, pp. 15–16.

9. See W. Enfield, *An Essay towards the History of Leverpool*, Warrington, 1773, pp. 20–40. Peet, *Liverpool in the Reign of Queen Anne*, p. 16.

10. T. Baines, *History of the commerce and town of Liverpool, and of the rise of manufacturing industry in the adjoining counties*, London, 1852, p. 416.

11. Baines, *History of the commerce*, p. 492. Further estimates of population in the eighteenth century may be found in M. Gregson, *Portfolio of fragments relative to the history and antiquities of the County Palatine and duchy of Lancaster*, 3rd Edition, London, 1869, p. 160.

12. Enfield, *An Essay*, pp. 23–24.

13. Enfield, *An Essay*, p. 24.

14. C. W. Chalklin, *The Provincial Towns of Georgian England*, London, 1974, Appendix VI, Table 2, p. 338.

15. Population in 1750 estimated at approximately 25,000, and in 1773 at 37,000. From Eyes' map of 1785, the township measured 2,300 yards from east to west, 4,420 yards from north to south, and 10,400 yards in circumference. Bounded to the west by the river Mersey, to the east by Low Hill and Everton, to the north by the township of Kirkdale and to the south by Toxteth Park, the whole area covered approximately 2,202 acres of which about 1,000 acres belonged to the corporation and the rest to individuals.

16. Edward Baines, *History, Directory, and Gazetteer of the county Palatine of Lancaster*, vol. I, Liverpool, 1824, p. 149.

17. A. J. Rawling, 'The Rise of Liverpool and Demographic Change in part of South West Lancashire, 1661–1750', unpublished PhD thesis, University of Liverpool, 1986, pp. 79, 20–32, 107.

18. Calculated from E. A. Wrigley and R. S. Schofield, *The Population History of England 1541–1871*, London, 1981, Tables A3.3, A2.1 and A2.2, by Rawling, 'Rise of Liverpool', pp. 81, 88.

19. Based on figures calculated by J. Langton and P. Laxton, 'Parish registers and urban structure: the example of late-eighteenth century Liverpool', *Urban History Yearbook*, 1978, pp. 74–84.

20. French demographers were some of the first to use the technique successfully. For example, see E. Gautier and L. Henry, *La population de Crulai*, Paris, 1958. For the English village of Colyton, see E. A. Wrigley, 'Family limitation in pre-industrial England', *EcHR*, 2nd series, 19, 1966, pp. 82–109.

21. For example, see R. A. P. Finlay, *Population and Metropolis: The Demography of London 1580–1650*, Cambridge, 1981. For demographic parameters derived from the reconstitution of 26 locations see E. A. Wrigley, R. S. Davies, J. E. Oeppen and R. S. Schofield, *English Population History from Family Reconstitution 1580–1837*, Cambridge, 1997.

22. An early summary of problems and some general comments on the reliability of family reconstitution methods are given in T. H. Hollingsworth, *Historical Demography*, London, 1969, pp. 181–95. See also S. Akerman, 'An evaluation of the family reconstitution technique', *Scandinavian EcHR*, 25, 1977, pp. 160–70; S. Ruggles, 'Migration, Marriage, and Mortality: Correcting Sources of Bias in English Family Reconstitutions', *Population Studies*, 46, 1992, pp. 507–22.

23. Rawling, 'Rise of Liverpool', p. 68.

24. For a detailed discussion of the form, quality and typicality of the Liverpool parish registers, the application of family reconstitution techniques, and the use of additional sources such as nonconformist event registers, see F. Lewis, 'The Demographic and Occupational Structure of Liverpool: a study of the parish registers, 1660–1750', unpublished PhD thesis, University of Liverpool, 1993, chapters 4 and 5.

25. For graphical representation of burial totals see Lewis, 'Demographic and Occupational Structure', Figure 6.3 p. 164.

26. Stillbirths recorded in Enfield, *An Essay*, p. 31. Baptism total taken from J. Gore, *Gore's Directory for Liverpool and its environs*, Liverpool, 1805, pp. 86–87.

27. For an overview of infant mortality rates from 26 English locations see Wrigley et al., *English Population History*, pp. 217–42.

28. L. Henry, *Manuel de démographie historique*, Geneva, 1967, pp. 125–29; E. A. Wrigley, 'Mortality in pre-industrial England: the example of Colyton, Devon, over three centuries', in *Population and Social Change*, ed. D. V. Glass and R. Revelle, London, 1972, pp. 247–49.

29. For example, see Wrigley, 'Mortality in pre-industrial England', pp. 269–70. The problems of fitting mortality values to life-table estimates is touched upon by Finlay, for a number of London parishes; *Population and Metropolis*, p. 86.

30. R. S. Schofield and E. A. Wrigley, 'Infant and child mortality in England in the late Tudor and early Stuart period', in *Health, Medicine and Mortality in the Sixteenth Century*, ed. C. Webster, Cambridge, 1979, pp. 61–95.

31. A. J. Coale and P. Demeny, *Regional Model Life Tables and Stable Populations*, Princeton, 1966.

32. Wrigley et al., *English Population History*. Table 6.21, p. 295.

33. See Wrigley et al., *English Population History*, Table 6.14, p. 262.

34. London parishes: calculated from Finlay, *Population and Metropolis*, Table 5.4, p. 90. Four English parishes: calculated from E. A. Wrigley and R. S. Schofield, 'English Population History from Family Reconstitution: Summary Results 1600-1799', *Population Studies*, 37, 1983, Table 14, p. 179.

35. J. Knodel and H. Kintner, 'The impact of breast feeding patterns on the bio-metric analysis of infant mortality', *Demography*, 14, 1977, pp. 391–409.

36. See Lewis, 'Demographic and Occupational Structure', Figure 6.11.

37. R. Davis, *The Rise of the English Shipping Industry in the Seventeenth and Eighteenth Centuries*, London, 1962, pp. 113–14, 133–45; M. Rediker, *Between the Devil and the Deep Blue Sea*, Cambridge, 1987, p. 82.

38. Finlay, *Population and Metropolis*, pp. 103–05.

39. For a variety of definitions of maternal mortality used in family reconstitution studies see Wrigley et al., *English Population History*, p. 309.

40. R. Schofield, 'Did the Mothers Really Die? Three Centuries of Maternal Mortality in "The World We Have Lost"', in *The World We Have Gained. Histories of Population and Social Structure*, ed. L. Bonfield, R. M. Smith and K. Wrightson, Oxford, 1986, pp. 232–33.

41. *Manual of the International Statistical Classification of Disease, Injuries, and Causes of Death*, vol. 1, Geneva, WHO, 1977, p. 772.

42. Schofield, 'Did the Mothers Really Die?', pp. 242–50, 232–33, Table 9.5, p. 248, best estimate value.

43. Wrigley and Schofield, 'English Population History from Family Reconstitution', p. 181.

44. J. Bongaarts, 'Intermediate fertility variables and marital fertility', *Population Studies*, 30, 1976, pp. 227–41. See also C. Wilson, 'The proximate determinants of marital fertility in England, 1600–1799', in Bonfield et al., eds, *The World We Have Gained*, pp. 203–30.

45. Wrigley and Schofield, *Population History of England*, p. 254.

46. R. L. Brown, 'The Rise and Fall of the Fleet Marriages', in *Marriage and Society*, ed. R.B. Outhwaite, London, 1981, p. 126 and Table III.

47. Wrigley et al., *English Population History*, Table 5.3, p. 134.

48. Lewis, 'Demographic and Occupational Structure', pp. 229–30.

49. See Rawling, 'Rise of Liverpool', pp. 91–125, 180–90; Langton and Laxton, 'Parish registers and urban structure', pp. 74–84.

50. See D. E. Ascott and F. Lewis, 'Motives to Move: reconstructing individual migration histories in early-eighteenth century Liverpool', in *Migration, Mobility and Modernization in Europe*, ed. D. Siddle, Liverpool, 2000, pp. 90–118.

51. Rawling, 'Rise of Liverpool', pp. 91, Figure 5.1, 92, Figure 5.2, 94, 180–90, and Table 5.7, p. 124.

52. See Lewis, 'Demographic and Occupational Structure', Figures 4.16 and 4.17.

53. W. Irvine, ed., *Marriage Licences Granted within the Archdeaconry of Chester in the Diocese of Chester*, RSLC, *1661–67*, 65, 1912; *1667–80*, 69, 1914; *1680–1691*, 73, 1918; *1691–1700*, 77, 1923; W. A. Tonge, ed., *Marriage Bonds of the Ancient Archdeaconry of Chester, now Preserved at Chester*, RSLC, *1700–06/ 07*, 82, 1933; *1707–11*, 85, 1935; *1711–15*, 97, 1942; *1715–19*, 101, 1946.

54. St Helens Local History and Archives Library: Hardshaw meeting register on micro-film of LRO MFI/51.

55. Lewis, 'Demographic and Occupational Structure', p. 246, Figures 8.2 and 8.3.

56. Apprenticeship records: LplRO 352/CLE/REG 4/1. See Rawling, 'Rise of Liverpool', pp. 181, Figure 8.1, 182.

57. See 'Women in the Port Town Economy' in chapter 3 below.

58. D. Souden, 'Movers and Stayers in Family Reconstitution Population', *LPS*, 33, 1984, pp. 11–28.

59. Souden, 'Movers and Stayers', p. 13.

60. Souden, 'Movers and Stayers', pp. 11–13. For further criticisms of this approach see K. D. M. Snell, 'Parish Registration and the study of labour mobility', *LPS*, 33, 1984, pp. 33–34; R. S. Schofield, 'Traffic in Corpses: some evidence from Barming, Kent 1788-1812', *LPS*, 33, 1984, pp. 49–50.

61. Souden, 'Movers and Stayers', pp. 23–27.

62. G. W. Oxley, 'The administration of the old Poor Law in the West Derby Hundred of Lancashire, 1601–1837', unpublished MA dissertation, University of Liverpool, 1966; Rawling, 'Rise of Liverpool', pp. 186–88.

63. Snell identifies such shortfall in burial registration as a major flaw in Souden's approach, based on inferred residence from parish registration. Snell, 'Parish Registration', pp. 33–34. Further comments are found in Schofield, 'Traffic in Corpses', p. 49.

64. For example, see D. E. Ascott, 'Wealth and Community: Liverpool, 1660–1760', unpublished PhD thesis, University of Liverpool, 1996, Fig. 4.4: 'Burials, home and away, recorded in Anglican Registers'; H. Peet, ed., *Liverpool Vestry Books 1681–1834*, vol. 1, Liverpool, 1912.

65. F. Lewis, 'Studying Urban Mobility: the possibilities for family reconstitution', *LPS*, 55, 1995, pp. 62–65.

66. J. Touzeau, *The Rise and Progress of Liverpool from 1551 to 1835*, Liverpool, 1910, p. 327.

67. Touzeau, *Rise and Progress of Liverpool*, p. 388.

3

Occupation: Structure, Mobility and Succession

From contemporary accounts and from the extensive literature covering aspects of the port's development, particularly from the later eighteenth century onwards, Liverpool's oceanic trading role in the regional, national and international economy has been well recognised. However, characterisation of Liverpool solely as a 'port town' overlooks the detailed composition of the broad economic base that developed in the period 1660–1760, and perhaps the variety of this economy can in no better way be gauged than by the diversity of trades and occupations practised by the town's inhabitants.

Occupation is a well-established tool of early modern historians, who often face a lack of more direct evidence for economic activity and social structure. Little material is available on the major industries or services of most towns: there are few business archives or centrally collected statistics before the later nineteenth century, and often the only quantitative approach to economic activity is to assess the number of people working in particular trades. Fortunately, various sources exist in which the recording of individuals' occupations was required or encouraged for identification purposes, and analysis and critique of this material has produced an extensive range of historical work.[1]

The first section of this chapter offers a brief survey of the optimum sources for an occupational study of Liverpool followed by the adoption of an appropriate method for classification and analysis of complex employment patterns. The need for refinement of the selected approach is then considered with particular reference to employment in the maritime sector, which was crucial to Liverpool but not necessarily prominent in the aggregate analysis of key sources. The rest of the chapter adopts a more qualitative multi-source linkage technique in tackling other questions that are central to understanding work and society in a rapidly growing and changing town – women's employment, and the difficult but fundamental issues of occupational plurality, mobility and stability.

Evidence and Interpretation

Systematic occupational analysis requires sources that are long-running, consistently high in quality and continuity of recording, and without significant bias or omission of particular sectors of the community. The two sources best meeting these criteria for early modern Liverpool are parish registers and probate material. Although varying in completeness, occupational information was recorded in each throughout the seventeenth and eighteenth centuries. These records also offer the opportunity to analyse occupational change at both the aggregate and individual level and to compare occupational trends between the two sources.[2]

Although purely intended as a chronicle of births, marriages and deaths, many parish registers also record the occupation of the male adults involved, whether fathers, bridegrooms or the deceased (women were recorded almost exclusively by marital status). There was, in fact, no requirement to record occupation in the baptism register until Rose's Act of 1813 and, although the recording of occupation may have become more consistent from 1754 under Hardwicke's Marriage Act, it was not obligatory. Subject to swings in consistency and quality, parish registers are generally a useful, long-running source of information and in many studies have provided a reasonably adequate route into the occupational structures of the parish they served.[3] In the case of Liverpool, this task is made more rewarding by the relatively high standard and consistency of registration from the early eighteenth century onwards.[4] Prior to the early years of the eighteenth century, conclusions must be more speculative given that there are considerably fewer register entries from which to draw, and registration quality, in terms of stated employment, was highly erratic.[5]

Probate material is the second key source of occupational data. A will usually contained occupational or status information in its preamble. Testators customarily began with statements identifying themselves and including an occupation or status. The terminology of this did not always equate with the opinions of the friends or neighbours who drew up an inventory, or of the officials who raised other probate documents, but differences were usually of degree. Women, unfortunately, used only their marital status. Clearly, testamentary evidence has drawbacks of exclusion and bias in that only a fraction of the populace is represented by testators. The will-making population will be weighted towards property-owning older men – propertied, because only those with property could leave it and the expense of probate would have been avoided by lesser people; older, because will-making tended to be a deathbed activity; and men because, by law, only free adult males and unmarried women 'of sound mind' could make wills.

The wills of all testators self-designated as 'of Liverpool' are analysed.

These may include mariners of foreign origin and unspecified association with Liverpool, and local people all of whose real estate was in adjoining townships and who appear to be the individuals described in parish burial registers as 'of' that same place. Excluded are an indeterminate number of business and professional men who participated in the social and economic life of Liverpool but invested their money and moved their abode to estates elsewhere, thus being lost to the ranks of Liverpool testators.

Never intended as records of employment, numerous problems arise in using probate material and parish registers as sources for occupational analysis. For example, self-image might lead a testator to claim a different title from that accorded him in the burial register. With event details often written up in the parish registers at a later date, it was not inconceivable that the parish official, having time to contemplate the true identity of his subject, diminished or embellished the said individual's position accordingly.

Occupational titles are also known to have undergone change through time and to have varied geographically. This problem is particularly vexing in considering the employment structure of a town experiencing rapid economic development, where the traditional labels given to small-scale craftsmen could later hide functional standing. For example, the difficulties in defining wholesale and retail activities are notable.[6] Any grouping of occupations must therefore be flexible and sympathetic to the period in question and to the changing structures and the emerging rationale behind an early industrialising economy.

Both parish registers and wills usually provide only one occupational designation per entry, when it has been generally recognised that the town workers of pre-industrial England often performed multiple tasks and had a variety of subsistence alternatives. Evidence from Liverpool probate documents would suggest that the workforce had a wide variety of employment sources open to them and many undertook a number of income-generating activities. Occasional examples of dual occupation create some confusion over the true emphasis of employment type. This may be by name, as in 'slater and plasterer', or over the nature of a particular trade. A recurring example is the 'ship's carpenter'. Is he a sailor who performs carpentry tasks aboard ship or is he essentially a craftsman who finds his working environment aboard a vessel? From extended record linkage covering significant periods in the individual's working life, it is often possible to probe the true nature of occupational labels and identify the essential character of employment. However, this can only be achieved for a limited subset of the population and so careful consideration must be given to such cases when considering placement within a classification scheme. Employment descriptions may be accompanied or replaced by social status or socio-occupational labels. Such designations tend to occur at both extremes of the social scale and have the dual effect of masking true occupational identity while offering some indication of social standing.

A further problem is that the surviving sources omit many economically active people. This inadequacy is acute as regards female employment. Both wills and parish registers are overwhelmingly limited to recording marital status, although there may be incidental occupational information within an individual's probate documents. Only a handful of parish register entries record female occupation in its own right, thus providing one of the least fruitful sources in gauging the nature and extent of female participation in the workforce, a problem common to many studies of occupation based upon register entries.[7] In addition, the occupations of some men were not recorded. Casual workers, men between jobs, or those at points in the life-cycle where employment was still undecided or even at an end would not necessarily record occupation. Such situations can often be supposed in the parish registers, particularly in marriage and burial records. The problem is less acute when considering willmakers since occupation or status was often included in probate material such as inventories or accounts.

Register evidence must also be considered in terms of religious denomination.[8] Anglican parish register coverage in Liverpool was generally of a high standard, at least from the early eighteenth century onwards, with very few years omitted or of suspiciously low quality. However, only those recording vital events in the Anglican parish registers are included in the following occupational analysis. The strong nonconformist body in the region, particularly from the early to mid decades of the eighteenth century onwards, meant that Anglican parish registers record a smaller percentage of births and deaths in southwest Lancashire than the national average – 97 per cent of deaths and just under 84 per cent of births for the period 1660–1760 in Liverpool.[9] Among the willmakers of the period are included nonconformists of various persuasions constituting almost 8 per cent of the total. However, nonconformity did not necessarily mean that individuals went unrecorded in the Anglican registers: Presbyterians and Roman Catholics were recorded, particularly for burial, in Anglican registers.[10]

Though the recording of occupation would seem at times to have been consistently good, what of the actual range of occupations involved? From a mere handful of core activities in mid-seventeenth-century Liverpool, economic diversification and specialisation within trades and sectors led, here as elsewhere, to a burgeoning variety of employment opportunities by the mid-eighteenth century. To enable observations to be made on the occupational structure of the town this assemblage of trades and occupations must be broken down and classified into groups based upon some underlying principle.

Several difficulties arise in devising a classification system that is logical in its aim and structure and yet suitable for, and sympathetic to, the character of the particular population in question. This study uses a version of Langton's classification scheme.[11] The eight basic occupational categories of this scheme are outlined in Figure 3.1, with categories sub-divided according to type of material processed or goods manufactured. These broad bands can be further disaggregated according to specific raw material employed. From this, some crude notions of wealth and status can be gained; an obvious example would be between goldsmiths and pewterers. Non-manufacturing headings are similarly broken down according to type of service rendered or role fulfilled, with separate sections dealing with specialist retail and specialist wholesale activities. A further ninth category has been added to accommodate those unidentified.

The use of such a comprehensive classification system in this context has several advantages. Once applied to the Liverpool data, direct comparisons can be made with a number of other contemporary locations.[12] Considering Liverpool's transition from a modest settlement in the seventeenth century to a major provincial centre by the mid-

Figure 3.1 *Occupational classification scheme*

I Primary occupations	*IV Transport*
A. Agriculture	A. Ocean and inland
B. Fishing	B. Land
C. Mineral Extraction	
II Building	*V Dealing*
A. Houses etc.	A. Specialist retail
B. Roads	B. Specialist wholesale
	C. Itinerant
	D. Indefinite
III Manufacture	*VI Public & professional service*
A. Tools and instruments	A. Public service
B. Shipbuilding	B. Professional service
C. Clothing	
D. Victualing	*VII Menial and domestic service*
E. Iron	
F. Non-ferrous metals	*VIII Status or other description*
G. Earthenware	
H. Glass	*IX Unidentified*
I. Furs and leather	
J. Glue, tallow	
K. Wood	
L. Textiles	

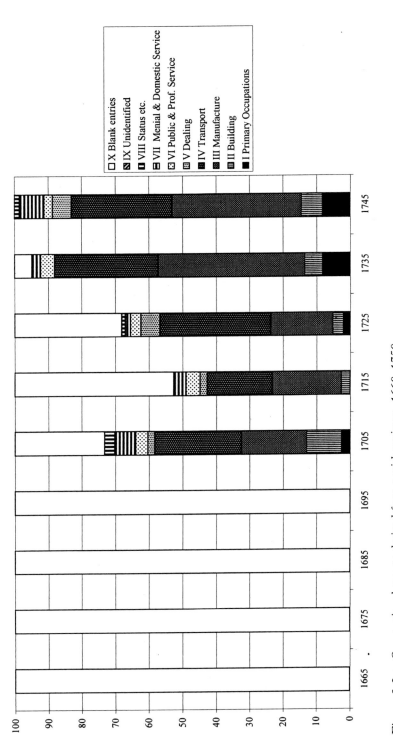

Figure 3.2.a Occupational groups derived from parish registers, 1660–1750
Adult male marriage

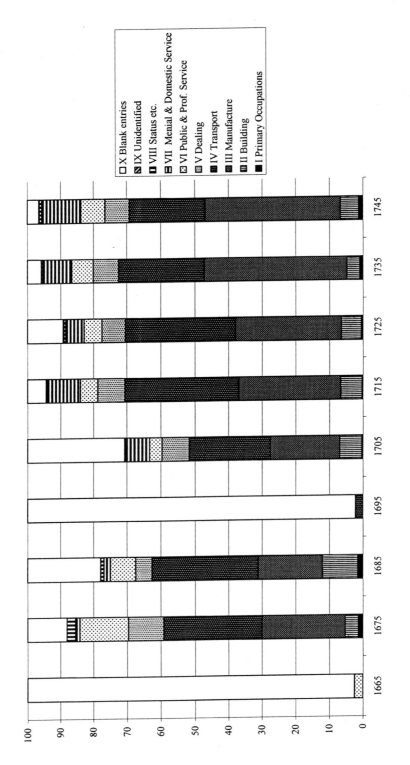

Figure 3.2.b *Occupational groups derived from parish registers, 1660–1750*
Child baptism – burial

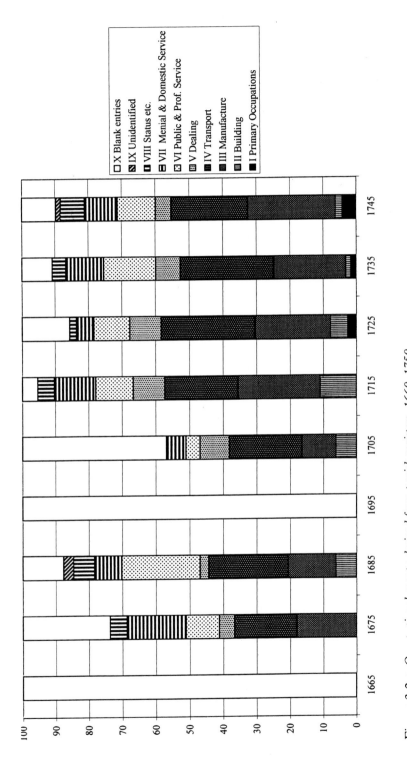

Figure 3.2.c *Occupational groups derived from parish registers, 1660–1750*
Adult male burial

eighteenth, the classification scheme is both detailed and flexible enough to accommodate the changing nature of the economic profile. With simplification, a recurring theme in the literature on classification, the beauty of this scheme lies in its comprehensive structure and provision for breaking broad categories down to quite minute proportions so that even individual professions can be scrutinised. It thus allows for both generalised statements and very specific observations to be made on the occupational structure through time.

In the case of the parish registers, a general overview of those recorded with occupation in the registers can be gained from a simple head-count, grouped according to the classification categories outlined above. This approach works reasonably well for marriage and adult burial registers since an individual was relatively unlikely to record more than one marriage or adult burial in the space of a year. Complications emerge when the approach is applied to records relating to individual children, since it was quite possible that a child could be both baptised and buried within a twelve-month period and thus leave multiple references to the father's occupation in respective parish registers. Therefore, if using combined child baptism and child burial registers, it becomes necessary to sift out such multiple references Although time-consuming, the exercise proves revealing. For example, before adjustment, 840 occupations are recorded in the 1735 baptism/burial composite register profile. After adjustment the number falls to 735, a loss of 105, some 12.5 per cent of the original total. The resulting profile is perhaps most representative of the working population since it contains the greatest number of entries of a register type per year and those individuals represented were probably in the most active period of their employment years. The three profiles are shown in Figure 3.2 for mid-decade years.[13]

Though the three register profiles confirm a similar overall distribution and character of employment types, certain subtle differences in the pattern of occupational distribution can be seen between the register sources. The profile based upon adult male burial records exhibits similarly high proportions in the manufacturing and transport categories, although in relative terms the percentage of entries in the latter category is not as high as in the two other profiles. Some downward bias may be attributed to sailors and mariners lost at sea. The intermediate profile, a composite of father's occupation recorded in child baptism and child burial entries, is perhaps most revealing. The following discussion particularly highlights some of the detailed categories that are subsumed in the larger classification. For further clarification, information from marriage registers is included where appropriate, and the profile of willmakers (Figure 3.3) is juxtaposed with that derived from adult male burials for another comparative perspective.

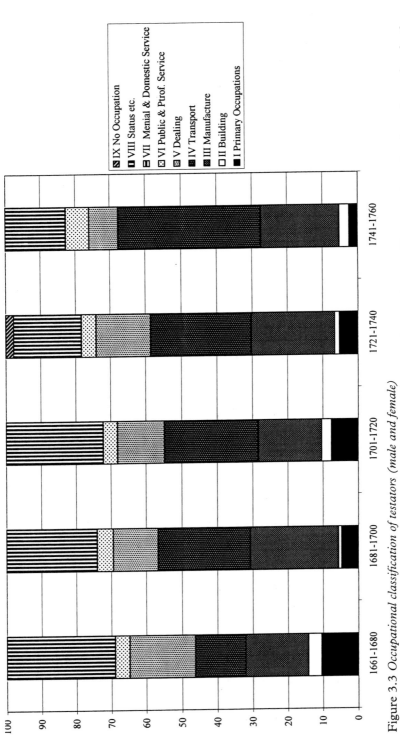

Figure 3.3 *Occupational classification of testators (male and female)*

Note: the overwhelming majority of women are classified by marital status – spinster, wives or widows – and are therefore subsumed under the status category

Liverpool Employment: a Broad Profile

By far the most dominant single category of Liverpool occupation is that of 'transport', in particular 'ocean and inland' containing the sailor/mariner group, with 20 to 30 per cent of the workforce over the whole 90-year period. Transport appears even more dominant in the testamentary profile, because of the large number of testators lost 'at, or beyond the sea', and who were therefore not buried in Liverpool.[14] Seventy-two are known as such, out of a total of 492 willmakers without a burial record and in potentially seagoing occupations. Although seafaring testators are known to have included transients of several nationalities, the majority of deaths abroad were of Liverpudlians. More detailed discussion of the maritime sector will be offered in the following section.

The next major group is that of 'manufacture' which produces broadly similar profiles in testamentary and adult male burial sources. Among testators this sector varied only within the range 18 to 23 per cent from 1661–1760. However, the manufacturing category in adult male burials exhibits the greatest difference from the profile based on child baptism and burial records. 'Manufacturing' in the latter had more than 40 per cent share in 1735, marginally less ten years later. A number of influential categories emerge from that optimum source.

Though integral to the success of the trading fleet, shipbuilding in eighteenth-century Liverpool was not practised on the scale found in other eighteenth-century ports, in particular Newcastle and Bristol.[15] It experienced varying fortune, maintaining between 8–10 per cent of the manufacturing workforce from the 1720s onwards. Producers of ancillary products, such as rope, enjoyed sustained success from the beginning of the eighteenth century. At the base of that sector, sailmakers enjoyed a more modest but consistent share over the same period possibly because Warrington, twenty miles upriver, specialised in sailmaking.

Metalworking, in both base and precious materials, fluctuated around the 1 per cent mark in the eighteenth century, with anchorsmiths in the former category and gold- and silver-smiths in the latter. Woodworking, principally joiners and carpenters, was an increasingly buoyant sector by the mid-eighteenth century. Such workers were probably assured of almost continuous employment, owing to the building boom in the south of the town and the erection of docks and warehouses from the 1700s onwards. However, much of the accompanying unskilled casual labour is contained within 'menial and domestic service' and is therefore not so immediately apparent. Also evident in the larger profile, and associated with the building sector, were the skilled trades involved in building construction; the masons, bricklayers and brickmakers.

Clothing manufacture provided one of the mainstays of the manufacturing sector. Shoemakers and cobblers were found in large numbers, a characteristic common to many pre-industrial towns. Indeed, it is thought that the shoemakers of Liverpool were not only supplying the domestic market, but also producing for export to the colonies.[16]

Tool and instrument manufacture, including the innovatory watch- and clock-makers of the period, and those producing nautical instruments, maintained a steady employment share of around 5 per cent from the late seventeenth to the mid-eighteenth century. Another local specialism, earthenware production, held from 1 to 3 per cent of the manufacturing workforce from the second decade of the eighteenth century onwards, although by the late eighteenth century the industry generally was in decline.[17]

Food and drink preparation, including the refining of imported sugar cargoes, though fluctuating in extent, was one of the chief manu- facturing groups, complemented by those in food and drink production and purveyance. Much of this success was no doubt attributable to the many ale-house keepers and brewers of the town. Such consumption habits were complemented by the wares of the tobacconists, a group that proliferated in the eighteenth century, supplied by Liverpool's trade links and geared to the growing market for luxury goods.

Primary occupations appear to have played a minor role throughout the period, although contact with the agricultural hinterland was maintained by those wishing to register vital events in Liverpool. In particular, the profile based upon male marriage entries indicates a relatively high proportion of agricultural workers, confirming that hinterland agricultural workers came to the town to celebrate marriage. Evidence from wills shows some discrepancies, with the proportion of agriculturalist testators declining unevenly through the period from a maximum 10 per cent, while burials in this category grow from nothing to a maximum of 6 per cent in the 1740s. There are two elements of explanation. First, testators used 'yeoman' as a label of status, but they were often registered for burial under another, occupational label. Secondly, testators in this sector frequently owned land in adjoining townships and were buried in neighbouring parishes, and therefore did not appear in the Liverpool burial registers.

The categories of 'dealing', including 'specialist wholesale' and 'specialist retail', constitute two of the occupational groups most difficult to identify as previously suggested; thus totals classified under the general wholesale heading appear somewhat depleted. However, in the child baptism/burial source 'retail' food and drink varied from 2 to 7 per cent over the period, with minor shares held by 'cloth and clothing', and other materials. The relatively high proportion in the 'specialist wholesale indefinite' category (between 1 and 5 per cent) may be explained by the inclusion of merchants, and to a minor extent, factors and dealers. Unfortunately, tracing the rise of this body from the parish registers is somewhat frustrated by the use of labels such as 'Mr' or 'Esquire' rather then the direct designation 'merchant'. Linkage of merchant testators to their burial records suggests that registration tended to favour civic status in preference to occupation. In a period when the ranks of councillors and aldermen were increasingly filled by merchants, these individuals appear in wills as merchants but in parish registers under public office, explaining why the dealing sector never looms as large in the burials as among testators. This reflects a national trend remarked elsewhere.[18]

Obviously, this creates the opposite trend for those in 'public and professional service' especially during the seventeenth century – these individuals are over-represented in burials and under-represented in wills. 'Public and professional service' also contained the majority of port officials and custom inspectors, and held between 1 to 2 per cent of the workforce, from child baptism/burial records, throughout the eighteenth century. Like the merchant category, the increasing share of this group can be traced from the early eighteenth century onwards when the demand for a bureaucratic and business infrastructure grew. 'Church, law and education' maintained a small but influential share, along with the doctors and physicians of the period.

However, those with a 'status' ascription are not best represented by the otherwise optimum source: at 1 to 2 per cent in the seventeenth century and declining thereafter, they contrast with just under 10 per cent reached in adult burials and male willmakers. Inflation of status through the period could have been reflected in all registers but gentility becoming increasingly ascribed to wealth would favour older men with years of accumulation.

At the other end of the social scale, 'menial and domestic service', dominated by household servants, rose from 1 to 2 per cent to reach 10 to12 per cent by 1745, and although quantified here in terms of male workers, it was also a major employment source for women. As would be expected, less than 1 per cent of testators were in this category, and none before 1721. This is the sector in which the greatest discrepancy was anticipated and where it is most attributable to the wealth bias of testators.

This broad profile demonstrates the range of occupation in Liverpool, and establishes the framework for closer analysis. Clearly, all the sectors described above could be subjected to more detailed investigation, but Liverpool belies the assertion that 'to look at the pre-industrial towns is thus to look at an unspecialised economy'.[19] Indeed it has been stated that Liverpool 'shifted significantly towards being a major manufacturing town during the early canal age … and then back again to a more monolithic seaport'.[20] A particular focus on employment related to Liverpool's port function is most necessary and follows in the next section.

The Maritime Sector

While enabling comparison with the economic structure of other early modern towns, the occupational classification applied above is less adequate for revealing the port aspects of the Liverpool economy. As stated earlier, shipping, seagoing and maritime activities warrant definition and identification in their own right and to enable comparison with other studies of port populations.[21] Throughout the period nearly every aspect of Liverpool's economic life was touched by the sea, but the importance of this aspect may be overlooked if occupations relating to maritime activity are scattered among diverse classification categories. Certain groups will be obvious by their influence; for example, the sailor/mariner cluster swells the size of the 'transport' category. However, many craftsmen such as shipwrights, sailmakers and coopers, were also seagoing although lost in the general throng of 'manufacture'. The first element of the term 'public and professional' undoubtedly concealed seafarers behind their civic function, while the second element encompassed ships' surgeons. More importantly 'dealing' included merchants who were, for at least half the period, likely to have emerged from the ranks of master mariners and to be still engaged in seagoing trade.

Seafaring was, however, only one aspect of the port function. As specific crafts and trades had distinct shipping associations, so certain services such as waterside carting were port-orientated. The totality of port administration by Customs personnel must also be included. With this in mind, a number of occupations that would seem to epitomise the maritime influence on Liverpool's economic structure have been re-classified and are assembled under three broad groupings, shown below.[22]

Group 1 sailors and mariners
Group 2 those involved in the building and outfitting of vessels
Group 3 those involved in the administration of the port and related businesses

Although overwhelming by their considerable presence, sailors and mariners constituted but one element of the town's maritime community. To further investigate those involved in the port and its business, three profiles have been constructed for mid-decade years based upon male burial, male marriage and child baptism-burial (adjusted) occupation entries categorised according to the 'port classification'. Results shown in Figure 3.4 are expressed as percentages of the total number of register entries (including blank entries) for particular years.[23]

As with the larger classification scheme, slight differences between register types can be seen, but across each of the three profiles the overall impression is one of dominance by the sailor/mariner group throughout the period. From a general increase in the overall share of the three categories combined within the total profile, it is also possible to gain a clearer understanding of the timing of Liverpool's engagement in large-scale oceanic ventures. This dramatic shift from small-scale trading and coastal traffic to oceanic passage is most obviously reflected in the growing presence of the port business and administration sector from the early decades of the eighteenth century onwards, and in the sustained share of those trades and industries supporting the shipping fleet within the total workforce.

Curiously, within the profile based upon male marriage records, no entries are found in the 'Port Administration' category from the 1720s onwards, perhaps reflecting the importance of such occupations and the need to employ seasoned workers, in particular older adult males, shown to be dominant in this sector in the third figure: adult male burials.

The application of this classification to testators (Table 3.1) reveals that over the whole period more than half the male willmakers were employed in a port-related occupation, predominantly that of mariner. As would be expected, however, the nature of maritime employment made it less likely that mariners would be buried in the town, so there is a discrepancy between the figures in Table 3.1 and the adult male burial figures in Table 3.2. Mariners do appear in a higher proportion in the figures for child baptism and burial.

Mariners accounted for a third to a half of testators throughout the period after 1680. In the first twenty years, 1661–1680, the much lower proportion of mariners may be attributable to the relative unimportance of the port, which is mirrored in the lack of administrative personnel: the number of such Customs officials grew steadily, particularly in the eighteenth century. Between 1741 and 1760 the mariner group grew threefold over the previous twenty-year period and reached 50 per cent of testators, a reflection of Liverpool's mid-eighteenth-century maritime capacity.

The shipbuilding and allied trades did not increase markedly in numbers until the last forty years of the period, although the category's share of testators was greatest between 1661 and 1680, which seems due to the generally low numbers in that period cohort. Nonetheless the proportion of port-related trades does run counter to the thesis of a relatively unimportant port function in the post-Restoration years. There are several possible explanations for shipbuilding and associated

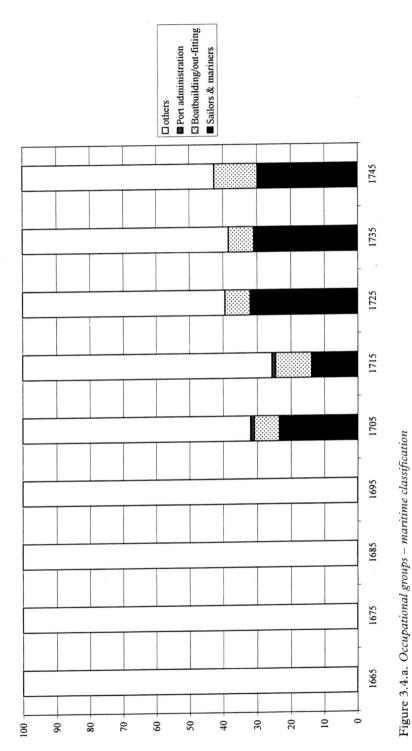

Figure 3.4.a. Occupational groups – maritime classification
Adult male marriage

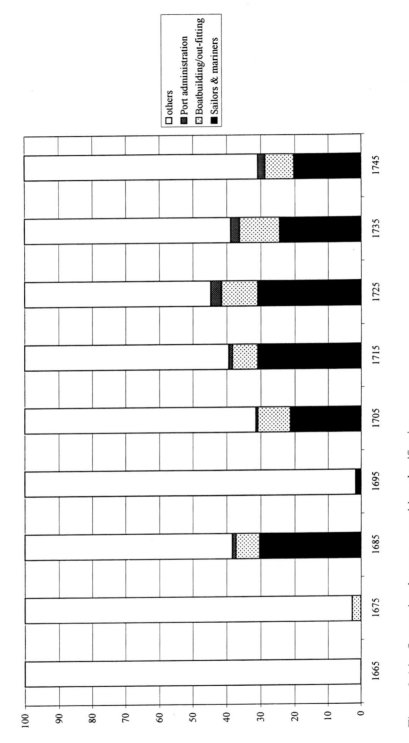

Figure 3.4.b. *Occupational groups – maritime classification*
Child baptism – burial

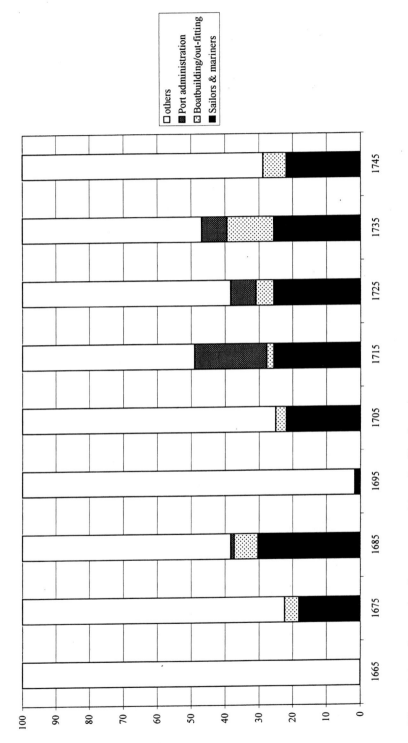

Figure 3.4.c. *Occupational groups – maritime classification*
Adult male burial

Table 3.1 *Testators in port-related occupations expressed as percentage within period cohorts*

	1661–80		1681–1700		1701–20		1721–40		1741–60		1661–1760	
	N	%	N	%	N	%	N	%	N	%	N	%
Mariners	11	18	39	34.5	70	35.3	124	35.6	372	50.9	616	42.5
Trades	6	9.8	9	7.7	9	4.5	24	6.9	44	6.0	93	6.4
Adminis-tration	–	–	1	0.9	4	2.0	5	1.4	14	1.9	24	1.7
Others	44	78.2	64	57.9	115	59.2	195	56.1	301	41.2	718	49.4
Total testators	61		113		198		348		731		1451	

Source: Liverpool men's wills 1661–1760; Ascott, 'Wealth and Community', Table 4.1.

Table 3.2 *Decedents in port-related occupations (percentage terms)*

	1665	1675	1685	1695	1705	1715	1725	1735	1745
Mariners	–	16.7	24.2	–	22.4	25.0	23.7	25.0	21.2
Trades	–	0	9.1	–	3.5	2.4	4.6	13.5	7.8
Administration	–	0	0	–	0	1.2	6.9	7.7	0
Others	–	83.3	66.7	–	74.1	71.4	64.8	53.8	71.0
Total burials	20	6	33	17	85	84	131	104	193

Source: Lewis, 'Demographic and Occupational Structure of Liverpool', Figure 3.4
Note: occupational data deficient for 1665 and 1695.

trades appearing disproportionate to the later growth of the port. For example, the 'loss' of ropemakers under the status usage of 'yeoman' seems prevalent around the turn of the century; the surge in urban building after 1720 may have absorbed or disguised in the records those with dual proficiency, such as the carpenters; and lastly, although ships were built for the Royal Navy, Liverpool was never a naval port with all the auxiliary activities. Moreover, shipbuilding did not in general increase in parallel with trade as the eighteenth century advanced because, as previously stated, Plantation-built vessels were appreciably cheaper for all but the 1730s.[24]

'Boatbuilding and outfitting' includes from 5 to 10 per cent of testators, but the somewhat greater range of 3 to 13 per cent of decedents. The difference may be related to wealth or testamentary practice, insofar as not all those buried would have made wills. It is also affected by the vagaries of occupational ascription in the registers, where 'carpenter', for example, could be 'house carpenter' or 'shipcarpenter'. Information within the testamentary evidence invariably resolved that conundrum among testators.

'Administration' only features in the burial records in 1715, 1725 and 1735 increasing from 3 to 9 per cent, whereas testators feature in all periods except 1660–1680, increasing in number from one to fourteen individuals, but never constituting more than 2 per cent. The discrepancy may be attributable to the structure of the Customs service and recruitment of its different levels of personnel. The senior Customs officers were required to be men without local connections, some of whom chose to be buried whence they came, while others were buried as 'gentleman'. This would account for the existence of wills but lack of burials in the first half of the period. There was more local recruitment to the lower-echelon Customs posts, which proliferated in the eighteenth century. Such individuals were more likely to have local burial and less likely to leave wills. Otherwise, and even more simply, it might be that Customs personnel did not die in the particular years in focus.

Seagoing was necessary for many other than the obvious mariners. Some wills made specific mention of voyages: for example, the merchant Morecroft Kirks was mentioned in a letter of 1744 as 'going abroad to Jamaica'.[25] Mariners used the formulation of consigning their bodies 'to earth or sea' in the preambles to their wills, as did tradesmen and professionals whose occupations involved seafaring. A total of 838 men (57 per cent of testators) were thus identified. As would be expected, most were seafarers (726), but a significant minority had other occupations.

Mariners had a propensity to make wills that was connected with the obvious dangers of their occupation. These wills are particularly valuable in giving information about individuals who might otherwise have left no trace in Liverpool records. The corrective which this testamentary population makes to an under-representation of mariners in the burial records is salutary, not so much in its size as in drawing attention to the shortfall. Accordingly, in view of the possible influence on many aspects of subsequent analysis, it seems essential to highlight the size and significance of this group. The maritime influence was paramount in Liverpool in absolute numbers and in the importance of this influence to many facets of the town's development. The mariner group epitomises Liverpool's rise from a concentration on coastal trade in 1660 to becoming the leading provincial port in the overseas trade of the later eighteenth century. The predominance of the maritime sector also had considerable implications for Liverpudlians who did not go to sea. Most obviously, a large number of absent maritime male workers created a particular occupational environment for women, and the next section considers this in more detail.

Women in the Port Town Economy

Perhaps one of the most unfortunate omissions of the pre-statistical era for the modern economic historian is the recording of female employment and thus an adequate understanding of women and their role in the workforce.[26] The direct evidence for women's occupations is minimal in Liverpool. In the parish registers between 1660 and 1750, female employment is rarely stated. In almost 20,000 marriage and burial records combined, less than 20 state female occupation. Evidence relates to midwives, occasional reference to those in service, a number of woman housekeepers referred to by those in lodgings, and a few isolated curiosities: Liverpool could boast a *comedian* and *brewer* among its female workpeople. From such evidence, a very limited indication of female participation in the workforce is confirmed. It is also impossible to identify whether the employment that women stated was full- or part-time.

Although doubtless very under-recorded, domestic service appears the largest employment sector, with 11 cases out of the total 17. The importance of this sector for women is further emphasised when the relative share of males within the domestic service category is considered. By the beginning of the eighteenth century the parish registers give the impression that approximately 7 per cent of the male workforce was engaged in menial or domestic service. In the following decades, although undergoing some fluctuation, this relative share rose to almost 12 per cent, thus highlighting the category as one of significant importance in the employment profile of adult males within the Liverpool workforce. A comparison is possible with the proportion of London's population in domestic service between 1660 and 1750: the ratio was close to four women to every man for much of the period.[27] Earle's small sample of London women between 1695 and 1725 revealed that 70 per cent worked full- or part-time, of whom 25 per cent, predominantly younger women, were domestic servants.[28] Enumerations of provincial towns during the late 1690s reveal a notable predominance of women in domestic service.[29] Women's employment of necessity might have had a more significant service element in the maritime economy of Liverpool than in larger towns with less vulnerable male employment.

Direct evidence for female employment in the probate material is also limited. Apart from legacies to servants, it is largely restricted to the later years when some female beneficiaries of indigent seamen were identified as 'landlady' or 'huckster', as in the wills of Antonio Roredrigu (1751) and Henry Roney (1749).[30] Thus the economic activity of female testators is recovered piecemeal and usually indirectly. Cicely Cooke, a deserted wife, was an exception. Hyperbole notwithstanding, the covering letter with which she prefixed her will chronicles her success as a baker.[31] Indirect evidence is therefore indispensable for discovering women's economic activity but must be utilised with due care. Items in a probate inventory may point to the occupation of the deceased, but there is danger of error in making such deductions: a 'midwife's stool and instruments' might mean that Margaret Heald was a midwife, but the high value of her estate at £817.7s. suggests either little need to practise or great skill and profit.

Evidence of businesswomen is also thinner than in other places. Liverpool never developed a strong guild system to generate records of women free to trade as 'feme sole', which was still occurring in London at this date.[32] Indeed, Katherine Cottingham, applying in 1703 'to follow the trade of milliner', was the only woman seeking permission to trade in Liverpool during the half century after the Restoration.[33] Alice Summerset's millinery apprenticeship is not recorded as her mother's will of 1738 suggests.[34] However, Mrs Gildus may well have been shopkeeping while her husband practised surgery, as his inventory included 'an account of Mrs Esther Gildus shop goods [haberdashery]'. In Liverpool it could be yet another instance of the difference between law and practice, remarked both in Britain and abroad.[35] In 1708 four women were charged on 'stock' and a further eight women were rated for shops.[36] Other female shopkeepers can be identified from inventories which included stock-in-trade: Jane Howard's haberdashery stock, valued in 1679, comprised over 80 per cent of her £43.10s.11d personalty; in 1741 Mary Farrington had a mere £2 worth of 'thread and other shop goods'. Elizabeth Catterall, who was the widow of John, variously chapman and glover, left similar evidence. She bequeathed to her son 'stockins in the shop', and he in turn was buried in 1720 as 'William Catteral, hosier'.

Brewing in the eighteenth century was undertaken by private households as well as in large-scale purpose-built brewhouses.[37] Women's involvement in commercial brewing is also revealed: Joyce Scaresbrick was undoubtedly responsible for the brewing enterprise while her husband sailed the seas, and he eventually left her the wherewithal. John Scaresbrick described himself as a mariner in his will, but a quarter of his inventoried wealth was in brewing utensils and ingredients, and his burial record describes him as a brewer. The bequests and instructions left by male testators identify this occupation for other widows, and in several instances suggest that they practised while wives. Richard Rimmer left brewing gear and malt to his widow, Anne. Margery Mackmullen and Margaret Gallaspy, both of whose inventories point to commercial brewing, had also been married to seafarers. A commercial role as brewer or maltster is suggested by the inventories of eight women exemplified by Phoebe Winfield, who had brewhouse equipment valued at £28 and malt worth £60.[38]

Apart from brewing, the businesses to be continued by widows throughout the period included those of a pewterer, for which Alice Jones was left all necessary equipment in 1658; a pipemaker, the option offered by Edward Lyon in 1708; and the butcher's business of James Mercer in 1749, 'if she [Mary] can do it Without Wast and Diminution thereof'.[39] Jane Harper continued the cooperage of her late husband, Richard, for fifteen years after his death in 1720. Anne Bushell maintained shipping interests for ten years after the death of her husband, William. The mercantile activities of Anne Yewdall continued for at least five years after the demise of Jeremiah.[40] Elizabeth Sheilds, although demoted to 'silversmith' when taking over the business of her goldsmith husband, Robert, also traded for thirteen years. She was patronised by the local gentry and took her own apprentice.[41] Cicely Cooke was paid for bread by the Vestry in 1752, and 'Mrs Eaton, bookseller' charged the Vestry annual sums from 1711 to 1722. She was Ann, widow of Joseph Eaton, who had himself supplied books and stationery from 1693 to his death in 1710.[42] Few others were accorded an occupation and whether payments to women were incidental earnings or for a full-time occupation is impossible to gauge. A number of named women were paid to care for pauper children or the sick during the late seventeenth century, after which this ever-growing parish burden was recorded as a lump sum. Elizabeth Kaye apparently did church laundry from 1719 to 1758.[43]

The economic success of some of these women can be assessed from their own wills and inventories. Widows may have been best placed to further family fortune and continue the wealth creation of their husbands by virtue of their entitlement to 'thirds', possibly the largest single share of an estate. The impressive Anne Bushell had maintained if not enhanced the share of shipping interests left to her by her husband. William Bushell's inventory of 1676 recorded 'parts of 8 ships and a lighter', but his will specified parts of three named ships to his sons: thus the six ships named in Anne's will ten years later were either different vessels or included a further purchase. Roger Jones left equipment, stock and raw materials worth £196 in 1658, but seven years later, his widow, Alice, left similar items on a lesser scale to approximately two-thirds the value. Elizabeth Sheilds' estate included 'all appurtenances of the gold-smiths business' but was not appraised. Elizabeth, like so many others, 'may have run the business for years but she was described in her will simply as widow'.[44] Another successful widow was Margery Formby, with a 16-room establishment including a cellar stocked with sack, wine, beer and ale. She was in a position during life to celebrate the Corporation's purchase of the town's fee farm by adding a silver tobacco box to the civic plate, and in death she augmented this with a silver tankard to be engraved: 'A gift from Margery Formby to the town of Liverpool'.[45]

Whereas explicit evidence of distinct occupations can be recovered for some women, data available for other economic activity are also valuable. Women's roles in various fields of investment and in the capital market were key contributions to economic development, and as significant as orthodox occupations. Such roles for women are thought to suggest that 'wealthier women had long found trade an unappetizing option'.[46]

In particular, there is substantial evidence of women as rentiers. Much of their multiple property holding, both in Liverpool and elsewhere, was let or sublet. This economic role of women has been analysed in London, where 'widows quite clearly dominate the female property market, especially the ownership of houses, from which they could draw a rental income'.[47] In Liverpool the 1708 rate includes 68 women assessed for property tenanted by others.[48] It is apparent that many women held property in their own right by inheritance or by purchase when not under coverture. Jane Alcock left a leasehold 'message and tenement in Dublin'. This may have been left to her outright by her first husband, John Eccleston, because all realty of her husband, Edward Alcock, was left to their mutual children. Jane also left appreciable further 'real' estate: in southwest Lancashire, a property at Aughton and the rents of land in Crosby; in Liverpool, four leasehold messuages with tenements, three houses and two crofts, three lands in the Townfield, three butts belonging to one messuage presumed a burgage, a 'new building and garden', all the rents of a house and shop leased to her stepson-in-law, and the rents of another two houses. Jane identified her undertenants, six of whom can be traced in the Hearth Tax of 1666, which identifies the properties concerned as a mixture of one- and two-hearth houses.[49]

Conglomerate holdings can be illustrated by that of Elizabeth Clayton, who had to make a codicil in 1745 to amend her will, of 1740, by inclusion of recent freehold and leasehold acquisitions in Whiston, Lancashire. Her will listed specific messuages, tenements and lands held by different tenures in Liverpool, where she also had a ropewalk and buildings. She named a cottage in Parr and land purchased there. There was no detail of the 'messuages, lands, tenements and mortgages taken out' for her daughter, Sarah, nor of 'all other real estate and mortgages freehold and copyhold' which were left to trustees. Two items of the realty which Elizabeth had inherited from her husband, William, and which she in turn left to her daughter, Sarah, were developed by the latter.

Specific investment can be identified: around the turn of the century Margaret Williamson had laid out £700 in new buildings and improvements on an 'estate in Liverpool descendible to my son Robert Williamson which was his ancestors on his father's side'. Women also developed land and invested in property on a smaller scale. Hannah

Wright, who had been widowed with five children in 1708, left, in 1731, 'a peice of ground in fee simple in Edmund street ... whereupon I have built one house to the front of the said street and two small houses backwards'. Involvement in development is suspected of testators who left blocks of property like that of Mary Huddleston. She left 'ten houses on the North side of the Lower End of ... Lord street, two houses in a certain alley or passage leading from Aldmn Rainford's house at the lower end of Castle Hey to the said houses above and a plott of ground in the above alley'. Sarah Clayton created Clayton Square and surrounding streets, on land leased from the Corporation of Liverpool. This land was first leased by her father in 1690, renewed by his widow in 1718 and 1738 and by Sarah in 1746 and 1751, at which time development was mooted of the square and streets to be built by Sarah. The area can be identified by street names from family and affines: Clayton, Leigh, Houghton, Parker, Tyrer and Case.

Women also held shares in 'industrial' concerns: Ann Clieveland had an interest 'in Allom works at Pleasington, near Blackburn'; her daughter, Alice, inherited shares in the saltworks at Dungeon Point;[50] the entrepreneurial Sarah Clayton exploited coal-bearing land at Parr, Lancashire, in partnership with her nephew Thomas Case.[51] A woman also had an option on developing local infrastructure: Robert Barrow left it 'to the discretion of my wife whether to sell my share in the Dry Dock now building'.

Several studies have revealed women to be fundamental to the loan market in various locales.[52] It has been suggested that in late eighteenth-century towns women made up 20 per cent of the loan capital traded.[53] In Liverpool men and women left almost the same proportion of inventories containing debts due to the testator (65 and 64 per cent respectively), and over 80 per cent of these women had more than £10 due to them. The gender difference was that 61 per cent of testatrices had over half their personalty in credits, in contrast to only 37 per cent of testators. In fact 24 of the 43 women who held bonds or bills had over 65 per cent of their personal wealth in this form.[54] There are exemplars of the continuation, if not increase, of this situation to the end of the period (after inventories become uncommon). One such was Joan Howard who had the bulk of her estate 'out at interest' in 1757.

Certainly the data from late seventeenth- and early eighteenth-century Liverpool suggest significant property ownership and rentier activity by women. The importance of women as sources of capital is also endorsed by the evidence of this study. A very notable contribution was apparently made by them to the loan market which fuelled all facets and levels of 'take off' in the local economy. Women continued to be significant in the financial areas of urban property and bond holding, later augmented by share ownership. However, the actual wealth of women was greater than their control over it as a consequence of the growth of trusts.[55] Women also undoubtedly had as important an economic role in the lower strata of the burgeoning port as they did in later periods when they are evident as itinerant hawkers, pedlars and stalwarts of a 'black economy' during the absence or underemployment of their menfolk.[56] Indeed, in Liverpool as elsewhere, women were a vital component in the family economy in various roles at all social levels.

In this study the role of women in work and other economic activity has been made accessible to a degree by sophisticated multi-source linkage. This approach can also correct another major weakness of conventional occupational study, which is to ignore the tendency of individuals to change either the description of their employment, or the employment itself, at different points in their lives. Given the highly mobile and fragile nature of the port-town economy, the final section of this chapter turns to an assessment of how those issues are reflected in the occupational record.

Occupational Mobility, Stability and Networks

The economic role of the individual was central in the pre-industrial, as in the medieval, town. Yet the occupational term applied to any one person could conceal a range of activity since multi-occupation was a common phenomenon.[57] It was also rare that within any given population all individuals maintained a single occupational label throughout a lifetime. By necessity, the broad profile offered above portrays the occupational make-up of the town in static, single-label terms; indeed, the use of a structural classification scheme necessitates this approach. It is more likely that a variety of occupations, reflective of age, experience and opportunity, would be practised.

Employment mobility can take a variety of forms and be measured over a number of timescales. Individual mobility can be assessed to some degree by charting change of occupation through time. Without consideration of individual timescales, it is problematic to gauge the context of the occupations stated. Some changes in occupational label appear to be the result of natural progression through life, from skilled or semi-skilled, highly active employment to more general work, often loosely described as labouring. Examples would include the shift from maltster to brewer to labourer, or horse hirer to stable keeper to labourer. Other progressions appear to be the result of either upward or downward movement, according to economic fortune; for example, draper to linen-draper to merchant; or chandler to merchant. Also evident is the growing specialisation within certain trades, such as instrument, watch- and clock-making; for example, watchmaker to watch-case maker.

Of course, change in employment description may have resulted from genuine employment change – whether in an upward or downward direction – or it may have been caused by synonymous use of a number of labels for one particular employment type. In addition, although the parish clerks entrusted with the task of accurately recording information tended to serve for long periods, thus ensuring reasonable continuity of expression, slight changes in the interpretation of particular employment labels may have been introduced over time. Construction of individual biographies enables some distinction between poor recording practice and actual change in circumstances.

There can be a relationship between occupational mobility and multiple occupation. Whereas in some cases the latter may have manifested as continual by-employment, in others apparent occupational mobility may have resulted from a more gradual change of career than the distinct occupational designations suggest. A spectrum of occupations may have been differently weighted in the individual over time.

In Liverpool there was a mercantile element in all sectors because of secondary interest in trade, similar to that noted in seventeenth-century Bristol where 'all men that are dealers even in shop trades launch into adventures by sea'.[58] Liverpool examples of this phenomenon included Thomas Matthews, a tailor who had a stock of 'shipp biscake' to the value of £2.15s., and Cuthbert Watkinson, a gunsmith who had 'cloth and yarn at sea' worth £165.

The most common mobility in Liverpool during this period was allied to adventuring at sea. This was less an employment change than a career progression in which mariners might survive to become masters and ultimately merchants. Examples are legion, particularly in the first half of the period. Some men, however, metamorphosed more distinctly: Jasper Mauditt was an attorney who represented the Council in London during the late seventeenth century but made his will as 'merchant' in 1714; John Pemberton, senior, was an apothecary when purchasing the freedom of Liverpool in 1655, as was his subsequent apprentice and future son-in-law, William Bassnett. Both men became very prosperous merchants. Another extreme instance of such occupational diversity was Zachariah Cook. By his will of 1699 he was a Liverpool merchant, but he left as a specific bequest 'all my instruments of steel belonging to chirurgery'. It is presumed that he was the 'Zach Cork' admitted as a freeman in 1697 by apprenticeship to Dr Norris.[59] In these cases it appears that trading interests, initially run in tandem with the original profession, eventually became paramount.

Occupational mobility across the generations is evident in Liverpool among the 'commercial aristocracy', which was developing during this period. Here as elsewhere there were younger sons of titled, or at least landed, families: Edward Tarleton, mariner/merchant, grandson of the recusant owner of Aigburth Hall; William Clayton, Esq., second mercantile generation of a Lancashire county family, and married into a Cheshire one; Samuel Powell, merchant, from 'Stannage Park, Radnorshire'; Roger Brooke, merchant, younger son of the baronial family of Norton Priory, Cheshire. Various sources reveal also that the merchants of Liverpool came from the range of backgrounds described by Minchinton.[60] Thus in Liverpool, as well as those mentioned above, there were Edward Cardwell, son of a tanner, 1708; Robert Turner, son of an innkeeper, 1709; Thomas Bright, son of a gentleman, 1709; Benjamin Foster, son of a clothier, 1710; John Blackburne, son of an esquire, 1739; Richard Royle, son of a tailor, 1740.[61]

Another confusion, identified in the aggregate, may be clarified by the alternative angle of this record linkage approach: production and sale, as well as great difference of scale, could be subsumed under the same label.[62] 'Wholesale' and 'retail', although developing, were not the distinct modern concepts. The potential for confusion is compounded by lack of demarcation. This might be more than simply selling items outside the stock of a certain trade, or an agriculturalist engaging in industrial by-employment. Kindred activities were commonly combined as in the case of Daniel Birchall, who defined himself as 'gentleman', was buried as a 'Notary Public', and was also a bookseller and publisher.[63]

Problems can undoubtedly be introduced when a classification scheme perforce unites occupation and status in one system. The major quandaries, in the application above, occurred because of the all-encompassing facility of the scheme. Occupation, as in an income-generating activity, can be concealed when an individual was referred to by his civic title of 'alderman' or 'bailiff'. Similarly, self-description as 'gentleman' or 'Esquire' was ceasing to signify landed rental income or armigerous status during this period. William Clayton was an important Liverpool merchant, although categorisation based on the title in his will would allow choice between 'Esq.' and 'M.P.' Therefore an individual assigned to 'status or other descriptions' might be, in fact, a merchant and thus 'dealing', or perhaps a Customs official and thus 'public and professional service'.[64] A Liverpool example was Maxwell Hamilton, gentleman, whose burial record places him in the Customs service as 'landwaiter'. Thus the title ascribed by appraising neighbours or the parish clerk did not always match the heights of a testator's self-perception. (Personal modesty, unique in this study, was shown by John Martindale. He styled himself 'yeoman' but was accorded 'gentleman'.) The primary sector, for instance, is weighted in the aggregate classification by the inclusion of 'yeomen' with no agricultural pretensions:

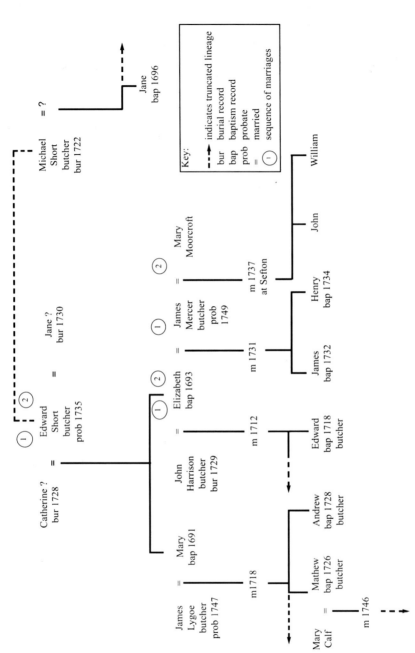

Figure 3.5 *Short family linkage*

William Gandy may have possessed rural patrimony in Over Whitley, Cheshire, but in Liverpool he was acting as scrivener or perhaps as attorney. This is shown in probate evidence by his drafting of the wills of at least 60 townsfolk between 1675 and 1708. Robert Seacome, also 'yeoman', was identified as landlord of the 'Woolpack' by the diarist, Nicholas Blundell.[65] Neither Gandy nor Seacome had any farm stock or gear and thus seem to be using a status title.[66]

There were also combinations of by-employment and yeoman title: Alan Woods, yeoman, was also a linen weaver, and John Bamber, yeoman, was a ropemaker. A variation on dual employment is the case of Jacob Stringer, a linen weaver prior to his parochial appointment as parish clerk. His will of 1751 suggests that he ran the two jobs in tandem. George Tarvin affords another instance of office-holding and craft occupation. He was granted freedom as a 'weighter [waiter] in the Customs house' but also allowed to use 'silk glove forms' in the practice of his craft.[67]

A straightforward occupational designation could conceal unexpected economic interest: Richard Gallaway was a shipwright but left property in Jamaica and named slaves. Less exotic were the ancillary activities of tobacco merchants and sugar bakers with involvement in the production of such commodities: Foster Cunliffe and Samuel Danvers are examples.[68] More generally, 'multiple occupation' might include varying degrees of property investment, infrastructure development and capital provision. These were diversifications of established men or the retired, but nonetheless significant in economic terms.

As this discussion suggests, multi-source record linkage facilitates not only the construction of detailed biographies for individuals but also the reconstruction of their various associations, in this instance within an occupational base. Tracing through a number of generations can recover continuity of employment type, with a son perpetuating the father's occupation or trade, or the construction of trade networks between relations.

The links between mercantile families and others of the urban elite have habitually been reconstituted since the first antiquarian interest.[69] The 'great and good' leave a strong imprint in all classes of record: personal, fiscal, religious and political. Links within lower status occupations are, however, less obvious and thus particularly interesting recoveries. A sample of these will be explored below.

Figure 3.5 exemplifies a grouping which constituted an occupational dynasty of butchers in the town for some sixty years. Whether the first generation, Edward and Michael Short, were brothers, cousins, or had some other relationship is uncertain, but the birth dates of their children suggest that they were of an age. In 1708 they were occupying premises in neighbouring streets: Michael as a ratepayer in Juggler Street, Edward

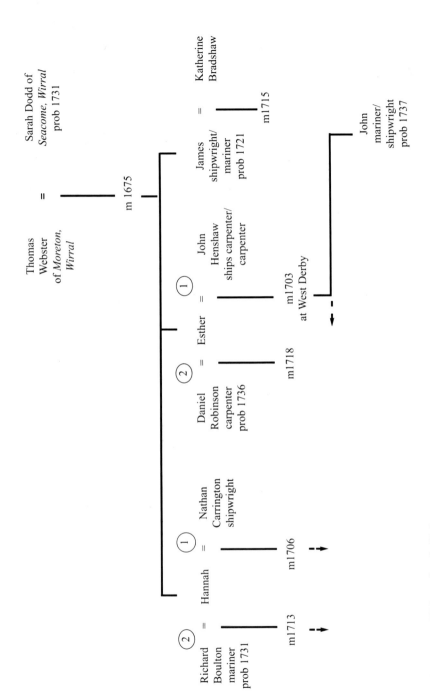

Figure 3.6 *Webster family linkage*

as tenant of two landlords for 'an old house' and 'a Slaughter House' in Tithebarn Street.[70] In the next generation Edward's two daughters married three husbands, all of whom were butchers. Were these men who saw their father-in-law 'as the chief means of their advancement'?[71] Two of them, James Lygoe and James Mercer, seem to have been from other families of butchers; the former was laterally linked, the latter might have been nephew to the namesake whose children's baptisms record him as a butcher. James Mercer, who married Elizabeth Harrison, née Short, took 'Mary Moorcroft' as his second wife, but her relationship, if any, to Liverpool butchers of that name cannot be verified. This Mary, mentioned above, was to carry on the butcher's trade 'for the further benefit' of minor children but the slaughterhouse was willed to her stepson, Henry, as soon as he was of age. James Lygoe who married Mary Short had, among twelve children, at least two sons who were butchers in Liverpool in the 1750s.

Address and occupation were common denominators in a more lateral network of seagoing craftsmen, inconsistently identified in the sources as 'mariner', 'carpenter', 'ship carpenter' and 'shipwright'. This illustrates both the problem of identifying seafarers as mentioned above, and the solution offered by multi-source linkage. In the reconstructed network, Sarah Webster could be described as the spider in the centre of a web of close kin (Figure 3.6). She was rated in Redcross Street in 1705 for her own house and those of three tenants, one of whom, by 1708, was her son-in-law, Nathan Carrington, shipwright. Another son-in-law, John Henshaw, ship carpenter, was also rated in 1708 for stock in Redcross Street.[72] In 1731 Sarah's daughter, Hannah Boulton, filed her second husband's will for probate. Richard Boulton, mariner, must have succeeded Nathan Carrington to wife and property in Redcross Street. Richard's other executor was Daniel Robinson, shipwright. No relationship was stated for the two men but Figure 3.6 shows a lateral affinal link: Daniel Robinson was second husband to Esther Henshaw, née Webster. James Webster, variously described as mariner and shipwright, and son of the house-owning Sarah, also lived in Redcross Street. Occupational links are evident both vertically and horizontally throughout this network.

Another occupational dynasty of such craftsmen manifests upward mobility down the generations. Roger James, senior, was a shipwright, admitted a burgess in 1657.[73] Ten years later he was one of few tenants adjudged 'a very honest man' by his landlord, Sir Edward Moore, by which time he had moved from a three-hearth house in Chapel Street to a house in Fenwick Street with land in Fenwick and Bridge Alleys.[74] Roger, junior, and his brother, Robert, were also shipwrights who died within a year of each other while in their early thirties. Roger was already able to make generous provision for his very young children. His younger son, Edward, also became a shipwright, and one who in turn left considerable real estate to *his* minor children. The elder son, John, took the favoured route of mariner to merchant, and prospered to the extent of marrying into the commercially important Tarleton clan in 1722.[75] It is noteworthy that, although only Roger James, senior, left adult children, there was sufficient accumulation through the generations to maintain the craft dynasty and achieve upward mobility.

Descendants of the bricklayer, William Bibby, demonstrate that mobility could be both positive and negative within a family. Although termed 'bricklayer' William was not in modern parlance a 'brickie'. Indeed he was the contractor responsible both for the supply of lime and for brickwork between 1708 and 1715 for the construction of the first commercial wet dock.[76] However, his eldest son was buried as 'labourer', whereas in direct contrast a grandson was deemed 'gentleman'. There may be unique personal circumstances or general norms behind these examples. The son, Charles, was possibly deficient in some area – incompetent, feckless or profligate. Nothing is specified in his father's will but Charles alone received an annuity rather than a share. The grandson, Charles Ward, while termed 'gentleman', was probably still involved in the family trade with father, uncle and brother all bricklayers, and his own son a plasterer.[77] He probably exemplifies the eighteenth-century tendency to accord gentility to any man of some fortune: 'In our Days all are accounted Gentlemen that have Money ...'[78]

Maintaining an occupational dynasty not infrequently demanded a 'bridging' role by a widowed mother. Mary Fleetwood epitomised this function. She was widow of James Fleetwood, glazier, who died in 1710 when their own sons were infants and children of their previous marriages still young. Mary apparently took over the business because 'Widow Fleetwood' or 'Mary Fleetwood' occurs in Vestry accounts from 1711, and in 1716 is identified as 'Mary Fleetwood, glazier'.[79] Her 'man' or her son/s did glazing and associated work at Little Crosby Hall from 1712 to 1728, when the Diurnal closes.[80] Mary obviously continued to run the business after her sons reached adulthood, presumably till her death in 1730 when James, the elder son, was first paid by the Vestry.[81]

Another occupational linkage role of women is exemplified in the Fleetwood family: Mary's stepdaughter married a glazier. He was not recorded as an apprentice of her father, although that Dick Whittington syndrome was quite common. Variations of daughters marrying into their father's trade are frequent findings within these reconstructed occupational networks in Liverpool. In the few examples cited above it occurs among butchers, ship carpenters, bricklayers and glaziers. It was also a common phenomenon of both daughters and widows among the mercantile elite as it has universally been.[82]

Thus there was consolidation and continuity alongside fragmentation and mobility. Both dynastic strategies and demographic accidents can be explored by multi-source record linkage, adding depth to the one-dimensional occupational analysis afforded by classification applied to individuals' single entries in parish registers or probate records. Indeed, in conclusion, this methodology of combining aggregate and individual level analysis not only confirms the general picture portrayed by contemporary writers and those who have studied Liverpool's economy from a variety of sources and perspectives, but also offers the potential to extend knowledge of poorly represented groups, such as women, within the urban economy. From the early 1700s the diversity of trades, manufactures and services offered by the town clearly delimited it as not only a major port, but also as a town with an enclave of high-class craftsmanship, a place for administrative and business acumen and a centre of conspicuous consumption, in step with the trends and fashions of the time. Whether this generated sufficient work opportunities to absorb the constant inflow of both skilled and unskilled migrants is another matter. Clearly apparent by the mid-decades of the eighteenth century were a growing number of displaced persons, transitory strangers, the poor and those requiring parish relief. Although such individuals defy categorisation and often even enumeration, their mere existence confirms that Liverpool was a town of growing stature, attracting both the economically useful and redundant alike.

Notes

1. For relevant synthesis, see J. M. Ellis, *The Georgian Town 1680–1840*, Basingstoke, 2001, chapter 3.

2. J. Patten, 'Urban occupations in pre-industrial England', *TIBG*, new series, 2, 1977, p. 311.

3. For example see E. J. Buckatzsch, 'Occupations in the Parish Registers of Sheffield, 1655–1719', *EcHR*, 2nd series, 1, 1948–49, pp. 145–50; A. L. Beier, 'Engine of manufacture: the trades of London', in *The Making of the Metropolis: London 1500–1700*, ed. A. L. Beier and R. Finlay, London, 1986, pp. 141–67.

4. See A. J. Rawling, 'The Rise of Liverpool and Demographic Change in Part of South West Lancashire, 1660-1760', unpublished PhD thesis, University of Liverpool, 1986, pp. 126–43; J. Langton and P. Laxton, 'Parish registers and urban structure: the example of late-eighteenth century Liverpool', *Urban History Yearbook*, 1978, pp. 74–84.

5. F. Lewis, 'The Demographic and Occupational Structure of Liverpool: a study of the Parish Registers, 1660–1750', unpublished PhD thesis, University of Liverpool, 1993, Figures 4.10, 4.12, 4.14 and 4.16.

6. See Patten, 'Urban occupations', pp. 304–05; also P. H. Lindert,

'English Occupations, 1670–1811', *JEcH*, 40. 4, 1980, p. 692.

7. For example, E. A. Wrigley, 'The changing occupational structure of Colyton over two centuries', *LPS*, 18, 1977, p. 17.

8. J. T. Krause, 'The changing adequacy of English Registration, 1690–1837', in *Population in History*, ed. D. V. Glass and D. E. C. Eversley, London, 1965, p. 382; E. D. Bebb, *Nonconformity and Social and Economic Life 1660–1800*, London, 1935, p. 45.

9. Rawling, 'The Rise of Liverpool', p. 68.

10. D. E. Ascott, 'Wealth and Community: Liverpool, 1660–1760', unpublished PhD thesis, University of Liverpool, 1996, pp. 174–78, Table 4.3.

11. J. Langton, 'Industry and Towns 1500–1730', in *An Historical Geography of England and Wales*, ed. R. A. Dodgshon and R. A. Butlin, London, 1978, pp. 186–87. For more details on the use in this study see Lewis, 'Demographic and Occupational Structure', Appendix 1.

12. For example D. J. Hibberd, 'Urban inequalities: social geography and demography in seventeenth century York', unpublished PhD thesis, University of Liverpool, 1981; S. M. Schwarz, 'Population, economy and society in North-East Lancashire, circa. 1660–1760', unpublished PhD thesis, University of Liverpool, 1989; E. Baigent, 'Bristol Society in the Later Eighteenth Century with special reference to the handling of fragmentary historical sources', unpublished DPhil thesis, University of Oxford, 1985.

13. The table of overall sample sizes can be found in Appendix 3.

14. See Ascott, 'Wealth and Community', p. 132.

15. R. Davis, *The Rise of the English Shipping Industry in the Seventeenth and Eighteenth Centuries*, London, 1962, p. 62; K. Morgan, *Bristol and the Atlantic Trade in the Eighteenth Century*, Cambridge, 1993, p. 40.

16. M. M. Schofield, 'Shoes and ships and sealing wax: eighteenth century Lancashire exports to the colonies', *THSLC*, 135, 1986, pp. 61–82.

17. J. Mayer, *History of the Art of Pottery in Liverpool*, Liverpool, 1871, p. 24.

18. P. Borsay, 'The English urban renaissance: the development of provincial urban culture *c.*1680–*c.*1760', in *The Eighteenth-Century Town, 1688–1820*, ed. P. Borsay, Harlow, 1990, pp. 175–79.

19. J. Patten, *English Towns 1500–1700*, Folkestone, 1978, p. 163.

20. Langton and Laxton, 'Parish registers and urban structure', p. 82.

21. Cf. the predominantly naval ports of Portsmouth and Plymouth, P. J. Corfield, *The Impact of English Towns 1700–1800*, Oxford, 1982, pp. 44–46; the concentration of mariners and ancillary trades in Stepney, M. J. Power, 'The East London working community in the seventeenth century', in *Work in Towns 850–1850*, ed. P. J. Corfield and D. Keene, Leicester, 1990, pp. 103–20; and, most appositely, Newcastle upon Tyne, J. M. Ellis, 'A dynamic society: social relations in Newcastle-upon-Tyne 1660–1760', in *The Transformation of English Provincial Towns 1600–1800*, ed. P. Clark, London, 1984, pp. 217–20.

22. For more detail see Lewis, 'Demographic and Occupational Structure', Appendix 2.

23. For sample sizes see Appendix 3.

24. R. Stewart-Brown, *Liverpool Ships in the Eighteenth Century*, London, 1932; Davis, *Rise of the English Shipping Industry*, pp. 66–68.

25. R. Jarvis, *Customs Letter-Books of the Port of Liverpool 1711–1813*, CS, 3rd series, 6, Manchester, 1954, p. 58.

26. See the classic text, A. Clark, *Working Life of Women in the Seventeenth Century*, ed. A. L. Erickson, London, 1992, especially introduction and bibliography pp. vii–lv. Also, for this period, P. Earle, 'The female labour market in London in the late seventeenth and early eighteenth centuries', *EcHR*, 2nd series, XLII. 3, 1989, pp. 328–53.

27. T. Meldrum, 'London Domestic Servants, 1660–1750', paper delivered to the Pre-Modern Towns Conference, Institute of Historical Research, November, 1993.

28. Earle, 'Female labour', pp. 338–44.

29. D. Souden, 'Migrants and the population structure of later seventeenth-century provincial cities and market towns', in *The Transformation of English Provincial Towns, 1600–1800*, ed. P. Clark, London, 1984, p. 152 and Table 17.

30. Source references for all testamentary evidence cited in the text are in Appendix 2. For clarification of references to individuals and families in chapters 3–6, e.g. Clieveland and Clayton, see the index.

31. Ascott, 'Wealth and Community', Appendix IV.

32. See P. Earle, *The Making of the English Middle Class*, London, 1989, p. 160.

33. Ref. 2873 in FREEMEN, a file of Liverpool grants of freedom, 1650–1708, created from Liverpool Town Books and deposited in 'The Liverpool community 1660–1750' at the Data Archive, University of Essex.

34. See Chapter 4 below. There was only one female apprentice recorded in the Liverpool Register and she was not Alice Summerset. Cf. the contrasting incidence averaging 10 females per annum in Bristol records 1625–1635 (c.3 per cent of all apprentices 1600–1645). I. K. Ben-Amos, 'Women apprentices in the trades and crafts of early modern Bristol', *Continuity and Change*, 6. 2, 1991, p. 229.

35. See S. Sogner and H. Sandvik, 'Minors in law, partners in work, equals in worth? Women in the Norwegian economy in the 16th to the 18th centuries', *La donna nell'economia. Secoli XIII–XVIII*, Prato, 1990, pp. 633–53.

36. H. Peet, ed., *Liverpool in the reign of Queen Anne, 1705 and 1708, from a rate assessment book of the town and parish*, Liverpool, 1908, pp. 53–108.

37. P. Clark, *The English Alehouse*, London, 1983, pp. 99–101.

38. For women's contribution to rural malting see B. Todd, 'Freebench and free enterprise: widows and their property in two Berkshire villages', in *English Rural Society 1500–1800*, ed. J. Chartres and D. G. Hey, Cambridge, 1990, p. 189.

39. For the role of widows in continuing businesses see Earle, *Making*, Table 6.2 and p. 171.

40. See Liverpool Port Books, for example PRO: E190/1375/8/ ff 8,10, and 13.

41. See J. J. Bagley and F. Tyrer, eds, *The Great Diurnal of Nicholas Blundell of Little Crosby, Lancashire*, vol. 2: 1712–1719, RSLC, 112, Manchester, 1970, p. 59; Liverpool Apprentice Books: LplRO 352/CLE/REG/4 17.9.1713 Thomas, s. of George Mankin of Milewater to Elizabeth Sheilds, silversmith.

42. H. Peet, ed., *Liverpool Vestry Books, 1681–1834*, vol. 1, 1681–1799, Liverpool, 1912, pp. 153 and 26–86.

43. Peet, *Liverpool Vestry Books*, pp. 82–175.

44. This universal experience has been observed of early modern Oxford. M. Prior, 'Women and the urban economy: Oxford 1500–1800', in *Women in English Society 1500–1800*, ed. M. Prior, London, 1985, p. 96.

45. Noted in T. Baines, *History of the commerce and town of Liverpool, and of the rise of manufacturing industry in the adjoining counties*, London, 1852, p. 334.

46. A. Vickery, *The Gentleman's Daughter: Women's Lives in Georgian England*, New Haven and London, 1998, p. 5. See also Chapter 4 below.

47. Earle, *Making*, pp. 169–70.

48. Peet, *Liverpool in the reign of Queen Anne*, pp. 53–108.

49. Hearth Tax, 1666, PRO: E179/250/9.

50. For details of Alice's inheritance see Chapter 4 below.

51. T. C. Barker and J. R. Harris, 'The Early Coal Magnates', in *A Merseyside Town in the Industrial Revolution*, ed. T. C. Barker and J. R. Harris, Liverpool, 1954, pp. 24–30.

52. For urban moneylending, see R. T. Vann, 'Wills and the family in an English town: Banbury, 1550–1800', *Journal of Family History*, 4, 1979, p. 366; Earle, *Making*, p. 174.

53. C. W. Chalklin, *The Provincial Towns of Georgian England*, London, 1974, p. 242.

54. Ascott, 'Wealth and Community', p. 308.

55. See C. Hall, 'Strains in the "firm of Wife, Children and Friends"? Middle-class women and employment in early nineteenth-century England', in *Women's Work and the Family Economy in Historical Perspective*, ed. P. Hudson and W. R. Lee, Manchester, 1990, p. 110.

56. For the later eighteenth century see S. Haggerty, 'Trade and trading communities in the eighteenth-century Atlantic: Liverpool and Philadelphia', unpublished PhD thesis, University of Liverpool, 2002, chapter 3; for early twentieth century see P. Ayers, *The Liverpool Docklands*, Liverpool, n.d., pp. 10–11, 37–43.

57. P. J. Corfield, 'Defining urban work', in Corfield and Keene, eds, *Work in Towns*, pp. 213–20; Lindert, 'English Occupations', p. 706.

58. Roger North, quoted in W. E. Minchinton, 'The Merchants in England in the Eighteenth Century', *Explorations in Entrepreneurial History*, 10, 1957–8, p. 64.

59. For Jasper Mauditt see T. Heywood, ed., *The Norris Papers*, CS, 9, Manchester, 1846, p. 47; John Pemberton, freedom 1655 (ref. 98 in FREEMEN, see fn. 33 above); William Bassnett, 'apothecary', freedom 1693 (ref. 1999 in FREEMEN) as apprentice to JP senior; 'merchant' in marriage licence 1698. See W. Irvine, ed., *Marriage Licences Granted within the*

Archdeaconry of Chester in the Diocese of Chester, 1691–1700, RSLC, 77, 1923, p. 188; Zach Cork, freedom 1697 (ref . 2228 in FREEMEN).

60. Minchinton, 'Merchants in England', p. 62.

61. Liverpool Apprenticeship Books: LplRO 352/CLE/REG/4. Cf. merchant recruitment in G. Jackson, *Hull in the Eighteenth Century*, London, 1972, pp. 99–106.

62. A. L. Merson, 'A calendar of Southampton Apprenticeship Registers, 1699–1740', *Southampton Record Series*, 12, 1968, pp. xxi–xxii.

63. Will of Robert Huddlestone; A. J. Mott, 'On books published in Liverpool', *THSLC*, 13, 1861, pp. 110, 121.

64. See A. J. Tawney and R. H. Tawney, 'An occupational census of the seventeenth century', *EcHR*, 5, 1934, p. 32.

65. Bagley and Tyrer, *The Great Diurnal*, vol 1, p. 58.

66. Cf. Newcastle upon Tyne 1660–1729, Ellis, 'A dynamic society', p. 220.

67. Ref. 1256 in FREEMEN, see fn. 33 above.

68. See J. W. Tyler, 'Foster Cunliffe and Sons: Liverpool Merchants in the Maryland Tobacco Trade, 1738–1765', *Maryland Historical Magazine*, 73. 3, 1978, pp. 246–79; will of Samuel Danvers, sugar baker.

69. M. Gregson, 'The Pedigree of the Claytons of Fullwood, connected with the Tarletons, Houghtons, Cases, Hardmans, Earles, and many other Families in Liverpool', in *Portfolio of Fragments relative to the History and Antiquities, Topography and Genealogies of the County Palatine and Duchy of Lancaster*, 3rd edition, London, 1869, pp. 167–70.

70. Peet, *Liverpool in the reign of Queen Anne*, pp. 59 and 73.

71. R. A. Houlbrooke, *The English Family 1450–1700*, London, 1984, p. 44.

72. Peet, *Liverpool in the reign of Queen Anne*, pp. 34, 91–92.

73. Stewart-Brown, *Liverpool Ships*, p. 113; ref. 118 in FREEMEN, see fn. 33 above.

74. Hearth Tax, 1663. PRO: E179/250/8; Heywood, *Moore Rental*, p. 112.

75. See Chapter 4 below.

76. For his partnership as revealed in litigation see M. Clarke, 'Thomas Steers', in *Dock Engineers and Dock Engineering: Papers Presented at a Research Day School 13.2.1993 NMGM*, Liverpool, 1993, p. 9.

77. H. Peet, 'Abstracts of deeds relating to the sale of pews in St Nicholas's Church, Liverpool', *THSLC*, 73, 1921, pp. 221–22.

78. N. Bailey, *Dictionarium Britannicum*, London, T. Cox, 1730.

79. Peet, *Liverpool Vestry Books*, pp. 67–74.

80. Bagley and Tyrer, *The Great Diurnal*, vol. 2: 1712–1719; vol. 3: 1720–1728, RSLC, 112, 1970; 114, 1972.

81. Peet, *Liverpool Vestry Books*, p. 102.

82. Cf. for medieval Yorkshire, J. I. Kermode, *Medieval Merchants: York, Beverley and Hull in the Later Middle Ages*, Cambridge, 1998, pp. 80–81; for eighteenth-century London, Earle, *Making*, pp. 189, 192.

4

Family and Friends: Inheritance
Strategies in a Mobile Population

Attitudes to wealth are important indicators for historians studying past societies. Recent research has demonstrated the centrality of non-subsistence acquisition in the lives of people far below the monied elite, and the existence and importance of complex patterns of consumption in all social classes.[1] The fact that much of this work can be given the shorthand label 'getting and spending' points to its importance in understanding the very basics of life, but also highlights aspects which need further investigation: in particular, 'preserving and passing on'.

Strategies for maintaining and securing wealth across generations promise to shed at least as much light on society as the acquisition of wealth and its disposal on goods and services. As noted in the Introduction above, some work has been done on the former question in rural societies and manufacturing towns, but little has been done on major ports, and early modern Liverpool offers important evidence. Liverpool, as has been discussed in earlier chapters, had a mobile population with a high level of in-migration and itinerant occupations. It also generated significant mercantile wealth from the later seventeenth century, but witnessed periodic slumps and lean periods, as is common in towns with such economic profiles.[2] Individuals and families who acquired new wealth faced considerable uncertainty and some dislocation from the wealth-transmission strategies of earlier generations.

This chapter begins by briefly outlining the major constituents of Liverpudlians' wealth and considers the concerns that motivated strategies for the preservation of that wealth. Testators were determined to avoid not only intestacy, but also other divisions of estates that would for some reason leave family members vulnerable. The friends and relations charged with overseeing the execution of a will played a key role in this, and the choice of these people is analysed in the second section. The third part of the chapter reviews patterns of bequest and strategies for wealth transmission and financial security in Liverpool, paying particular attention to the different priorities and circumstances of male and female testators. The final section brings various threads together in a number of case studies, which emphasise the subtlety and complexity of family structures and the motives behind attitudes to wealth and its preservation across the generations.

Getting and Passing On

The pattern of wealth holding in Liverpool assessed by this study is that indicated by testamentary evidence, which, in the absence of universal private account books or comprehensive taxation records, offers the clearest available insight into the diversity of wealth holding during this period. A total of 1,769 wills survive of those granted probate between 1660 and 1760, drawn up by 1,451 men and 318 women describing themselves as 'of Liverpool'.[3] Testamentary evidence is not, of course, without problems: it provides only a 'snapshot' of property at the time of will making, is biased towards older, wealthier males, and offers no consistent valuation of estates. Nevertheless, wills were written to preserve and direct the distribution of wealth, and therefore serve as an invaluable source for the analysis of the priorities and concerns of testators.

Wealth could be held in many forms, which became more varied and complex in an urban setting during the long eighteenth century. The mercantile element in the wealth of men engaged in all economic sectors has been noted in Chapter 3. Fragmentary evidence suggests that some women also had significant commercial interests, albeit few of them by comparison with other parts of northern Europe.[4] However, the debt/credit nexus was more conspicuous, and has long been seen as fundamental to the burgeoning economic activity of the eighteenth century.[5] It was ubiquitous in Liverpool. Notwithstanding anything else, debt was the most universal category, other than household goods, in the Liverpool inventories of this period. It was the item of major value in total personal estate. These credits to testators, and the debts which are mentioned in wills as encumbering estates, are particularly important.

Real estate held by Liverpudlian testators during the years 1660–1760 was apparently of every tenure, held in widely different places, acquired by many means, and owned for different reasons over various lengths of time.[6] It is notable that almost half those giving detail of their realty had property outside Liverpool, although perhaps less remarkable when considered in conjunction with the scale of in-migration. The sub-letting of property was an important aspect. Thus real estate was perhaps a more significant component in the wealth of Liverpudlians than their commercial preoccupations would suggest. It is obvious though that clear-cut divisions, however neat for historians, would have meant less to Liverpudlian testators who apparently left widely disparate wealth held in a variety of forms. Certainly the spectrum of wealth was extended over time as Liverpool's growth was reflected by increase in both affluence and poverty. That spectrum is best exemplified by the mariner grouping, ranging from deckhand to virtual merchant, although women also left a wide range of wealth. Despite being legally restricted in their property-holding while married, women were represented in all aspects of wealth holding. Testatrices, although relatively few, were notable for realty and credit.[7] At different degrees of affluence testators seem to have owned a blend of assets either by accident or design. Diverse wealth holdings reflect a complex society and economy in which individuals had many opportunities for accumulation and exchange. Wills express testators' wishes concerning wealth disposal but not the estates' capacity to fulfil them. When considering patterns of bequest it is helpful to review first how an estate would have been divided in the case of intestacy. This indicates what the testator was seeking to alter by leaving a will.

Different elements of property were subject to different diktats.[8] The descent of freehold land was governed by the rules of primogeniture under the common law. Copyhold land devolved according to custom, but almost all Liverpudlian testators sought control by 'surrender to the use of a Will'. Leaseholds, for lives and for years, were treated differently during part of this period but, by 1741, as chattels, were regulated by the terms of the lease and rules governing personal estate.[9] Personalty was subject to a division of one-third to the wife, two-thirds to the children, confirmed by the 1670 Act for the Better Settling of Intestates' Estates.[10] Individuals who were satisfied with these provisions may have waived their rights of testation.[11]

The motivations and anxieties of testators are revealed in general statements or in the conditions placed upon inheritance. The desire to preserve or enhance the estate prompted testators to particular instructions, some of which sought ongoing control over disbursement or beneficiaries. Constraints were often idiosyncratic but there were many common concerns.

General statements of intent range from the persuasive to the punitive. The *raison d'être* of a will might be spelt out, as by Mrs Jane Alcock who made hers in 1666 'for setting of peace and amitie among my children and friends'. Her complex family structure with children by two husbands as well as stepchildren was not uncommon among testators, and others made similar statements. Some testators extolled or enjoined filial support: in 1745 William Beckett had a son 'whose goodness and dutifulness to us I can never sufficiently commend and hope he will continue the same to his dear mother for the future'. Richard Kelsall desired, in 1749, that 'my three dear sons ... will be aiding and assisting their dear mother'. Some testators feared familial strife to the extent of a general threat such as that made by Catherine Walsh in 1705: 'any beneficiary disputing [the will] loses the bequest'. Others even required an undertaking that one particular beneficiary should not 'molest' the executor or other legatees: the widowed Anne Phelps made her son's £5 legacy of 1709 contingent upon him signing a release to his sister, and not molesting her.

The concern of a testator was that the estate should fulfil his ultimate intentions. He wanted to safeguard against possible diminution and against the consequence of his wife's remarriage, which loomed large in testators' considerations. Therefore testators employed life-grants to wives to maintain property for children. In Liverpool, 351 (40 per cent) of those benefiting their wives made such grants, an appreciably higher proportion than elsewhere. The commonplace that remarriage declined from the seventeenth century *may* be less true of Liverpool, and that divergence from a national norm may be yet another instance of Liverpool's singularity being related to its port function. Seafarers were the numerically dominant group among Liverpudlian testators (49 per cent of the total), and their distinct attributes were influential. The perils of seafaring were a spur to mariners' willmaking, and the likelihood of a high rate of early widowhood accounts for a striking incidence of life-grants.

A stronger protection was to make bequests contingent on continuing widowhood. Contemporary comment suggested that this was from concern to preserve the patrimony of minor children, which if in the hands of their mother would transfer to her new husband, as would her life-interest in property.[12] Therefore testators had recourse to pre-cautionary measures. In Liverpool these varied from demanding that an inventory be taken and a bond entered by the new husband, through the most common requirement that the widow relinquish real and personal estate in return for an annuity, to the extreme of the widow being 'Intirely cut off', as Thomas Finney threatened in 1749.

The attitudes of Liverpudlian testators contrast markedly with those of testators in rural Terling 'where there are few examples of conditions in the event of remarriage'.[13] Liverpudlians diverge also from metro-politan practice. Earle found reduction or rescinding of widows' legacies unusual in London.[14] However, in small-town Hinckley, some 29 per cent made their wives' legacies contingent on widowhood.[15] In Liverpool 123 testators made their widows' inheritances contingent upon widow-hood, while a further 64 additionally stipulated chastity: a total of 22 per cent of benefiting wives were thus constrained.[16]

The level of constraint varied over the period: whereas over half the testators of the 1660s made life-grants to their wives, 38 per cent did so in the 1700s and one-third in the 1740s. In the 1660s the same proportion, over half, made bequests contingent on widowhood, and three of the seven testators charged their wives with the upbringing of children. Each of these contingencies was applied to 18 per cent of wives in the 1700s, whereas in the 1740s only 14 per cent of testators stipulated widowhood, and less than 3 per cent of bequests were contingent on raising the family. It is noteworthy that the largest group of wills, that for the 1740s, has the lowest level of contingent legacies. These estimates refine the overall figures of contingencies on wives' bequests between 1660 and 1760: 40 per cent life-interests; 22 per cent on widowhood; 10 per cent on raising minor children.

The incidence of limitation on widows in Liverpool was higher than elsewhere in England.[17] However, this seems attributable to small sample size in some cases, and to the rural/urban dichotomy. Indeed, *increasing* rates of limitation were imposed in America over time: 16 per cent on widows' land in late seventeenth-century Maryland, rising to 31 per cent by the mid-eighteenth century; 36 per cent in Pennsylvania between 1685 and 1756.[18] In apparent contradiction, however, of any fear of wives' future conduct, many testators appointed their wives as executrices. In fact, women retained control over property in their charge as executrices, whereas property held in their own right would pass to future husbands upon remarriage. The incidence of this in Liverpool is explored below.

Trust and Control

Appointment of executors was a critical consideration for any willmaker because control of the estate would be granted to such nominees by the appropriate ecclesiastical court. Indeed it has been suggested that communally active individuals were sought as executors.[19] Existing historiography notes differing expectations of executors over time, place and social class.[20] Liverpool data allow some investigation: the bald statistics are that, for 1,769 wills, 2,152 executors were appointed and 1,063 executrices. Many of the nominated executors had multiple appointments, and 2,307 individuals are believed to have been nominated in total.

The incidence of multiple nomination ranged from some 219 individuals appointed twice, to one notable man, Bryan Blundell, who was appointed executor under 20 wills. Blundell (1675–1756) was a wealthy mariner/merchant, frequent office holder and generous philanthropist, with wide networks of kith, kin and association. Between the extremes of nomination fall two prominent merchants (father and son, John Pemberton), who were appointed under a total of 17 wills, and were conspicuous as executors for testators beyond their immediate kin. Nonconformity was obviously the significant factor in these multiple appointments – six testators were definitely dissenters, and two more had another known nonconformist as executor. One testator can be presumed to have been motivated by mutual connection with Chester. Most interestingly, two wills indicate a business link between the testator and his Pemberton executor.

For Liverpool testators, blood relations and affines made up 54 per cent of executors, with 37 per cent of unspecified relationship, and 9 per cent acknowledged as friends. These figures equate with those for towns in south Lancashire and Cheshire between 1701 and 1760.[21] Thus 46 per cent, if not unrecognised kin, would be either 'community brokers' or 'friends and neighbours' of comparable status or similar occupation to the testator.[22] Liverpool apparently had examples of both but did not noticeably favour either. However, differentiation based on notions of occupational hierarchy may require revision in the light of reconstituted networks of, for example, kinship and religious affiliation. Liverpool's significant nonconformist congregations were largely excluded from civic and vestry office, and have therefore not been obvious to historians as 'community brokers'. At the same time, it is dangerous to assume that two individuals with the same occupational label shared similar status: the term 'mariner' was applied to both ordinary seamen and ship masters.

Historians' differing methodologies preclude comprehensive comparisons of like with like. This is exemplified by the question of wives as executrices. Liverpudlian testators designated their wives as executrices for a total of 643 wills (74 per cent). The wife was sole executrix in 258 cases, and acted jointly in the others: this is relatively low compared with other urban incidence and indeed with all rates for the seventeenth century.[23] In fact the period again seems a key variable. Appointment in Liverpool varied over time as it did in colonial America, where the rates, hitherto corresponding with those in England, declined dramatically during the eighteenth century.[24] There is apparent corroboration from eighteenth-century English evidence for Birmingham and Sheffield, where only around 30 per cent of metalworkers appointed executrices, of whom most would have been their wives.[25]

The closer analysis of Liverpool data reveals a decline over time from 55 per cent of wives as executrices (1660–1680) to 34 per cent (1740–1760). Indirect comparison can be made with the 38 per cent of townsmen in Cheshire and south Lancashire who nominated nuclear family (wives and/or children) between 1701 and 1760.[26] In Hinckley only 24 per cent of executors were wives and/or children, but that was between 1750 and 1839, and the testators in question included bachelors and widowers.[27] A calculation based on all Liverpool testators gives 44 per cent nominating wives (without including nominated children).

Several elements may have a bearing on the rate of Liverpudlians' wives as executrices. The most obvious factor is the influence of seafarers, which, as mentioned above, would be peculiar to port towns. Two characteristics of seafaring testators are germane: many were unmarried young men, and many were raising wills to benefit their creditors. In neither case was a wife appointed executrix. There have been suggestions elsewhere that the 'middling sort' did not believe their wives capable of acting alone; that men were sparing their wives the responsibility; or that wealthier ones were afraid of their widows' remarriage.[28] The appointment of overseers may be seen as also curtailing the autonomy of the widow as executrix. Overseers and trustees were the other appointees under wills, although only nominated by a minority of testators in Liverpool.

Overseers were designated throughout the period but under only 3 per cent of wills, with greater incidence in the seventeenth century. The dearth of overseers might be a northern phenomenon; Selby and rural Yorkshire had the only comparable incidence.[29] However, the period again seems more significant than location, because in early seventeenth-century Southwark, for example, no fewer than 38 of 50 men making wills between 1620 and 1626 appointed overseers.[30] For a later period in Banbury, a 'decline in the use of overseers after the Civil War' was found.[31] The status of the Liverpool overseers somewhat belies the assertion that 'very few overseers were described as men in authority'.[32] Assistance rather than supervision may have been the testator's intention, but undoubtedly many overseers had status to use authoritatively if necessary: of the 39 men chosen, two were clerics, 15 designated 'Mr', five gentlemen, five aldermen, and two Esquires. It has been said that 'women were never appointed overseer'.[33] However, in Liverpool one *was* – a redoubtable merchant widow, Mrs Anne Bushell.

Overseers occurred less frequently and trustees more often during the course of this period. The relative balance may be indicative of two discrete strategies working independently or in tandem: that executors required neither oversight nor the associated patronage, and/or that formal trusts were needed as the sophistication of legal provision percolated to a burgeoning provincial town where wealth was accruing to an unprecedented extent.

About 10 per cent of both testators and testatrices created trusts. The vast majority of trustees were men but over 10 per cent were women, which falls between the proportions of Birmingham at 8 per cent and Sheffield at 21.5 per cent.[34] All three places confute an assertion that 'women were ... virtually never trustees'.[35] The fact that Liverpool's female trustees were appointed with increasing frequency towards the end of the period may be characteristic of greater financial experience and competence in a certain stratum. It also validates the idea of a relaxed interval in a repetitive cycle of varying severity of patriarchal control.[36] Correspondingly, there is little evidence of the economic opportunity afforded to male family members employing the capital of trusts while administering funds on behalf of their female relations as happened during the nineteenth century.[37] Trustees appointed in eighteenth-century Liverpool were not predominantly family members: less than a third were identified in any degree of kinship to the testator.

Trustees might also be executors. Executors were appointed to the virtual role of trustees under 107 wills when estates were vested in them for liquidation and subsequent administration. Their informal role was usually of shorter duration than that of formal trusteeship. However, executors' ongoing responsibility is epitomised by the case of Robert Ashbrooke, mariner, probate 1692. His real estate was still in executors' hands in 1708.[38] In Liverpool it would seem that more executors than trustees had potential use of decedents' estates. The executors' power varied in its duration and in its autonomy, which could be considerable if the testator relied on the executors' judgement. Instructions to 'put out at interest' all or part of an estate indicate executors' access to capital monies. This was significant in the financing of particular trades when resources from craftsmen and others, who had become much more distinctively urban, were less likely to be invested in mortgages. Executors within the testator's trade and those of the mercantile elite had other investment opportunities. The phenomenon seems to be emergent in Liverpool by the mid-eighteenth century, although seen more generally as a somewhat later occurrence.[39] Thus Liverpool testators might be employing distinct wealth-enhancing strategies in their choice of executors. For example, Robert Williamson, mariner and alderman, stated that 'a considerable part of my said estate is in parts of shipps which are at sea'. He believed '[they] cannot be improved but by adventuringe them' and instructed that his 'said executors shall from time to time sett the said shipps to freight or sell them at their discretion'.

All functionaries nominated, whether in Liverpool or far afield, would have been intended to secure estates in their charge and to ensure the transmission of wealth as the testator willed. Apparently, however, more than such safeguarding was hoped of a significant number, and members of the Liverpool community made active use of this available capital in the continuing expansion of the town's economy.

Patterns and Strategies

It has been suggested that 'the difference between women's wills and men's wills is in large part the difference between matrimony and patrimony'.[40] The implication is that while matrimony suggests lateral ties of kinship – thence similar dispersal of property – patrimony suggests property descending. In other studies, patterns of bequest have

Table 4.1 *Relationship of beneficiaries to testator, 1661–1760, expressed as percentage of total no. of wills (1,451)*

Relationship by blood	N	%	Relationship by marriage	N	%	Non-familial	N	%
Son	656	45	Wife	869	60	Unspecified	236	15
Daughter	480	33	Stepchild	34	2	Godchild	30	2
Grandchild	185	13	Son/daughter-in-law	90	6	Friend	109	7
Great-grandchild	8	1	Sibling-in-law	87	6	Servant	65	4
Parent	166	11	Parents-in-law	12	0.8	Partner	3	0.2
Sibling	493	34	Niece/nephew-in-law	6	0.4	Tenant	5	0.3
Niece/nephew	265	18	Grandchild-in-law	3	0.2	Clergy	11	0.7
Aunt/uncle	46	3				Charity	111	8
Cousin	101	7						
Kin	120	8						

Source: Liverpool wills 1661–1760; Ascott, 'Wealth and Community', Table 6.1.

been demonstrably related to the gender of the testator/testatrix.[41] The most obvious difference between the wills of men and women must be those resulting from the restrictions placed upon willmaking by women. Therefore while they were the most frequent beneficiaries under men's wills, spouses would rarely feature in the wills of women: 96 per cent of Liverpudlian testatrices being either widows or spinsters.

The received opinion is that benefit under wills of the early modern period was likely to be concentrated within the nuclear 'family of procreation'.[42] Male and female willmakers had different relationships to their favoured beneficiaries. Women willmakers were predominantly widows and as such were free of many of the pressures upon men's testation. Widows' children were more likely to be adult and already endowed from patrimony, or even already dead. Many women were therefore more free, by the nature of their position, to bequeath according to inclination rather than familial responsibility.

Tables 4.1 and 2 show an analysis of the data according to beneficiaries' relationship with the testator/testatrix. Of 1,451 testators, 60 per cent acknowledged their wives, whereas husbands benefited under only three wills, although named in four of the 12 wills raised by wives. Otherwise blood relations dominated, albeit with marked gender differences: women recognised sons and daughters almost equally, whereas men favoured sons. Women favoured sisters over brothers while men treated them almost equally. Women were twice as likely to remember nephews and nieces. Overall, women favoured *female* blood relations,

Table 4.2 *Relationship of beneficiaries to testatrix, 1661–1760, as percentage of total no. of wills (318)*

Relationship by blood	N	%	Relationship by marriage	N	%	Non-familial	N	%
Son	147	46	Husband	3	1	Unspecified	216	68
Daughter	141	44	Stepchild	11	3	Godchild	16	5
Grandchild	110	35	Son/daughter-in-law	45	14	Friend	8	2
Great-grandchild	4	1	Sibling-in-law	41	13	Servant	33	10
Parent	16	5	Parents-in-law	4	1	Master/mistress	4	1
Sibling	130	41	Niece/nephew-in-law	6	2	Tenant	8	3
Niece/nephew	128	40	Grandchild-in-law	3	1	Clergy	14	4
Aunt/uncle	7	2				Charity	56	18
Cousin	42	13						
Kin	64	20						

Source: Liverpool wills 1661–1760; Ascott, 'Wealth and Community', Table 6.2.

with the exception of their parents. Twice the percentage of men remembered their mothers as remembered their fathers. Testatrices reversed this.

An appreciably higher percentage of testatrices left legacies to affines, and proportionally more women left to *female* affinal relations, although women's apparent gender preference was not demonstrated in relation to sons- and daughters-in-law. More women than men remembered stepchildren.

The most pronounced contrast between women's and men's wills is in their 'diffuse' nature reflected in beneficiaries of unstated relationship, remembered by almost 70 per cent of women but only 15 per cent of men, although half of the latter indicated friendship which was specified by a mere 2 per cent of women. The friendship invoked in men's wills was almost exclusively describing executors, overseers or trustees. Servants and tenants were remembered by few people but nonetheless predominantly by women; masters and mistresses by women only. Clergy received bequests from 3 per cent more women than men, while charities were supported by 10 per cent more women than men: 18 to 8. This survey of Liverpudlian wills therefore reinforces previous studies which have indicated the 'diffuse' nature of women's wills in recognising a wider circle of beneficiaries, of whom a greater proportion would be female and more would appear to be from outside the family circle.[43]

Although wives were the most numerous beneficiaries under men's wills, their interest, as has been noted, was frequently limited to life. To

Table 4.3 *Division of realty among children under wills from period cohorts, by testator's gender*

	1660s		1700s		1740s	
	Men %	Women %	Men %	Women %	Men %	Women %
To eldest son only	–	–	23.8	28.7	28.6	20.0
To eldest son more than other children	–	–	19.0	7.1	7.9	10.0
To elder sons only	33.3	–	4.8	–	3.2	–
To sons but only had sons	16.7	–	–	14.3	4.8	–
To son(s) nothing to daughters	–	–	4.8	–	1.6	–
To sons and daughters	50.0	50.0	9.5	7.1	23.8	–
To daughters but only had daughters	–	–	19.0	14.3	14.3	10.0
To daughter(s) nothing to sons	–	–	4.8	14.3	–	30.0
Not left to children	–	50.0	4.8	7.1	–	20.0
Sold and added to personalty	–	–	9.5	7.1	15.9	10.0
Total number of testators	6	3	21	14	63	10

Source: Liverpool wills, in period cohorts 1665–1669; 1705–1709; 1745–1749; Ascott, 'Wealth and Community', Table 6.8.

assess the degree of bias in favour of particular relations and variations over time, an evaluation of three cohorts has been made, those of all extant Liverpudlian wills of the 1660s, 1700s and 1740s. Bequests to children were of greatest long-term significance, and their share of real estate – freehold, copyhold and, for these purposes, leasehold – is shown in Table 4.3.

The major devisees were eldest sons of testators. By the end of the period almost a quarter of devises were to both sons and daughters. When these devises were of specific items, they were largely under the wills of men who had multiple leasehold properties and thus were strictly bequest rather than devise. There is an impression that the testators making such distribution were unlikely to have gentry links, and an equitable pattern of distribution has been attributed to a 'business culture' as opposed to a 'gentry culture'.[44] Otherwise they reflect equal distribution of unspecified real estate. Realty was left by men to their daughters most frequently when there were only daughters. The property when described was invariably leasehold, but if freehold it would have been expected to go to daughters as co-parceners rather than to a collateral male relative.

Table 4.4 *Division of personalty among children under wills from period cohorts, by testator's gender*

	1660s		1700s		1740s	
	Men %	Women %	Men %	Women %	Men %	Women %
To eldest son more than other children	–	33.3	20.8	11.7	19.7	30.0
To eldest daughter more than younger daughter(s)	10.0	–	4.2	5.9	–	10.0
To son(s) more than daughter(s)	–	–	–	–	–	–
To daughter(s) more than son(s)	20.0	–	12.5	23.5	–	10.0
To one daughter more than other children	10.0	–	33.3	29.4	19.7	20.0
To younger children more than older	30.0	–	12.5	17.6	17.1	10.0
Equal division among children	30.0	66.7	16.7	11.7	38.1	20.0
Insufficient information to establish hierarchy	–	–	–	–	5.3	–
Total number of testators	10	3	24	17	63	10

Source: Liverpool wills, in period cohorts 1665–1669; 1705–1709; 1745–1749; Ascott, 'Wealth and Community', Table 6.7.

Liverpool's pattern of devise by testatrices displays the tendency found elsewhere of women leaving real estate to males rather than females.[45] Women were, however, more likely than men to leave realty to daughters in preference to sons when the existence of both was acknowledged. The reason was sometimes stated: the dispossessed son was feckless or long absent. Prior provision for sons under a father's will is also a possible reason. Individual women could have simply preferred to provide a home for the child, a daughter, in greatest need.[46]

The pattern of bequests to children, agglomerating all personalty, is shown in Table 4.4. In the 1660s younger children received more than their older siblings as often as the share was equal. In the 1700s one daughter or an eldest son had the lion's share more often than there was an equal division. However, both those figures in the 1700s include the instances of only children, which may have precluded an otherwise equitable division. The incidence of younger children receiving more personalty than their elders should be associated with the age/life-stage of the recipients or with the corresponding devise of realty. In the first instance younger children were receiving, either actually or apparently, a share equal to shares previously disbursed among their siblings. The 'hotchpotch' of intestacy was being operated by the testator: this took into account any sum advanced to the child of an intestate during the parent's lifetime, before reckoning the share in residuary estate. Taken in conjunction with the devise of real estate, the disproportionate shares of personalty frequently seem a compensation for all real estate going to the eldest son. When a son was so favoured the estate seems substantial and real property was frequently encumbered to provide cash portions for other children. This practice of the landed classes was copied most conspicuously by the upper echelons of Liverpudlian testators.

Testators appear to favour equitable distribution of personalty most obviously in the 1740s, when a marked predominance is associated with a significant increase in total estates being liquidated and placed at interest, which is in turn allied to a higher incidence of all benefiting children being minors.

The analysis of women's distribution of personalty is hampered by the very low number of wills, but nonetheless Table 4.4 suggests a gender difference in disbursement. Testatrices seem to have recognised their daughters more substantially than testators did and to have favoured daughter(s) over other children, most evidently in the 1700s.

At the primary level of devise and bequest, especially by testators, the stem family predominates, with an apparent focus upon the nuclear family of reproduction where its members survive. Within that framework there is much evidence of personal preference or unstated force of circumstance.

There was an imbalance throughout in that women left a disproportionately higher share of bequests than was warranted by their percentage of the wills, further to which they favoured female beneficiaries, especially in their diffuse disbursements. The careful allocation of many small sums or keepsakes among family and friends is considered indicative of both women's personal feeling towards their possessions and towards the recipients, who were frequently other single women.[47] However, men without close family made similarly 'diffuse' wills; indeed two men each left more than 40 legacies. Women were apparently more ready to make wills reflecting personal discretion with regard to both close family and the wider circle of friends. The wealth of a testator must also influence testamentary inclusion, as in the cases of Bryan Blundell and Elizabeth Clayton, who could afford to look beyond immediate family already well endowed, and who each probably had a central role to wider kin during life as in death.

Charity seems related to both wealth and family circumstance. Unless obviously wealthy, there was less likelihood that a testator with close dependants would leave charitable bequests. Charitable bequests provide significant evidence of migration into Liverpool by frequently indicating the testator's parish of origin. The focus of charity altered during the period 1660–1760: an initial predominance of bequests to the poor and to the church changing in later years to bequests for specific institutions – the Bluecoat School, or the Public Infirmary. Nonetheless there was an overall decline in charitable provision. This should perhaps be set against *inter vivos* philanthropy because the institutions mentioned above were supported by annual subscription as well as outright gift. Possibly there was an alteration in the pattern of charity rather than the inclination to give.

Before Death Do Us Part: Lifetime Giving

While historians have their best evidence for patterns of wealth transmission by bequest, it is also essential to stress the strategies employed for transferring property before death. Such familial provision began long before willmaking unless death was untimely. Indeed, half the resources of the seventeenth-century Essex clergyman, Ralph Josselin, were expended on his children during his lifetime, as revealed by a combination of will and accounts detailing the expense of education, apprenticeship, marriage portions and transfer of goods and land.[48]

A marriage settlement might provide not only for the wife when widowed but also for unborn children – although a settlement nullified a future widow's entitlement to 'thirds', it gave the increased security of constituting a debt and thus first call on the estate. Settlements were frequently made to safeguard the inheritance of children when their mothers remarried. Such instances may warrant only allusion in a will, and thus distort the apparent pattern of provision to an unknown extent. William Valentine's will of 1689 affords an extreme example of an estate obscured by pre-marriage settlement:

> whereas I have hertofore sealled Awriting for the use of my said wife which is of sufficient worth and According to my estate for her Mentenence which thing was done Neare to the time of Our Maridg I for Bere to bequeath Any moore unto her.

The settlement on a second marriage might provide for the children of a man's previous union, as in the case of John Nichols, who rehearsed in his will of 1745 an agreement settling £1,000 on his three daughters and £200 on his new wife, and securing 'for her own use' one-third of his personal estate, 'the above £1,000 first deducted'. Women also initiated pre-marriage settlements to preserve for the duration of coverture not only the estates of existing children but also their own property rights.

Ensuring finance for settlements could require use of the debt and credit network, as shown in John Dutton's will. A reiteration of his marriage agreement was supplemented by the minutiae of calling-in, and putting-out again, monies to fulfil that agreement. The details give incidental information on the combinations of bond and mortgage; the range of status of those involved in this credit network; and the geographical area covered. John Dutton's strategy in 1745 epitomises the extra dimension given to the local loan-market by in-migrants who thus linked the personnel of Liverpool with that of their area of origin. In Dutton's case the circle of debt and credit extended from mid-Cheshire to Liverpool and its Lancashire hinterland.[49]

The child's 'start in life', which might otherwise have been supplied during a testator's lifetime, features in wills when a testator died young or could afford to be a doting grandparent. Thus forward planning for education, apprenticeship, setting-up in trade, or furnishing a marriage portion may be detailed in the will. Much forethought might go into such stratagems at all levels of society.[50]

Most frequently executors were enjoined 'to maintain and educate children according to their degree'. A number of Liverpool merchants educated a son for the professions. Silvester Richmond went further by acquiring the advowson of Garstang for the benefit of his son Richard who became vicar there in 1680 followed by son Henry in 1698.[51] The former eventually became rector of Walton, the latter rector of Liverpool. This securing of professional appointments, manifested in Liverpool by clerical, legal and medical, has been adjudged an eighteenth-century inheritance strategy of the propertied classes.[52]

Preparation for a worst-case scenario was made in 1711 by the yeoman, Will Gandy, who charged that his grandchildren be educated and apprenticed 'that thereby they may be able to support and maintain themselves if their temporal substance shall happen to be Wasted, spent or gone'. Similarly in 1718 Thomas Roby, gentleman, left money for his nephew's schooling and requested 'Aldmn. Cunliffe to take the lad to be an apprentice to the tobacco trade or a cooper wh'ether he likes best'.

Apprenticeship was supposedly in decline during this period except in servicing the upper strata of urban occupations.[53] Such servicing is thought to have been typified by the sons of county families enrolling in mercantile apprenticeships. In mid-seventeenth-century Liverpool the career ladder was frequently from mariner to merchant. This was the route of Edward Tarleton, senior, grandson of minor landed gentry. He became a Liverpool mariner/merchant, property holder, and civic dignitary. Resurgence of the family fortune in the Liverpool area enabled the eventual repurchase of the ancestral seat, Aigburth Hall, and subsequent relocation there by Edward's greatgrandson, John Tarleton (1718–1775).

Assuring apprenticeship was also a conspicuous consideration for many *urban* testators. Men with extremes of wealth could express the same purpose: in 1694 Thomas Willis left £100 to bind his grandson apprentice with a further £500 'to set him up in trade'.[54] Fifteen years later, not matching the munificence but with equal concern, Thomas Mercer wrote 'I have £7 by me which I would have you, my executor, to pay my funeral expenses ... and the remainder ... I think will bind my son into a trade.' Not only men gave thought to apprenticeships. In 1738 Elizabeth Summerset reviewed her strategy: 'whereas I have already given to my daughter Alice £40 as apprentice fee to learn the art of a milliner ... it is my will that ... Alice ... shall instruct [my daughter] Mary in the said trade and they joyn their fortunes ... into one Common stock for carrying on the said trade in Liverpool or elsewhere as soon as Alice is out of her time'. Madam Elizabeth Clayton had more largesse to bestow upon her descendants. She assisted with £100, of the £400 fee, to bind one grandson to 'William Tennant citizen and mercer of London' and left £100 in Trust until he came out of his time. She paid the full £250 fee to bind another grandson.

Formal apprenticeship was not the only means of provision as witnessed in 1747 by the will of George Parker, which stated: 'whereas I have some time ago given unto my said two daughters ... to carry on their business of shopkeeping now I give and bequeath the same unto them divided equally together with all stock book debts and Improvements they have already made ... not chargeable for the same ... neither chargeable for rent of the shop they now enjoy for three months after my decease'.

Another significant element in wealth transmission was the marriage portion, for which wills are an important if inconsistent source. Prior provision or future funding was mentioned by testators of diverse wealth and status, albeit mainly by those of substance and standing. The rector, Thomas Baldwin, specified in his will of 1751 an item of real estate as part of his younger son's marriage settlement. Since his elder daughter received only some items formerly her mother's, while the younger had 10 guineas for mourning, it seems likely that there had been appropriate provision on the occasion of their respective marriages. In 1714 William Clayton, merchant and MP, was more specific: £1,000 paid earlier to each of his sons-in-law as marriage portion was matched as legacy to each unmarried child. Craftsmen could be equally concerned to safeguard the future for their offspring. William Pryor, cordwainer, entered into a complex of bonds to ensure a settlement of property on his daughter by her future husband, after which Pryor would pay his son-in-law £60. Failing the completion Pryor rescinded the arrangement in favour of a direct payment of £60 to his daughter.

A further strategy for capital consolidation was kin-marriage. First-cousin marriage or sibling exchange both limited the 'leakage' of wealth from the family over the generations.[55] While lacking robust statistics, the impression is of frequent reinforcement of such family ties in Liverpool. There are examples of successive generations augmenting the association, and many instances of sibling exchange. In the Tarleton family examples of the former strategy include Frances marrying first her cousin Timothy, then Jonathan Livesley, with *their* daughters marrying two Tarleton cousins. Sibling exchange is best exemplified by James, Anne and Margaret Robinson marrying respectively Mary, Lawrence and Roger Dewhurst.

Broad strategies of wealth transmission and familial provision can be identified and analysed in the aggregate as above. However, generalisations about patterns of bequest are open to question, since there was a baffling multiplicity of inheritance practices. It is difficult to reduce the mass to patterns without undue simplification of known variables, and an acknowledgement that many variables must remain unknown. Bequests will follow some pattern based on a fusion of social mores and individual inclination tempered by testamentary restrictions, yet each will is the product of a unique combination of circumstances: economic, demographic and personal. Although these factors are key variables, exact wealth is irrecoverable from most wills, especially the portmanteau formulaic ones, and without family reconstitution it is impossible to be sure what accidents of demography or demonstrations of family favouritism are represented by the extant will. The final section will therefore demonstrate how the application of a variant of the family reconstitution technique enables deeper understanding of Liverpool's testamentary evidence.

Cases in Context

Wills, it must be remembered, are the product of individual priorities and circumstances, and the testator is under no obligation to place his wishes in context. There is rarely any explanation for a particular pattern of bequest, or sense of alternative strategies that might have been pursued. The individual, personal nature of the will makes it uniquely valuable to the historian, but also means that the full implications of any given will can rarely be assessed through study of that document alone – other, linked sources must be used to locate the will in its broader context. In particular, the group of *actual* beneficiaries needs to be assessed in terms of the *potential* kin group available to a testator.[56] Miranda Chaytor has communicated the complexities of kinship and illustrated that

> households ... were not fixed or isolated structures; the boundaries between
> them and the hierarchies within them were continually broken and rearranged

as marriages and deaths moved people between households, redefining their status and the relationships between them.[57]

Two techniques have been suggested for approaching these complex structures: microsimulation and family reconstitution. Microsimulation shows the relations available to an individual at different life-stages from fertility, mortality and nuptiality indices. The number of various degrees of kin is calculable by this means to recreate the widest demographic context.[58] Family reconstitution, on the other hand, reorganises vital event records into nuclear family units.[59] A variant of that methodology was therefore chosen for this analysis to establish not only the familial situation of an individual testator but also the interlinking of families in networks of kinship and association.[60]

Different family circumstances probably pertained in the cases of, for example, a man who left all to be divided equally among his children; a man who left to children but in very disparate proportions; and a man who left all to a wide circle of kin. For instance, the last willmaker may have had no immediate family and for that reason be making wider distribution, but what demographic pattern he reflects is unknown. He might be bachelor or widower, unmarried or much married, never have been a father or have outlived a large brood. What, for example, were the family circumstances of Liverpool merchant Hugh Patten, who left everything to wider family in Warrington, whence he came? His will of 1736 gives no hint of the reason for this uncommon pattern of bequest. Liverpool parish registers, however, reveal that Patten had two wives and ten children, all of whom predeceased him, and are therefore unmentioned in his will.

In 1708 Patten's mother-in-law, Anne Tarleton, also left an unusual will, showing inconsistent treatment of her two daughters and her grandchildren. One daughter, Anne, received the considerable bequest of the 'great cedar chest' and half of residual personalty while the other, Sarah, did not benefit. The testatrix gave opposite treatment to her grandchildren: Anne's three children are unmentioned, but Sarah's received half their grandmother's residual personalty. The will gives no reason for the starkly different treatment. It might be surmised that one daughter was under coverture whereas the other was currently widowed and seen as in need. However, record linkage establishes Anne Moone already benefiting as the widow of both George Lewis, and Robert Moone and finally becoming Anne Williamson. *Her* will exemplifies unequal distribution by widows favouring daughters over sons, and primarily the unmarried daughter – with freehold property and specific personalty – before division of the residue.

Linkage also reveals equitable treatment of the two Tarleton daughters, Sarah and Anne, by their father, Edward. He left properties to revert to them after his wife's death. In 1708 Anne Tarleton was rated for these in a Chappel Yard enclave of widows, which included her daughter, then Anne Moone.[61] This example demonstrates how much more can be understood of property holding and the data of rate assessments from the reconstruction of kinship networks.

Another mercantile family making unequal distribution epitomises the vulnerability of mercantile wealth through contrasts between the bequest patterns of father and son, Richard Houghton. In 1712 the senior left personal estate valued at nearly £22,000, of which the junior received a disproportionate share. The whole of considerable realty went to junior, albeit with encumbrances. The elder Richard left bequests to wider family, servants and charity, with £1,000 each to younger children plus a share equal with their mother and elder brother in residual personalty. He expressed concern over education, explicitly decreeing that his second son, Henry,

> be brought up a scholar and as soon as he shall be fittly qualified with good schoole learneing then that he have what further education may be convenient at some of the Colleges of Oxford or Cambridge til he be capable of some benefice or Imployment ... to be paid from interest on £1,000.

Any shortfall was to be made up by the testator's widow or eldest son without 'breaking into his [Henry's] said legacy'. Reconstruction of the kinship network reveals the boy as a grandson of Silvester Richmond, and possibly benefiting from a unique provision made by the latter who, in 1691, had left the advowson of Garstang to be administered for family advantage.[62] *His* executors were to fill vacancies 'with a suitable grandchild or great-grandchild, and *no* strangers'.

Richard Houghton, junior, could offer no such largesse and restricted bequests to lineal descendants. In 1746 he detailed rich real and personal estate but envisaged debts consuming the latter and requiring sale or mortgage of the former, which was charged with finding a mere £100 each for the young children of his second marriage. His first family received only mourning rings, being 'handsomely provided for and portioned as well from their mother's as out of my settled estate'. Grandchildren had just a guinea each. The token bequests resulted from 'the great and heavy losses in Trade I have lately sustained'. Not only is distribution demonstrably unequal but family linkage also contrasts substantial with incongruously small bequests. The predicament of Houghton junior demonstrates how the insecurity of trade could decimate considerable inheritance.

Unequal distribution of estates was not the sole preserve of elite families such as the Tarletons and Houghtons. Much more modest estates were subject to similar concerns, and were divided to make best provision for the most needy family members. Indeed it can be argued that limited resources made discriminating provision even more crucial further down the social scale. In 1725 Jeremiah Arrowsmith, a tailor, left inventoried household goods worth just £18.12s.1d. to his wife as executrix, charged with 'educating and bringing up' a minor son and daughter after provision of only 12d. each to an older son and daughter. The will does not explain unequal distribution. However, the elder children were from a first marriage in Upholland, Lancashire, and were aged 23 and 18 respectively, considerably older than the nine- and seven-year-old offspring of Arrowsmith's second marriage, solemnised after he moved to Liverpool.[63] Arrowsmith was protecting the vulnerable younger children, his elder children being either set up in the world or expected to make their own way.

Arrowsmith differentiated among his biological children, but second families including stepchildren could cause still more complications. In 1710 Robert Sheilds specified that money surplus to their upbringing be divided among his three minor children. The will of his widow Elizabeth reveals, however, that he had a stepson, Alexander Lewis: Elizabeth's previous marriage was to Edward Lewis, goldsmith. Thus she may not have been continuing Robert's craft during her widowhood as much as maintaining a business which she brought to that marriage. Certainly Elizabeth left the goldsmith's enterprise to her son by the first union. The safeguarding of this inheritance, by a now irrecoverable settlement made before Elizabeth's second marriage, would explain the second husband's completely separate strategy in providing exclusively for his own children.

Proposed paternal provision for minor children could be improved by a maternal scheme. Combining the wills of Thomas Carter, gentleman, and his widow, Hannah, exemplifies this. His will of 1696 charged unspecified debts on the family home in Chapel Street, which he directed to be sold. Any residue after the clearance of debt was to be divided between his three minor daughters, whose maintenance and monetary legacies, at the age of 21, were charged to leasehold property in neighbouring Toxteth Park, which was left to his wife.

Hannah's will of 1709 recounts her strategies to resolve the situation (two previous widowhoods may explain her acumen and assurance). Thomas is stated to have been 'indebted to several persons … to the sume of £420 and upwards'. To pay this Hannah had been 'forced to borrow and take up at Interest' a total of £330. Only in 1709 had the Chapel Street property been sold for £380, from which the debts of £330 were to be paid. The leasehold, charged by Thomas with £350 for his daughters, was left by Hannah in trust for the use of one daughter in lieu of the £100 from her father.

The stratagems in operation above are illustrative of various aspects of the credit network. Hannah kept the family home by incurring debts in her own name to clear those of her deceased husband. The sources of

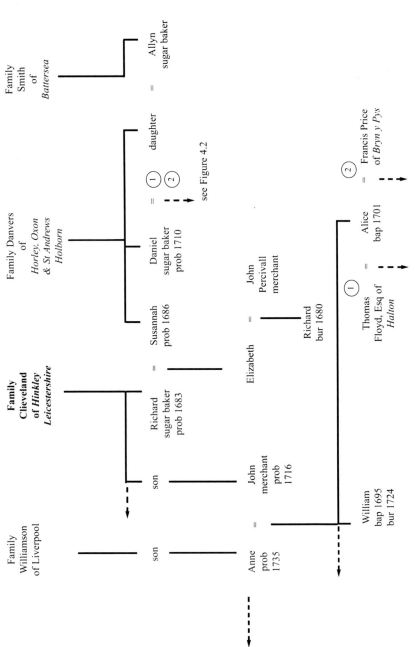

Figure 4.1 *Clieveland family linkage*

these monies illustrate two phenomena: inter-familial borrowing, in this case from the executors of Thomas Carter's deceased brother; and kinship areas of interest/influence, not only Liverpool but nearby Toxteth Park and Roby, where the family had connections. The factors behind each instance of the loan market in action are shown as complex and pertinent to the individual.

Testators had to be pragmatic and flexible to ensure that the more vulnerable family members were protected, and this is not always visible in their wills. In addition, many individuals benefited under more than one will, accumulating a number of bequests. Broad networks of bequest were particularly significant in Liverpool, because the highly mobile population retained links to their origins, and chains of wealth ran both ways. At the top of the social scale, Elizabeth Clayton's children and grandchildren in Liverpool are known to have benefited substantially under the will of her brother, who was Rector of Stoke Bruerne, Northamptonshire, when he died.[64] At the other end of the scale, and beneficiary of bequest *from* Liverpool, was Joseph Grayson whose uncle, David Greson [*sic*], left freehold properties in Liverpool to his nephews with instruction that 'none of the houses to be sold but to descend to the lawful heirs'. This was the magnet that pulled Joseph to follow his uncle to Liverpool from Rainford, Lancashire, and made Joseph one of few labourers to leave real estate.

Reconstruction of kinship and bequest networks gives an instant impression of general disbursement and concentration of bequests. It also reveals the specific accumulation of an individual who benefited under several wills. Such reconstructions of *mobile* commercial families are particularly revealing. The Clieveland family provide an excellent example (Figure 4.1). They entered Liverpool, flourished there, and left within the generations spanned by this study, taking, in the process, the control of appreciable amounts of real estate into 'foreign' (Welsh!) hands.[65]

Richard Clieveland and his brother-in-law, Daniel Danvers, were both distance migrants of gentry origin, who came as entrepreneurs from London.[66] They were among 'the several ingenious men settled in Liverpool which caused ... trade to the plantations and other places'.[67] Clieveland and Danvers considered their venture worth a very high purchase price for the freedom of Liverpool. They paid £40 each in 1682: only two of more than 1,500 freemen in the second half of the seventeenth century paid a higher sum.[68] They pioneered the new industry of sugar baking founded on West Indian imports. Family backing in the industry came from their affine links to the great London sugar-baking family, the Smiths of Battersea, albeit not in the form recorded by Moore in 1667: 'One Mr Smith, a great sugar baker at London ... worth forty thousand pounds ... came to treat with me'.[69]

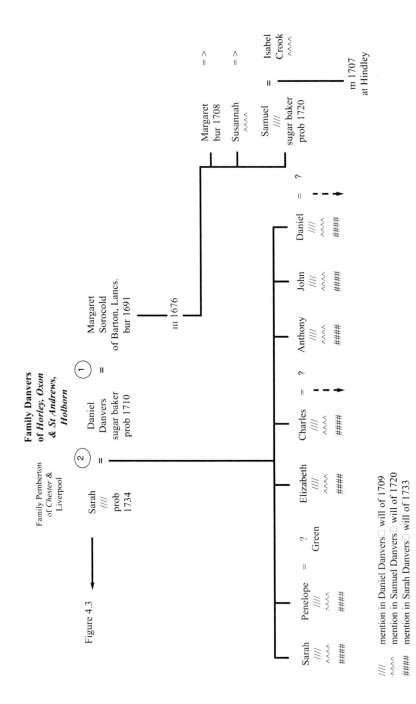

Figure 4.2 *Danvers family linkage*

The Clieveland/Danvers/ Smith interest group did build a sugar house but on an entirely different site from the one under negotiation with Moore.[70]

Substantial property was acquired. Richard Clieveland, first listed in 1673, was one of only four householders taxed for seven or more hearths, but whether he also had tenanted property then or later remains unknown.[71] There is no detail in his bequest of residual estate to his wife, Suzanna, and no mention of real estate in her will. Richard's joint bequest of £400 to his only child and her husband illustrates marriage portions and claims typicality in being conditional on the son-in-law settling 'an estate of inheritance in fee simple as is usually settled on a wife and issue in this Country for and upon the receipt of a £1000 marriage portion'.

Having no male heir, Richard adopted his nephew John, who joined him in Liverpool, married into the old-established local family of Williamson, and went on to represent Liverpool as MP from 1710 to 1713. Much of John Clieveland's wealth came from heavy involvement in overseas trading with both Ireland and the American Plantations.[72] In 1708 John was rated for two residential properties in Liverpool as well as five Townfield or Common holdings.[73] On his death, in 1716, he bequeathed to his children that same Liverpool property plus six parcels, recently purchased, of houses, warehouses and land. These included, outside Liverpool, the Manor of Birkenhead together with 'divers messuages, land, and tenements' in four North Wirral townships, and a share in the saltworks at Dungeon Point, six miles upriver from Liverpool. By the time John Clieveland's surviving daughter, Alice, left the town after marrying a Welshman, she had control of real estate within Liverpool, in the local area, and further afield. Alice brought to her second marriage not only the property left by her father, but also a share of the inheritance of her brother, William. This included the Manor of Birkenhead, of which a namesake of Alice's husband, Francis Price, was still Lord in 1839.[74] In addition Alice was left, by her mother, property outside Liverpool, in Wirral and east Lancashire, including an industrial interest in an 'Alum Works near Blackburn'.

The Clievelands may have profited handsomely from their move to Liverpool, but they clearly did not see their horizons restricted to the town. The *extra*-Liverpool dimension of many financial and commercial activities, including property ownership, serves as a reminder that some of the town's wealthier citizens operated on a broader canvas than can be recovered readily by historians largely reliant on limited local sources. This stratum, termed as 'genteel', was composed of lesser landowners, professionals, merchants and manufacturers.[75] The strategies of the mercantile Clievelands encapsulate key phenomena: entrepreneurial activity, marriages respectively cementing a business association and a

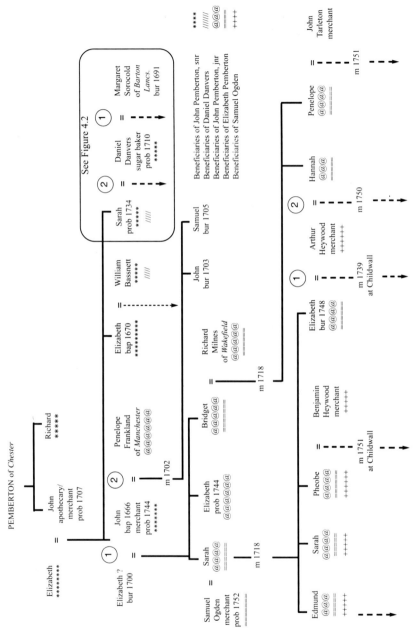

Figure 4.3 *Pemberton family linkage*

migrant into the urban establishment, the accumulation of town property and ultimate purchase of a manorial estate, and the dowering of a merchant's daughter into the landed gentry, which took the profits of all foregoing activity out of Liverpool.[76]

By contrast, associated families confirm a concentration of wealth within Liverpool. The aforementioned Daniel Danvers, brother-in-law and partner to the elder Clieveland, was himself a wealthy man. In 1682 he could afford £40 to become a freeman of Liverpool; in 1708 his house, warehouse, sugar-house and stock made the highest valuation, £450.[77] Danvers exemplifies the importance of incorporating life-stage into any wealth assessment of those rated in the fiscal records. In 1708 he was perhaps between 55 and 60: the children of his first marriage were all married (just), children of the second marriage were all minors, and Daniel himself was to die in 1710. Figure 4.2 shows his wealth passed to the next generation. With the exception of specific realty to the eldest son, all residual estate was divided equally among the second family at majority. They benefited subsequently under the wills of their half-brother and mother.

Danvers' nonconformist Pemberton affines (Figures 4.2 and 4.3) demonstrate further that Liverpool not only attracted the poor hoping to become rich, but also the well-off hoping to become richer. John Pemberton, senior, came from Chester to Liverpool in the 1650s to be an apothecary who turned merchant.[78] He was a burgess of Chester and held significant realty there which he devised fifty years later to his only son, John, together with 'a house and a small parcel of land in Virginia' and the reversion of two of his four Liverpool properties with the two fields 'leased from the towne of Liverpool'. John junior also received shipping shares and £110. His sisters, one of whom had married her father's apprentice, were to have a Liverpool house each on the death of their mother. Sixty-five pounds was left for pecuniary bequests, mainly to wider family within Liverpool.

The Liverpool valuation of John junior in 1708 was £350, and his considerable trading activities during that year were concentrated on Virginia.[79] His total wealth in 1737, when he made his will, cannot be appraised, but the document illustrates the domestic financial arrangements among the mercantile elite of the period. It is notable that he left that 'which I have not already settled'. His wife was to have £600 over and above £100 by marriage settlement, and 'all the money [not above £100] which she hath in her own hands and which I usually allow'd to be as her private purse'. John's unmarried daughter was left one-third of residual realty and personalty, £500 cash legacy, and '£1,500 to make her equal with marriage portion to daughters Ogden and Milnes', whose respective children received equal shares in the other two-thirds of residual estate after their own fathers had received £500 each. 'Daughter

Ogden' married within Liverpool nonconformity, but 'daughter Milnes' married the scion of a prominent dissenting family in Wakefield, who became Unitarians and prospered to the extent of gaining dowries of *c.* £100,000 with the daughters-in-law of the next generation.[80] Pemberton's joint executors (unmarried daughter and sons-in-law) had discretion to sell realty and were instructed to place personal estate at interest in Trust until the grandchildren were of age, which in several cases was probably before their grandfather's death.

The apparent loss of one-third of this fortune from Liverpool to Wakefield was mitigated by two of those heiresses taking Liverpudlian merchants as husbands. Great-granddaughters of John Pemberton senior were the heiresses sought by the Heywood brothers, Liverpool merchants descended from a southeast Lancashire family which had produced renowned nonconformist ministers. Indeed Arthur and Benjamin Heywood are examples of sibling-exchange marriage, which Arthur then compounded by a second kin-marriage to his deceased wife's cousin.[81] The Heywoods utilised part of their substantial wealth to found the earliest Liverpool bank to survive, and funded much nonconformist philanthropy in the wider region.[82]

These cases demonstrate the importance of moving beyond an analysis based on individual wills to a broader understanding derived from the reconstruction of networks, which often involved overlapping familial, residential, occupational, political, associational and religious elements. Although extremely labour-intensive, such an approach not only facilitates a more nuanced study of already visible elites, but casts new light on their middling and lower counterparts.

Conclusion

The specific examples, and the broader patterns identified in earlier sections of the chapter, demonstrate the sophisticated nature of wealth-preservation strategies in early modern Liverpool. The complexity of Liverpudlian provision needs to be assessed in the context of the town's development during the century after the Restoration, especially in its maritime connections. A range of indicators point to remarkable change and growth. Population increased exponentially from a very low base without pre-existing support systems: Liverpool lacked a medieval heritage of guild and parochial institutions which in other towns provided an underpinning, however rudimentary, for demographic and commercial expansion in the early modern era. In addition, in- and out-migration with possible separation from extended family, accompanied by high levels of male employment in dangerous occupations, created an uncertain environment for those contemplating the financial security of their families. Even quite lowly individuals sought to ensure some level of provision. More positively, opportunities for the acquisition of wealth in an expanding port town gave others sufficient riches to enable distribution beyond the immediate family.

Broadly speaking, therefore, the particular circumstances of the burgeoning town encouraged the widespread adoption of legal strategies for the familial preservation of wealth. These ranged from the most basic provisions of a will to the more complex forms of entails and trusts, or liquidation for investment. Not only did willmaking itself spread far down the social scale, but also wealthier Liverpudlians had early recourse to the more sophisticated strategies associated with the landed classes. The existence of wills from a broad range of testators is in itself indicative of the fragile, but also potentially lucrative, nature of life in Liverpool. However, the true complexity of the situation becomes apparent through the content of the wills, and – most importantly – through their contextualisation by network reconstruction.

Notes

1. J. Brewer and R. Porter, eds, *Consumption and the World of Goods*, London, 1993; L. Weatherill, *Consumer Behaviour and Material Culture in Britain 1660–1760*, London, 1988; M. Spufford, *The Great Reclothing of Rural England*, London, 1984; J. Thirsk, *Economic Policy and Projects: The Development of a Consumer Society in Early Modern England*, Oxford, 1978. For a wider view of cause and effect see F. Braudel, *Capitalism and Material Life, 1400–1800*, London, 1973.

2. Cf. K. Morgan, *Bristol and the Atlantic Trade in the Eighteenth Century*, Cambridge, 1993; T. M. Devine and G. Jackson, *Glasgow Volume 1: Beginnings to 1830*, Manchester, 1995. For a specific impact on Liverpool trade see L. M. Cullen, *Anglo-Irish Trade, 1660–1800*, Manchester, 1968, pp. 29–30.

3. Source references for all testamentary evidence cited in the text are in Appendix 2. For clarification of multiple references to individuals and families in Chapters 3–6, e.g. Clieveland and Clayton, see the index.

4. D. A. Rabuzzi, 'Women as merchants in eighteenth-century northern Germany: the case of Stralsund, 1750–1830, *Central European History*, 28. 4, 1995, pp. 441–42. I am indebted to Dr G. J. Milne for this reference.

5. P. Mathias, 'Capital, credit and enterprise in the Industrial Revolution', in *The Transformation of England*, ed. P. Mathias, London, 1979, pp. 88–90.

6. See D. E. Ascott, 'Wealth and Community: Liverpool 1660–1760', unpublished PhD thesis, University of Liverpool, 1996, pp. 235–61.

7. For a comprehensive study of wealth holding and restrictions see A. L. Erickson, *Women and Property in Early Modern England*, London, 1993.

8. J. and N. Cox, 'Probate 1500–1800: a system in transition', in *When Death Do Us Part: Understanding and Interpreting the Probate Records of Early*

Modern England, ed. T. Arkell, N. Evans and N. Goose, Oxford, 2000, pp. 14–37; for a distillation relevant to Liverpool in this period see Ascott, 'Wealth and Community', pp. 25–43.

9. Cox and Cox, 'Probate', pp. 31–32.

10. Erickson, *Women and Property*, pp. 178–86.

11. See Appendix 1 Sources and Methods: Testamentary records.

12. H. Swinburne, *A Briefe Treatise of Testaments and Last Willes*, 1590, pp. 299–301.

13. K. Wrightson and D. Levine, *Poverty and Piety in an English Village, Terling 1525–1700*, New York, 1979, p. 97.

14. P. Earle, *The Making of the English Middle Class*, London, 1989, p. 321.

15. P. Lane, 'Women, property and inheritance', in *Urban Fortunes, 1700–1900*, ed. J. Stobart and A. Owens, Aldershot, 2000, p. 183.

16. Some 12 testators even extended the same proviso to the legacies of their daughters and daughters-in-law, and one stipulated that a benefiting servant should not remarry.

17. Erickson, *Women and Property*, table 9.4, p. 167.

18. L. G. Carr, 'Inheritance in the Colonial Chesapeake', in *Women in the Age of the American Revolution*, ed. R. Hoffman and P. J. Albert, Charlottesville, VA, 1989, pp. 172, 177. The Pennsylvania figure combines data for contingencies on widowhood and children's minority: C. Shammas, 'Early American Women and Control over Capital', in Hoffman and Albert, eds, *Women*, p. 142.

19. S. D'Cruze, 'The Middling Sort in eighteenth-century Colchester: independence, social relations and the community broker', in *The Middling Sort of People*, ed. J. Barry and C. Brooks, London, 1994, pp. 181–207.

20. M. Berg, 'Women's Property and the Industrial Revolution', *Journal of Interdisciplinary History*, 24.2, 1993, p. 239.

21. J. Stobart, 'Social and geographical contexts of property transmission in the eighteenth century', in Stobart and Owens, eds, *Urban Fortunes*, Table 5.1 p. 113.

22. D'Cruze, 'The Middling Sort', p. 182; Stobart, 'Social and geographical contexts', p. 113.

23. Erickson, *Women and Property*, table 9.1, p. 158.

24. D. S. Narrett, 'Men's Wills and Women's Property Rights in Colonial New York', in Hoffman and Albert, eds, *Women*, p. 118.

25. Berg, 'Women's Property', p. 239.

26. Stobart, 'Social and geographical contexts', table 5.1, p. 113.

27. Lane, 'Women, property and inheritance', pp. 148–49.

28. Earle, *Making*, p. 315; Erickson, *Women and Property*, p. 159.

29. Erickson, *Women and Property*, table 9.2, p. 160.

30. J. Boulton, *Neighbourhood and Society*, Cambridge, 1987, pp. 237–38.

31. R. T. Vann, 'Wills and the family in an English town: Banbury, 1550–1800', *Journal of Family History*, 4, 1979, p. 366.

32. Erickson, *Women and Property*, p. 161.

33. Erickson, *Women and Property*, p. 229.

34. Berg, 'Women's Property', p. 238.

35. Erickson, *Women and Property*, p. 229.

36. S. Staves, *Married Women's Separate Property in England, 1660–1833*, Cambridge, MA, 1990, p. 229.

37. L. Davidoff and C. Hall, *Family Fortunes*, London, 1987, p. 209.

38. H. Peet, ed., *Liverpool in the reign of Queen Anne, 1705 and 1708*, Liverpool, 1908, pp. 80, 109.

39. B. L. Anderson, 'Provincial Aspects of the Financial Revolution of the Eighteenth Century', *Business History*, 11, 1969, p. 17.

40. Erickson, *Women and Property*, p. 213.

41. N. Evans, 'Inheritance, Women, Religion and Education in Early Modern Society as revealed by Wills', in *Probate Records and the Local Community*, ed. P. Riden, Gloucester, 1985, pp. 53–70; Erickson, *Women and Property*, p. 213; Berg, 'Women's Property', pp. 233–50; A. McCrum, 'Inheritance and the family', in Stobart and Owens, eds, *Urban Fortunes*, pp. 164–68. Contrary conclusions have been drawn by K. Wrightson, 'Kinship in an English Village: Terling, Essex 1500–1700', in *Land, Kinship and Life-Cycle*, ed. R. M. Smith, Cambridge, 1984, p. 325.

42. Wrightson, 'Kinship in an English Village', pp. 324–32; Vann, 'Wills and the family', pp. 346–67; D. Cressy, 'Kinship and kinship interaction in early modern England', *P&P*, 113, 1986, pp. 38–69.

43. V. Brodsky, 'Widows in Late Elizabethan London', in *The World We Have Gained*, ed. L. Bonfield, R. M. Smith and K. Wrightson, Oxford, 1986, p. 148; J. A. Johnston, 'The Probate Inventories and Wills of a Worcestershire Parish, 1676–1775', *Midland History*, 1, 1971, p. 32; Vann, 'Wills and the family', pp. 366–67.

44. C. F. Foster, *Seven Households: Life in Cheshire and Lancashire, 1582–1774*, Arley, 2002, p. 4.

45. Berg, 'Women's Property', p. 243.

46. S. D. Amussen, *An Ordered Society: Gender and Class in Early Modern England*, Oxford, 1988, pp. 91–92.

47. Berg, 'Women's Property', p. 243.

48. A. D. J. Macfarlane, *The Family Life of Ralph Josselin, a Seventeenth-Century Clergyman*, Cambridge, 1970.

49. Ascott, 'Wealth and Community', pp. 262–89 and Appendix VII.

50. E. P. Thompson, 'The grid of inheritance: a comment', in *Family and Inheritance: Rural Society in Western Europe, 1200-1800*, ed. J.Goody, J. Thirsk and E. P. Thompson, Cambridge, 1976, pp. 328–60.

51. See R. Trappes-Lomax, ed., *The Diary and Letter Book of the Rev. Thomas Brockbank 1671–1709*, CS, 89, Manchester, 1930, pp. 153–224.

52. Thompson, 'The grid of inheritance', p. 358.

53. P. Clark, 'Migrants in the city', in *Migration and Society in Early Modern England*, ed. P. Clark and D. C. Souden, London, 1987, p. 269.

54. The £100 premium was probably for a Liverpool apprenticeship, the highest rate for which in 1718 was £130, quoted in E. Hughes, *North Country Life in the Eighteenth Century*, London, 1952, p. 107.

55. These strategies are explored in P. D. Hall, 'Family Structure and Economic Organization', in *Family and Kin in Urban Communities, 1700–1930*, ed. T. K. Hareven, New York, 1977, pp. 38–61.

56. Cressy, 'Kinship', p. 56.

57. M. Chaytor, 'Household and kinship', *History Workshop Journal*, 10, 1980, p. 48.

58. For modern application of this technique developed by J. E. Smith see 'News from the ESRC Cambridge Group for the History of Population & Social Structure', *LPS*, 34, 1985, p. 11.

59. Cressy, 'Kinship', p. 56.

60. See Appendix 1 Sources and Methods: Testamentary records.

61. Peet, *Liverpool in the reign of Queen Anne*, p. 64.

62. See above, p. 120.

63. A. Brierley, ed., *The Registers of the Church of St. Thomas the Martyr, Upholland in the County of Lancaster*, LPRS, 23, Rochdale, 1905.

64. See W. F. Irvine ed., *A collection of Lancashire and Cheshire Wills not now found in any Probate Registry 1301–1752*, RSLC, 30, London, 1896, pp. 154–56. Thomas Leigh, rector, will date 1749.

65. D. E. Ascott and F. Lewis, 'Motives to Move: reconstructing individual migration histories in early-eighteenth century Liverpool', in *Migration, Mobility and Modernization in Europe*, ed. D. Siddle, Liverpool, 2000, pp. 103–04.

66. Peet, *Liverpool in the reign of Queen Anne*, pp. 32–33; 61–62.

67. The preamble to the Act which made Liverpool a Parish of itself, see H. Peet, ed., *Liverpool Vestry Books, 1681–1834*, vol. 1, 1681–1799, Liverpool, 1912, Appendix B, pp. 409–10.

68. Liverpool Town Books: LplRO 352/COU 3–6.

69. T. Heywood, ed., *The Moore Rental*, CS, 10, Manchester, 1847, pp. 76–77.

70. Smith did not, as Parkinson and others have suggested from the above source, complete the purchase mooted in the Rental. C. N. Parkinson, *The Rise of the Port of Liverpool*, Liverpool, 1952, p. 54.

71. Hearth Tax, 1673, PRO: E179/132/355.

72. For example, see Liverpool Port Books. PRO: E190/1375/8.

73. Peet, *Liverpool in the reign of Queen Anne*, pp. 59, 61, 71, 77, 115, 117.

74. J. Boult, ed., 'A Littoral Survey of the Port of Liverpool', *THSLC*, 22, 1870, pp. 188–90.

75. A. Vickery, *The Gentleman's Daughter: Women's Lives in Georgian England*, New Haven and London, 1998, pp. 13–14.

76. R. Grassby, 'Social Mobility and Business Enterprise in Seventeenth Century England', in *Puritans and Revolutionaries*, ed. D. Pennington and K. Thomas, Oxford, 1978, p. 358.

77. Calculated by T. Baines, *History of the commerce and town of Liverpool,* London, 1852, p. 351.

78. Heywood, *Moore Rental*, p. 93.

79. Baines, *History of commerce*, p. 351; Liverpool Port Book, PRO: E190/ 1375/8.

80. R.G. Wilson, *Gentlemen Merchants: The Merchant Community in Leeds, 1700–1830,* Manchester, 1971, p. 22.

81. See Figure 4.3 for relationships.

82. G. Chandler, *Four Centuries of Banking*, vol. 1, London, 1964, pp. 171– 90; P. O'Brien, *Warrington Academy 1757–86*, Wigan, 1989, p. 47.

5

Government

Liverpool is a town whose notoriety as a centre of the slave trade and considerable commercial success during the seventeenth and eighteenth centuries belies the fact that we know little about the townspeople or their society. This chapter focuses on the governors of that society. It approaches the subject by identifying the Liverpool men (and the very few women) named as town officers and councillors in the main town record, the Town Books, during the period 1650 to 1750.[1] The officers' names were listed in the election court on 18 October each year or in the first portmoot court of the year soon after; the names of councillors were listed after each council or assembly meeting. Some 6,593 names were recorded in the hundred-year period, many of them appearing repeatedly as individuals served year after year. From this number, 1,587 individuals were identified and added to a data set of those involved in the government of the town.[2] Few of them are ascribed occupations in the Town Books but, by linking them to Liverpool wills and adult male burials which frequently give such information, an analysis of the occupation profile of the governors can be attempted.[3] Further linking of names in port books and rates allows an insight into their economic activity. Conclusions about the character and development of political control in the town are thus possible and are important in explaining its dramatic development.

Recent historians have considered the political structure of towns in a wider economic and social context than the Webbs attempted in their pioneering work on English local government. Though the particular constitutional arrangements in towns differed from place to place, the result of local tradition and the dictates of Crown charters, the exercise of power was negotiated between the active freemen and town governments, which might in theory have represented freemen but, in practice, reflected the interest of a social or economic elite within the town or the political influence of a great local landowner. It has become common currency to talk about oligarchical government as normal in towns and of it intensifying in the late seventeenth and early eighteenth centuries as town corporations and national governments sought to restore order and uniformity after the dislocation of the English Revolution.[4]

This meant, in practice, an attempt to limit the participation of freemen in local politics and the vesting of power in the wealthy and politically reliable leaders of urban society. Town government, depending as it did on voluntary and largely unpaid service, had always tended to fall to the wealthy townsmen simply because they could afford it. In return they reaped the advantage of being able to promote policies which helped their activities. Their power was not unlimited. However autocratic a town charter encouraged governors to be, they had to act with a degree of consent from the town. Town freemen and others, employees, apprentices and women, were neighbours or friends and often had business or family connections with political leaders. Moreover, the smooth running of a town depended on the assistance of a substantial number of voluntary officials, such as jurors at borough courts and regulators of markets and the town environment. Pearl and Rappaport make a forceful case that London gained stability in the sixteenth and seventeenth centuries precisely because so many of its citizens were tied into regulating local affairs at parish and ward level.[5] The same was true in other towns too. Indeed, it is arguable that local government in England as a whole depended on just such involvement.

It is such issues that this chapter intends to investigate in the context of Liverpool. Who governed the town? What kind of people were they? How powerful were they? Such questions have a particular point for a town which was rapidly changing. After almost half a millennium as a small town Liverpool was on the verge of one of the more dramatic transformations in urban history. Its population increased from about 1,300 in the 1660s to 20–22,000 in 1750. Its long-standing coastal and Irish Sea trade was extended by voyages to the Americas from the 1660s, and to Africa from the 1700s. From being an insignificant port in the shadow of Chester it emerged to challenge and overtake provincial ports with long trading pedigrees such as Bristol, Exeter and Hull.[6] The government of the town reacted to the emergence of the port and helped to create it. Besides the political challenges which beset most English towns in an unstable period Liverpool had its own precocious growth to deal with as well. The following analysis will concentrate predominantly on government structure, the involvement of townspeople in running the town, and the changing character of the council. Politics and policy in the town are discussed in Chapter 6.

Officials

The quarterly portmoot courts in Liverpool frequently ended proceedings with the declaration 'We approve all ancient orders and laudable customs'. There is no doubt that they were conscious of a tradition of developed government. One aspect of the tradition was the large number of officials elected or appointed each year. On 18 October, St Luke's Day, a mayor, two bailiffs, a recorder, town clerk, serjeant-at-mace and water bailiff were elected. At a common council or portmoot court which followed more officials were elected: merchant appraisers; port customers; registers of leather and other regulators of crafts and markets, such as alefounders and leavelookers; the heyward, barleymen, scavengers and others who regulated town streets and the Common; and even a minister and clerk, ecclesiastical officials.[7] A complete list appears in Table 5.1.

Not all officials were elected each year. In fact, mayor and bailiffs aside, it is probable that many of the officials were appointed or confirmed.[8] Some were officials with particular qualifications and duties attracting stipends or fees and served during good service. The recorder and town clerk were obvious examples.[9] The minister of St Nicholas, a chapelry of the parish church at Walton, was confirmed each year.

The number of officials each year increased as time went on. In 1678 inspectors of inmates, 17 each year, were elected to monitor immigrants. In 1685 two sub-bailiffs appear. In 1722 six assistant constables were elected to help keep order, a number increased to 14 by 1750. The original 44 officials of 1660 grew to about 70 by the 1720s. Together with jurors at portmoot courts the number of active officials grew from 68 to 94. The ratio of officials to householders would have been about 1 to 4.4 in the 1660s, slipping to 1 to 18.6 by the 1720s.[10] Mid-seventeenth-century Liverpool shared the characteristic noted of London of being a much-governed town.[11]

Most towns were used to a complex array of officials. Sixteenth-century Exeter, for example, employed a group of over 30. Norwich employed about 50 officials in 1689.[12] What is surprising is that so small a town as Liverpool had a comparable quota. It may be that the number of officials does not simply reflect a town's size and political sophistication.[13] The large number of officials in Liverpool implied consent to town government and should have encouraged political stability. This is particularly the case since they were drawn from different sectors of the population, merchants, mariners and craftsmen (see Table 5.1).

The mayor and bailiffs were elected by all burgesses at the election court and their names were usually recorded in the Town Book in a bold hand, reflecting a perception of their importance.[14] They were genuinely elected officials, though how candidates for election were nominated is not clear. Moreover the three offices were usually filled by different individuals each year, only a small number returning to the office a second time: William Stanley, Lord Strange, mayor in 1662 and 1668; James, Earl of Derby, in 1707 and 1734; George Tyrer esq. in 1710, 1717 and 1730; Richard Gildart esq. in 1714, 1731 and 1736; Foster Cunliffe esq. in 1711, 1729 and 1735; and Bryan Blundell in 1721 and 1728 were exceptional.[15] The dates suggest that the practice was becoming more common in the early eighteenth century. A similar tendency occurs among bailiffs: only one bailiff repeated the office in the late seventeenth century whereas 13 did in the early eighteenth century.[16] It seems that the chief offices were becoming the preserve of a smaller number of men.

The mayor was the chief officer charged with maintaining the town's liberties, overseeing other officials and making policy with aldermen and councillors.[17] He was drawn from an economically and socially selective group, most mayors being described as gentleman or esquire (78 per cent of the total between 1650 and 1750), though from 1688 such titles became increasingly attached to the office whatever the social status of the incumbent. For a period after the Restoration we find aristocrats filling the office: Charles, Earl of Derby, in 1666, Thomas, Viscount Colchester, in 1667, William, Lord Strange, in 1662 and 1668. Several mayors in the 1670s and 1680s were, in contrast, townsmen, four merchants and four mariners.[18]

The two bailiffs were responsible for calling portmoot courts, empanelling jurors and enforcing court judgements.[19] The men elected were not unlike those who became mayors. About one-third of bailiffs went on to become mayor (61 of 190 between 1650 and 1750). Bailiffs were often described as gentlemen or esquire (57 per cent of the total between 1650 and 1750) though, unlike mayors, none was noble. Many were merchants or mariners in the period up to 1688: there were 17 merchants, 12 mariners, six craftsmen and three professionals. Below bailiffs but of similar status were the four merchant appraisers responsible for raising local taxes. They, too, were often merchants and many (122, or 66 per cent) went on to become bailiffs, and some even mayor. Occasionally they repeated the office (60 of the 183) after a few years.[20]

The two important 'professional' officials, recorder and town clerk, provided continuity of advice and record keeping for the mayors and bailiffs.[21] John Entwistle esq. of Wigan served as recorder, the legal adviser of the corporation, for forty-six years from 1662, to be succeeded by his son, Bertil, for a further seventeen years, and then by Thomas Ashurst esq. for nineteen years. John Winstanley had been town clerk, with responsibility for keeping of minutes of courts and council and other town documents, for twenty-two years when deprived of office

Table 5.1 *Liverpool Officers 1650–1750*

Office	Dates, if not 1649–1750	Elected at	Average tenure (years)	Common status
Mayor's group				
Mayor		Election court	1.1	Gent
Head bailiff		Election court	1.1	Gent
Town bailiff		Election court	1.1	Gent
Sub-bailiffs (2)	1685–1750	Common council	1.0	Craft
Recorder		Common council	14.6	Esq
Town clerk		Common council	14.6	
Serjeant at mace		Common council	7.8	
Swordbearer	1687–1750	Common council	10.7	
Beadle	1652–1750	Cc/ Portmoot court	6.2	
Order				
Assistant constables (14)	1722–1750	Portmoot court	1.5	Craft
Inspectors inmates (17)	1678–1714	Portmoot court	1.5	
Taxation				
Stewards of hall (2)	1649–1718	Common council	1.1	Mr
Merchant appraisers (4)	1649–1714	Portmoot court	1.4	Mr
Port				
Town Customer		Common council	6.0	
Sub-Customer	1649–1711	Common council	6.0	
Hallkeeper		Common council	9.3	could be female
Water bailiff	1674–1747	Election court	4.9	
Market				
Leavelookers (2)	1649–1714	Portmoot court	2.3	
Aletasters (2)	1649–1714	Portmoot court	1.0	
Registers leather (2)	1649–1714	Portmoot court	2.9	
Boardsetters (2)	1649–1676	Portmoot court	4.1	could be female
Boothsetters (2)	1649–1701	Portmoot court	4.1	could be female
Porters (7)	1649–1670	Portmoot court	5.9	
Streets and Common				
Heyward	1649–1736	Common council	6.8	
Barleymen (4)	1649–1714	Portmoot court	1.1	
Murenger	1649–1714	Portmoot court	3.0	
Scavengers (7)	1649–1714	Portmoot court	1.1	
Overseers of highway (2)	1649–1714	Portmoot court	1.3	

Church				
Minister	1649–1698	Common council	7.1	Mr
Parish clerk			10.7	
Sexton	1673–1750		8.6	could be female
Organist	1695–1750		16.0	Mr
Schoolmaster		Common Council	7.5	Mr
Usher	1680–1750	Common Council	7.5	Mr
Churchwardens (2)		Portmoot court		

Source: TOWNBOOK

under the Corporation Act in 1662. Samuel Fazakerley took over from 1664 till 1677, Thomas Sandiford and John Sandiford successively until 1704, and Ralph Peters for thirty-six years from 1707 until 1742.[22]

Lesser officials were drawn from lower-status occupations. After 1685 the majority of sub-bailiffs (70 per cent) were craftsmen, workers in wood, metal and cloth. Assistant constables were also overwhelmingly craftsmen (80 per cent). Port officials, the Customers and water bailiffs, were appointments from a small group of men with appropriate experience, as were officials charged with regulating livestock, such as heywards (livestock in the town field) and barleymen (livestock on the Common). Market regulators were also chosen for their experience: leavelookers (checking the wholesomeness of victuals), alefounders (testing beer and bread), and registers of leather (ensuring that only legally tanned leather was sold). Market boardsetters and boothsetters are a particularly interesting group, holding office for years on end and passing the role within families, including to women. William Chorley, boardsetter from 1653 to 1670, was followed by Ann Chorley for a further six years. Thomas Witter, boothsetter from 1655 to 1665, was succeeded by his widow until 1669, and Francis Witter, perhaps their son, until 1698. Mary Robinson succeeded Richard Robinson as hallkeeper and boothsetter from 1711 to 1721.[23]

These officials attempted to regulate the economic, social and religious life of the town, apparently conscientiously. Portmoot presentments of officials for not carrying out duties were exceptional: two boothsetters and two alefounders were presented in the mayoral year 1660–61, and the same number in 1662–63, for neglect of office.[24] The chief officials, and those keeping order and levying taxation, changed annually but others, recorders, town clerks and port and market officials, served for long periods. Administrative continuity must have resulted. It is significant that officers were drawn from different occupation and status groups. It is arguable that this helped communal stability.

Councillors

The council was at the heart of town government. In Liverpool it took a dominant role from 1580, when Mayor Edward Halsall established a council of 12 aldermen and 24 councillors as the governing body. It included the mayor, two bailiffs, recorder and town clerk *ex officio*. Each mayor became an alderman after his mayoral year and joined the 'mayor's brethren' or aldermen, and bailiffs became common councillors or 'bailiffs' peers' after their office. All councillors served for life and vacancies were filled by co-option if numbers were not kept up by the annual increment of a mayor and bailiffs.[25]

Such a structure was fairly typical of late seventeenth-century town constitutions. Councils of 12 aldermen and 24 common councillors were usual, though some towns had fewer and some more. Exeter, for example, had eight aldermen and 16 councillors, Norwich 24 aldermen and 60 councillors.[26] Two-thirds of towns were closed corporations with councillors serving for life and co-opting new members. In a minority of towns councillors served for life but an annual election of a mayor and chief officers allowed freemen some political voice. Liverpool in 1660 was one of these. In a very few councils there were open elections of chief officers and common councillors. London and Norwich are the best-known.[27]

Liverpool in 1660 had a mixed constitution. It had a council whose members served for life but was fed by freemen elections of a mayor and bailiff each year. However, it changed to a closed corporation in the late seventeenth century and remained so until municipal government in England was reformed in 1835. The constitutional change can be briefly described. In 1660 the town operated under a charter of Charles I of 1626 which did not mention a council at all though in fact a council of mayor, aldermen and common councillors continued to operate as it had since 1580.[28] The council was 'closed' by a charter of 1677, obtained in a comparatively quiet period for corporations between a group of early Restoration charters and the major re-issuing of charters after the Exclusion Crisis. The charter increased the council to 60 and, by prescribing 15 non-townsmen (i.e. local gentlemen), sought to build in a Royalist and Anglican majority. More significantly it closed the council to the electoral influence of freemen by transferring the right of electing the mayor and bailiffs from freemen to council.[29]

A third charter in 1695, a result of Whig agitation in the years following the 1689 revolution, reinstated a smaller council of mayor and 40 councillors and returned political autonomy to the town. However, a clause which declared that 'from these forty-one there shall be one honest and discreet man who shall be... the mayor... and two honest and discreet men who shall be... the bailiffs' confirmed the closed

Table 5.2 *Number of new councillors and aldermen in each decade*

	1650s	1660s	1670s	1680s	1690s	1700s	1710s	1720s	1730s	1740s
Councillors	32	30	32	35	40	28	9	11	21	21
Aldermen	9	9	7	6	8	13	8	6	6	0
Total	41	39	39	41	48	41	17	17	27	21

Source: TOWNBOOK.

council. The chief officers were to be drawn only from the council and Liverpool was confirmed as a closed corporation. Despite challenges in 1726, 1734, 1750 and in the 1790s, council hegemony held firm until 1835.[30]

The loss of open elections of mayor and bailiff and the consequent 'closing' of the council in 1677 became obvious in several ways. The first sign is the smaller number of men who became councillors. Table 5.2 sets out the number of new men joining each decade. From an average of 42 or more each decade in the late seventeenth century, peaking in the 1690s because of the number of new councillors introduced by the charter of 1695, the average falls to 25 in the early eighteenth century.

Furthermore, council oligarchy intensified in the early eighteenth century. A restricted group of men served as councillors and aldermen and served for longer periods. Some 45 men served more than twenty years on the council in the early eighteenth century compared with 16 in the late seventeenth century. Some conspicuous long-serving late seventeenth-century councillors are worth individual mention. Most significant was Thomas Johnson. Bailiff in 1663, merchant appraiser in 1665 and mayor in 1670, he withdrew from the council in 1677 when the new charter was granted but reappeared on the council with the charter of 1695, to be succeeded by his son Thomas junior.[31] Peter Lurting, merchant appraiser in 1649, bailiff in 1652 and mayor in 1663, retired with Johnson in 1677. Like Johnson he would not accept the charter of 1677 and asked to be excused from serving because of his age.[32] John Entwistle, a long-serving recorder, who resigned the post in 1709 when he was 84 years old, left a son to continue the tradition.[33] Edward Tarleton, mariner, was merchant appraiser in 1669 and mayor in 1682. He, too, was followed by a son, Edward, mayor in 1712.[34] Silvester Richmond, a medical man, mayor in 1672, left two sons who became local clergymen.[35]

Several of the more numerous long-serving councillors in the early eighteenth century command attention. The first is Thomas Johnson junior (Sir Thomas after 1708), son of the Thomas Johnson already described, a mariner and tobacco merchant, bailiff in 1689, merchant appraiser in 1691, mayor in 1695 and later MP for the town.[36] His close friend, Richard Norris, of the gentry family of Speke Hall connected by marriage to several Liverpool merchant families, was bailiff in 1695, merchant appraiser in 1697, mayor in 1700, deputy mayor in 1707, MP in 1708 as a fellow and staunch ally of Sir Thomas Johnson, and in 1718 high sheriff of the county of Lancaster.[37] Richard Gildart, son-in-law of Sir Thomas Johnson, was a councillor in 1707, merchant appraiser in 1708, bailiff in 1712, mayor three times in 1714, 1731 and 1736, and MP from 1734.[38] Foster Cunliffe became inspector of inmates in 1707, bailiff in 1708 and 1727, merchant appraiser in 1710 and mayor in 1716, 1729 and 1735.[39] Captain John Hughes was steward of hall in 1704, bailiff in 1710 and 1734, merchant appraiser in 1711, and mayor in 1727.[40] Silvester Morecroft was steward of hall in 1689, inspector of inmates in 1696, bailiff in 1700 and mayor in 1706, and the first treasurer of the corporation in 1716.[41] Captain Bryan Blundell, founder of the Bluecoat Hospital, became a councillor in 1720, was mayor in 1721 and 1728, and bailiff in 1735.[42] Thomas Steers, brought from London to build the Old Dock, was made dock master in 1717, became bailiff and councillor in 1719, merchant appraiser in 1721, water bailiff in 1731 and mayor in 1739.[43]

Such councillors were among the most active traders and political leaders in the town. They provided continuity and experience in town government and, despite some political tensions, created a powerful interest group which pushed forward the commercial development of Liverpool. The growing continuity on the council in the eighteenth century is very clear. Some 8 per cent (16 of the 208) of the late seventeenth-century councillors served more than twenty years; 37 per cent (45 of the 123) did so in the early eighteenth century. Their longer service may have been because they became councillors when they were younger than their predecessors though we have no reliable data about ages. They certainly did not spend a long 'apprenticeship' in office, serving an average of one office and waiting thereafter only a year before admission to the council. The seventeenth-century average was service in two offices and a five-year wait before admission.[44] Co-option rather than election of councillors after 1695 clearly made for swifter entry. The criterion for admission was no longer a vote given to candidates who had spent years serving in office but the acceptability of the family, wealth, or the business connections of council aspirants. Early promotion to the council had another effect. After new councillors had served as mayor they continued active council careers thereafter, serving again as mayor or standing for parliament rather than retiring quietly to the aldermanic bench as had happened in the seventeenth century. The Liverpool political system was based on an entrenched oligarchy after 1695.

Merchant Oligarchy

The concentration of power was not simply a matter of authority being vested in fewer hands. There was an economic dimension to oligarchy which is revealed by analysis of the occupations of councillors and officials. Only 251 (16 per cent) of the 1,587 individuals listed in the Town Books are described by occupation; a larger proportion, 28 per cent (438), are ascribed a status. The occupations of more councillors and officials can be traced in wills and adult male burials. Some 214 (13.5 per cent) were linked to testators and 374 (23.6 per cent) to adult male burials.[45] Such modest success casts an interesting light on the sources and on Liverpool society. It implies that less than one in seven town officers and councillors made a will which was proved in the period, a rather low ratio considering that this sample of the population contained the powerful and wealthy. Fewer than one in four were recorded as buried in the parish, which seems very low. St Mary's, Walton-on-the-Hill, the mother church of the town, remained a frequent place of interment even after St Nicholas was made parochial in 1699, and burials took place in other parishes too.[46] The tantalising propensity of many Liverpool men to be buried elsewhere provokes thought about the notion of a Liverpool community and what it meant to those who were part of it.

Such linkage boosts the number of councillors and officials who can be ascribed an occupation to 466, 29.4 per cent of the total. Together with the status afforded to a further 28 per cent of the total there is supplementary information about the character of over half the group. It is good enough by the standards of knowledge of early modern town populations to encourage analysis and the results are suggestive of the balance of power and influence in the town.[47] The 466 individuals with a known occupation followed 112 distinct avocations, a reasonable spread for a town often assumed to be monopolised by its port function.[48] They have been categorised into generic groups and the occupational profiles of officials and councillors together, of councillors, and of aldermen are displayed in Table 5.3.[49]

It is interesting that trading and seafaring occupations do not dominate. The largest occupational group is manufacturing, accounting for almost half the total, which suggests that Liverpool shared much in common with most early modern towns in the importance of its craftsmen. The large number of wood-based craftsmen include coopers (33) and blockmakers (10), shipwrights and ship carpenters (28) who comprised a formidable body of port-based craftsmen. They are balanced by toolmakers, especially watchmakers (10), metal and leather workers, and makers of clothing, among whom tailors (15) and shoemakers (14) were prominent. The low number of textile craftsmen involved in running the town is notable and rather unusual.[50]

Table 5.3 *Occupational profile of Liverpool townsmen in government, 1650–1750 (based on 29.4% with occupations identified)*

Occupation	All		Councillors		Aldermen	
	No.	*%*	*No.*	*%*	*No.*	*%*
Agricultural	13	2.8			1	3.3
Building	24	5.2	4	4.1		
Manufacturing:						
Tools	*15*		*4*			
Ships	*28*		*2*			
Clothing	*34*		*4*			
Victuals	*30*		*3*			
Metals	*16*		*5*			
Pottery	*6*		*1*			
Leather	*15*				*2*	
Tallow &c	*5*					
Wood	*62*		*1*			
Textiles	*10*					
	221	47.4	20	20.4	2	6.6
Transport:						
Sea	*34*		*14*		*5*	
Land	*11*					
	45	9.7	14	14.3	5	16.6
Dealing:						
Specialist	*51*		*17*		*4*	
General	*62*		*34*		*15*	
	113	24.3	51	52.0	19	63.3
Professional	45	9.7	9	9.2	3	10
Menial	2	0.4				
Doubtful	3	0.6				
Totals	466	100.1	98	100	30	99.8

Source: A computer file, TBINDEX, based on TOWNBOOK.

Dealers, about a quarter of the total, emerge as a significant but not dominant group. The general merchants (62), 13 per cent of the total, represent the ocean-going dealers characteristic of a port and it is significant that they are the single most numerous occupation. Among the specialist dealers, haberdashers, drapers, grocers and innkeepers stand out (14). They, too, provided for people engaged in trade. Transport workers, including mariners (33), make up less than 10 per cent of the total, certainly much less than their numerical significance in the town would warrant. A mariner on the high seas was perhaps unsuited to be a town official. Professional groups, which include a significant number of barbers (22), as well as clergy, lawyers and doctors, are as important as transport workers despite their modest numbers in the town, a demonstration of the use of literate skills in administration.

The occupation profile of councillors and aldermen is quite different. Whereas many of the officials of the town, registers of leather, aletasters, boardsetters, boothsetters and porters, were perforce drawn from the ranks of craftsmen, small traders and carriers, the real governors of the town were drawn from those with capital and position. Dealers played a major role in the council, making up half the councillors and almost two-thirds of aldermen. Though there are some craftsmen on the council, watchmakers, tailors, shoemakers, goldsmiths and whitesmiths, they comprise only a fifth of councillors and hardly appear at all as aldermen. Professional groups maintain representation of about 10 per cent on the council. Despite the low representation of mariners as officers their importance to the town is demonstrated by their representation on the council, and they provide more aldermen than any other group but merchants. In this case the occupational ascription of mariner might be misleading. Men who operated at the highest level in the town, such as Sir Thomas Johnson and Bryan Blundell, described themselves as mariners though it is obvious that they were major traders. There is no doubt that the commercial priorities of a growing port town are affirmed by the central importance on the council of merchants and mariners.

It comes as no surprise to find merchants in control of a town council in this period. They were usually the wealthiest citizens and needed facilities for trade. There was no better way of protecting their interests than involving themselves in town government. In most port towns merchants were well represented on the council. In early seventeenth-century Bristol, merchants occupied over 47 per cent (rising to 80 per cent if retail dealers are added) of council seats. Seventeenth-century Hull councillors were almost all merchants. Exeter merchants between 1688 and 1715 comprised 45 per cent of the council, and in Glasgow in 1711 the proportion of merchants was fixed at 52 per cent. In manufacturing towns, too, a similar pattern obtained. Some 86 per cent of the late seventeenth-century Leeds council, for example, were merchants.[51] The danger of comparing such statistics from very different towns is obvious and it would be foolish to read fine distinctions into these percentages. The strong presence of merchants on councils is, however, clear. Liverpool conforms to a general pattern.

There is one respect in which merchant representation during the period stands out, the intensification of merchant numbers on the council after 1700. Table 5.4 shows that merchants took command of the council at this time, their representation among councillors rising from 43 to 70 per cent and among aldermen from 58 to 73 per cent.

Table 5.4 *Occupational profile of Liverpool townsmen in government in late seventeenth and early eighteenth centuries (%)*

	All		Councillors		Aldermen	
	17th	*18th*	*17th*	*18th*	*17th*	*18th*
No.	*203*	*263*	*65*	*33*	*19*	*11*
Building	4.9	5.3	3.1	6.1		
Manufacture	38.4	54.4	27.7	6.1	5.2	9.0
Transport	15.3	5.3	18.5	6.1	21.0	9.0
Dealing	28.1	21.3	43.1	69.7	57.8	72.7
Professions	7.9	11.0	7.7	12.1	10.5	9.0
Menial	0.5	0.4				
Unidentified		1.1				
Totals	100	99.9	100.1	100.1	99.7	99.7

Source: TBINDEX.

Central in this takeover were overseas traders. Before 1700 they held only 14 of the 65 places on council and seven of the 19 aldermanic seats; after 1700 they filled 20 of the 33 council places and provided eight of the 11 aldermen. The charter of 1695 played a major role in this change because it named many merchants as councillors for the first time. Its importance in advancing the commercial interest in the town was as great as its confirmation of oligarchy.

The inflation of status ascriptions was one way councillors at this time signalled their exclusive position. 'Mr', 'gentleman' and 'esquire' came into much more common use after 1688 among particular officers, the mayor, bailiffs and merchant appraisers, for example. What is interesting is that councillors were increasingly styled 'gentlemen' rather than 'Mr', and aldermen 'esquires' rather than 'gentlemen', in the eighteenth century. The changes are shown in Table 5.5.

There may have been several influences at work: the increasing wealth of the Liverpool elite, the contemporary urban cult of pseudo-gentility and the increasing pomp of town government.[52] The use of status titles for particular officials was quite sudden. Mayors are styled gentleman or esquire from 1689, rather than being described by their occupation, and bailiffs follow suit. The steward of hall gains the distinction of a status title in 1689, and merchant appraisers and inspectors of inmates do so in 1697. The change may have been the result of a change in the town clerk who recorded them. In 1689 John Sandiford replaced Thomas Sandiford in office. Thus, social distinctions reinforced the increasing power exercised by councillors in Liverpool. Merchants took over control of the council and displayed their position by gentle titles. The impression

Table 5.5 *Changes in status ascriptions: Liverpool townspeople in government before 1700 and after 1700*

	All		Councillors		Aldermen	
	Pre-1700	*Post-1700*	*Pre-1700*	*Post-1700*	*Pre-1700*	*Post-1700*
Peers	4	1			4	1
Knights	3		1		1	
Esquires	27	48	9	14	17	31
Gentlemen	52	44	37	40	13	1
Mr	127	120	37	7	3	
Woman	4	4				
Widow	2	1				
Totals	220	218	84	61	39	33

Source: TBINDEX

of the rise of a small, powerful and visible group emerging to control and direct the growing town is strengthened.

Council Wealth

Behind the emergence of merchant oligarchy in Liverpool in the late seventeenth century lay a change in the economic character of merchants in the town described in Chapter 1. Great traders operating across the Atlantic as well as to Ireland and Europe appeared for the first time, and the volume of commodities carried increased dramatically. It was argued that the growth of trade towards the end of the seventeenth century was largely the result of the growth of a small number of great merchants prepared to engage in large-scale ventures. Among these, councillors were well represented and it is clear that they were well represented in the commercial revolution in Liverpool.

It is a reasonable proposition that a town's political elite should be wealthier than the townspeople they govern. Wealthy men gain access to the council more easily and political position no doubt gives them an advantage in business. This was not true for dissenters, of course, who were important in trade but after 1662 were debarred from council office. However, the form and extent of councillors' wealth varies over time. The trading activity of councillors in the 1660s, for example, was modest compared to their successors in the 1700s. This raises the question of what can be deduced about the economic involvement of councillors in different periods, not only in trade but in other capital enterprises. Because of the availability of sources which give evidence of trading activity, port books and plantation registers, and others which give an indication of command of property, hearth taxes and rate assessments, it is possible to attempt an answer to this question.[53]

The council cohort in the 1660s seems modest in its enterprise and assets. Some 31 per cent of the group engaged in overseas trade but in a small way, averaging 2.2 shipments in the year 1664–65 compared to the average of all merchants of 2.4. The largest trader on the council was John Walles, a master trading on his own account, who exported to Dublin eight shipments comprising 59 chaldrons of coal, 2.5 tons of rod iron and 20 cwt of nails. He was exceptional. Thomas Johnson accounted for only three shipments from Ireland in 1665: he imported four nags and 19 cattle in two shipments from Drogheda in June, and four barrels of beef from Carrickfergus the following February. No councillors stand comparison with the 12 busiest merchants that year: Richard Percival, for example, accounted for 21 shipments to and from Dundalk and Drogheda, William Webster for 26 shipments to and from Dublin and Drogheda.[54]

In contrast to such modest trade, councillors occupied grander houses than average if we can trust their average number of 3.4 hearths against 2.1 in the town as a whole. John Sturzaker, a sadler, accounted for six hearths on Water Street; seven other councillors were taxed on five hearths: William Accars, a currier on Dale Street, Thomas Andoe, a mariner on Chapel Street, Thomas Birch on Dale Street, William Eccleston on Dale Street, Samuel Fazakerley, town clerk, on Dale Street, Captain William Gardner on Chapel Street, and John Sandiford on High Street. Most councillors, 14 in all, were assessed for three or four hearths, Thomas Johnson among them living in Water Street. A few councillors accounted for below average numbers of hearths: Captain John Walles, the active trader, was assessed for two hearths, along with six others. Captain Thomas Bicksteth, Ralph Hall, a tidewaiter, and William Mulliney, serjeant at mace, each accounted for only one hearth. Whether much can be made of this evidence is doubtful. It certainly does not indicate ownership of property. The most that can be said is that most councillors lived in larger houses than average but few in very large or grand premises.[55]

The economic enterprise of the council cohort in the 1700s was altogether more ambitious. Some 50 per cent of councillors engaged in overseas trade compared with 31 per cent in the 1660s. Moreover, the scale of their business was substantial, averaging 18.3 shipments a year compared with only 5.9 among all overseas merchants.[56] Thomas Johnson junior, Sir Thomas from 1708, was responsible for some 98 shipments in 1708–09 compared with the three shipments of his father in 1664–65. He imported 383,000 lbs of tobacco in six ships from Virginia, and exported 8,084 bushels of salt, 34 cwt of nails, and smaller quantities of wrought iron, tobacco pipes, haberdashery, silk, paper and bridles. He imported 765 cwt of muscovado sugar and quantities of indigo, pimento and logwood in one ship from Jamaica, and exported leather, earthenware, silk and buttons to Barbados. He also continued his father's interest in the Irish trade. Some 13 ships from Dublin, Belfast, Sligo and Londonderry carried 107 cwt of linen yarn, 3,587 yards of linen cloth, 41 cwt of soap, and quantities of staves, iron, hides and tar. In return 21 ships exported 11,131 bushels of salt, 99 chaldrons of coal, 81 cwt of copperas and a variety of manufactures, nails, bed linen, haberdashery, leather goods, earthenware and pipes, to ten Irish ports.[57]

Johnson was among the most active merchants in the town in 1709 but some fellow councillors followed close behind. John Clieveland accounted for 54 shipments, including 14 from and two to Virginia, four from and 12 to West Indian islands, and eight from and ten to Ireland. He had to be forced to be mayor in 1703, his reluctance perhaps due to his desire to concentrate on business.[58] Foster Cunliffe, an apprentice of Sir Thomas Johnson, was an Isle of Man specialist. His 54 shipments included 18 shipments from and 11 to the island, but also 14 shipments from Virginia. William Squire, in partnership with Peter Hall, was responsible for 48 shipments, including ten shipments from Virginia, four from the West Indies, and 13 from and 14 to Ireland. Though there were greater traders who were not on the council, John Cunningham (128 shipments), Benjamin Hunter (88), Peter Clinton (72), and John Percival (70) the most conspicuous, there is no doubt that councillors were a well-established group within the trading elite.[59]

Councillors' involvement in trade was reflected in lower status officials who were also prominent traders at this time. Some 19 per cent were involved in overseas trade in 1708–09 compared to only 9 per cent of their precursors in 1665–66. They accounted for an average of almost 8.6 shipments against the overall mean of 5.9 in 1708–09. Their predecessors in 1664–65 had averaged only one shipment, well below the mean of 2.4. The decade after 1700 was a period when craftsmen who were town officials engaged in overseas trade alongside their merchant councillor superiors. Something of the ferment of trade which Sacks has argued characterised Bristol in the late seventeenth century seems to have gripped Liverpool also.[60]

Councillors' investment in property in 1708–09 was as significant as their involvement in trade. Real estate represented a lower-risk venture than trade and had a practical use in storing merchandise. Merchants often owned warehouses near quaysides and docks. The opportunity for large-scale investment in property greatly increased in the late seventeenth century when the Corporation won control of the Common from Lord Molyneux in 1672. It lay outside the medieval town to the south and east of the Liver Pool and townsmen began to take building leases of land close to the site where the Old Dock was later built. Liverpool entrepreneurs were able to invest heavily in property as well as in trade. Among them, councillors were prominent. By 1708 they were rated on an average of 5.2 properties against two among ratepayers as a whole.[61] Once again, Sir Thomas Johnson stands out. His 28 properties made him the largest property-owner in the town. He paid rates on 12 houses, a kiln and a barn in Dale Street, a house and warehouse in Covent Garden, seven closes on the Common, and a rope yard near the new church of St Peter. Alderman Tyrer accounted for 23 properties, aldermen Bicksteth, Clayton and Houghton 15 each, John Sandiford, town clerk, 14, and John Fells, mariner, ten. These seven councillors represent half the owners accounting for over ten properties. They seem to have been as active in acquiring property in the late seventeenth century as in trading.[62]

During the late seventeenth century a group of investors in trade and property transformed the character of the town, developing overseas trade and building the first suburb of Liverpool. Councillors were at the forefront of both developments. During the first half of the eighteenth century there are some indications that they may have changed their pattern of investment. A continued investment in property is obvious enough but commercial investment less so. The idea derives from the modest involvement of councillors in share-owning in plantation ships in the 1740s, used as a surrogate measure for trade because no overseas port book survives for the period.[63] Shares in plantation ships are, of course, not the same as investment in trade. They required capital rather than credit and represented a longer-term investment than the purchase of commodities. Moreover, plantation ships were only a proportion of the total tonnage using the port of Liverpool. Nevertheless they are one measure of investment in commerce. Some 39 per cent of councillors owned shares in plantation ships between 1743 and 1748. On average they owned shares in 4.3 ships compared with an average of 2.4 for the whole ship-owning group. Since the average councillor's share was an eighth of a ship rather than the overall shipowners' average of a fourth, councillors look to have been no more involved in shipownership than the generality. Only two councillors had shares in ten ships or more: James Gildart had shares in 14 and Foster Cunliffe in ten. There were 12 non-council shipowners who owned shares in more than ten ships, Arthur Heywood, John Hardman and James Pardoe notable among them. Councillor Richard Gildart, son-in-law and partner of Sir Thomas Johnson, held shares in only two plantation ships, an eighth share in the *Queen of Hungary* and a fourth share in the *Middleham*, both small snows. It would be stretching evidence to infer that Gildart and his fellow councillors had begun to disengage from active involvement in commerce but it is a possibility which needs further research.

Councillors had certainly not stopped investing in property. In 1743 councillors were assessed for an average of 8.1 properties compared to the overall ratepayers' average of 2.5. Whereas councillors had held twice the average property holding in 1708 they held three times the average by 1743. Richard Gildart is, again, a useful example. Unlike his apparently modest investment in plantation shipping, he was credited, in the rate of 1743, for almost twice the amount of property held by his father-in-law, Sir Thomas Johnson, in 1708. He paid rates on 63 properties, including Sir Thomas Johnson Buildings, 12 houses, five warehouses, a barn, tanyard, kiln, stable, four yards and 18 closes or crofts. Most of the buildings were in Dale Street in the medieval town, and in Duke Street, a new development on the Common.[64] Gildart may have been cautious about trade after his involvement with Sir Thomas Johnson's financial difficulties in 1723.[65] Might he be characterised as a third-generation merchant (after Thomas Johnson senior and Sir Thomas Johnson) who put more money into property than commerce, a gentlemanly capitalist?[66] His very active political career, three times mayor of the town and long-serving MP, might have distracted him from regular attention to trade. Equally it might be that the sources catch Gildart at a stage in his life when he would naturally have retired from active trading, for he was 72 years of age in 1743.

Nine councillors in 1743 owned ten or more properties in the town, a quarter of the 36 owners on this scale. Though there were more large-scale property-owners in the town in the 1740s the average councillor's property holding had risen much faster than ratepayers as a whole. There seems no doubt that they perceived real estate as a more vital investment than ships. The location of councillors' property is also revealing. By 1743 it tended to be situated on main streets in the old town. Some 29 per cent of councillors' property sat on prime frontage compared with only 13 per cent of that owned by town officials, the lower status group whose property sat mainly in side streets.[67] Councillors evidently purchased visible property. It fitted their status and political position.

The data on trade, shipping and property investment add substantially to an understanding of the changes in government in the town. As Liverpool became more commercial, the council changed in sympathy, increasingly dominated by merchants involved in long-distance transatlantic trade. By the first decade of the eighteenth century councillors' involvement in trade seems particularly intense and was shared by lower-status town officers. At the same time councillors accumulated property, and their continuing investment in real estate becomes very obvious by the mid-eighteenth century. It may be that they were less active in commercial investment by this date though a considered judgement on this must await further investigation.

The governing group in Liverpool became more exclusive, more powerful and more wealthy during the period, though at no time did they exercise unfettered hegemony. Throughout the period there were always non-trading representatives on the council. In the 1660s John Blundell, a Prescot gentleman, Charles, Earl of Derby, John Entwistle, the recorder from Wigan, and Samuel Fazakerley, gentleman of Allerton, provided a landed counterpoint to the trading interest. In the 1700s James, Earl of Derby, Joseph Eaton, bookseller, Bertil Entwistle, the recorder, and Ralph Peters, the town clerk, stand out. In the 1740s Thomas Ashurst, ex-recorder, Thomas Baldwin, the minister, William Barlow, attorney, Owen Brereton, the recorder, Sylvester Morecroft, postmaster, and Ralph Peters, the town clerk, made up an increasing professional middle-class group, some of them appointed for their particular skills rather than being elected.[68] Such councillors, however, were numerically less significant than the mercantile interest, especially in the middle period, the 1700s.

Control of a port by merchants is hardly surprising. It is a mechanism whereby the interests of trade are fostered. Whereas in Bristol, Hull and Exeter such control was long established, Liverpool followed suit at the end of the seventeenth century. The large number of active traders in the town was clearly an important influence. By 1709 the 186 traders who exported from Liverpool represented about 2.5 per cent of the town population of 7,500. In Hull the 116 exporters of 1702 accounted for only 2 per cent of its population of 6,000. Bristol's 247 exporters at a rather later date, 1775, represented less than 1 per cent of its larger population of over 30,000.[69] The widespread participation in and dependance on overseas trade in Liverpool must have strengthened the hand of merchants on the council.

The commercial and governmental revolution in Liverpool had a more immediate cause. The council which decided in 1708 to build the first dock contained 12 major traders: Robert Barrow, John Cleiveland, John Cockshut, Thomas Coore, Foster Cunliffe, John Earle, Richard Gildart, Francis Goodrick, Sir Thomas Johnson, Richard Norris, William Squire and George Tyrer. All but one were heavily involved in transatlantic trade. They made up the largest single interest group on the council and there can be little doubt that their political influence was crucial in persuading the council to decide on the risky enterprise of building a dock. Their position on the council was due to the granting of a new charter in 1695 which, in turn, resulted from a fortuitous political event, an electoral fraud, to be considered in detail in Chapter 6. The effect of the charter was to promote Thomas Johnson junior and nine great merchants to the council, still present in 1708 when the council decided to build the first dock.[70] Though the structure of government and commercial growth were vital, politics also had an important part to play in the town's evolution.

Notes

1. M. Power, ed., *Liverpool Town Books 1649–1671*, RSLC, 136, 1999; thereafter, the original books are in LplRO 352 MIN/COU 3–10.

2. This computer file is called TOWNBOOK and provides the data for the analysis of officials and concillors in this chapter. It is deposited in 'The Liverpool Community 1660–1750' at the Data Archive, University of Essex.

3. Will evidence: D. E. Ascott, 'Wealth and Community: Liverpool 1660–1760', unpublished PhD thesis, University of Liverpool, 1996; adult male burial evidence: F. Lewis, 'The Demographic and Occupational Structure of Liverpool: a study of the parish registers, 1660–1750', unpublished PhD thesis, University of Liverpool, 1993.

4. S. and B. Webb, *English Local Government from the Revolution to the Municipal Corporations Act*, London, 1908, I, pp. 303–403; Jonathan Barry, 'Introduction', in *The Tudor and Stuart Town*, ed. J Barry, London, 1990, pp. 24–32.

5. V. Pearl, 'Change and stability in seventeenth-century London', reprinted in Barry, ed., *Tudor and Stuart Town*, pp.139–65; S. Rappaport, *Worlds within Worlds: Structures of Life in Sixteenth-century London*, Cambridge, 1989, chapter 9; cf. critique by I. Archer, *The Pursuit of Stability: Social Relations in Elizabethan London*, Cambridge, 1991, pp. 14–17.

6. M. Power, 'The growth of Liverpool', in *Popular Politics, Riot and Labour: Essays in Liverpool History 1790–1940*, ed. J. C. Belchem, Liverpool, 1992, pp. 21–37; R.C. Jarvis, 'The head port of Chester and Liverpool its creek and member', *THSLC*, 102, 1951, pp. 75–80; D. H. Sacks, *The Widening Gate: Bristol and the Atlantic Economy 1450–1700*, Berkeley, 1993; Robert Newton, *Eighteenth-century Exeter*, Exeter, 1984; G. Jackson, *Hull in the Eighteenth Century*, London, 1972.

7. Power, *Liverpool Town Books 1649–1671*, pp. 111–12, for elections and appointments for mayoral year 1659–60; G. Chandler, ed., *Liverpool under Charles I*, Liverpool, 1960, pp. 106–09, for officials' oaths.

8. Webbs, *Manor and Borough*, I, pp. 303–06, for minor officials; pp. 309–27, for mayors, bailiffs, recorder and town clerk.

9. Town clerks were accustomed to pay the bailiffs an annual fee from the emoluments of their office. John Winstanley, clerk from 1641 to 1662, paid £10, Samuel Fazakerley, clerk from 1664 to 1672, £5: See Chandler, *Liverpool under Charles I*, pp. 282–84, 354–57; Power, *Liverpool Town Books 1649–1671*, p. 164.

10. Information from TOWNBOOK. The ratios assume 300 households from the 1660s hearth taxes, 1500 households in the rate in 1708, and, by projection, about 1750 households by 1720.

11. The ratio in London in the 1640s was low in inner-city wards, such as Cornhill, at one official to three households, and higher in outer-city wards such as Farringdon, at one to 18 households: Pearl, 'Change and stability', p. 154.

12. Kevin Wilson, 'Political organization in the sixteenth-century town', in *The Fabric of the Traditional Community*, Open University English Urban History 1500–1780, unit 6, p. 62; Webbs, *Manor and Borough*, I, pp. 541–42.

13. Christopher Friedrichs makes the point that 'even a small town like Liverpool in the seventeenth century had dozens of officials': *The Early Modern City 1450–1750*, London, 1995, p. 267.

14. The charter of 1626 laid down the process of election: J. Ramsay Muir and E. M. Platt, *A History of Municipal Government in Liverpool from the Earliest Times to the Municipal Reform Act of 1835*, Liverpool, 1906, p. 185.

15. For clarification of multiple references to individuals and families in Chapters 3–6, e.g. Clieveland and Clayton, see the index.

16. TOWNBOOK.

17. Webbs, *Manor and Borough*, I, pp. 309–17.

18. TOWNBOOK. Occupations of mayors traced in wills and burials.

19. Webbs, *Manor and Borough*, I, pp. 318–20.

20. TOWNBOOK. Occupations traced in wills and burials.

21. Webbs, *Manor and Borough*, I, pp. 321–27.

22. TOWNBOOK.

23. TOWNBOOK.

24. Power, *Liverpool Town Books 1649–71*, pp. 137, 150.

25. Muir and Platt, *Municipal Government in Liverpool*, pp. 87–88, 81–82, 85.

26. Webbs, *Manor and Borough*, I, pp. 360–65; II, pp. 531–32; Newton, *Eighteenth-century Exeter*, p. 34.

27. Webbs, *Manor and Borough*, I, pp. 368–89; II, pp. 531–32.

28. Muir and Platt, *Municipal Government in Liverpool*, pp. 92–93.

29. Another charter of 1685, part of the re-issuing of town charters by Charles II after the Exclusion Crisis, did not alter the number or method of election of the chief officers: J. Miller, 'The crown and the borough charters in the reign of Charles II', *EHR*, 100, 1985, pp. 67–79; Muir and Platt, *Municipal Government in Liverpool*, pp. 105, 107–08.

30. Muir and Platt, *Municipal Government in Liverpool*, pp. 111–13, 248, 125–32.

31. Career details from TOWNBOOK; for resignation in 1677, second mayoralty in 1695 and succession as mayor by his son, Thomas junior, see J. Touzeau, *The Rise and Progress of Liverpool from 1551 to 1835*, Liverpool, 1910, pp. 297, 337.

32. Touzeau, *Rise and Progress*, p. 297.

33. Touzeau, *Rise and Progress*, pp. 386–87.

34. Touzeau, *Rise and Progress*, pp.313, 344.

35. Touzeau, *Rise and Progress*, pp. 287–88, 319–20; see Chapter 4.

36. Touzeau, *Rise and Progress*, pp. 377–82; E. Cruickshanks, 'Sir Thomas Johnson', in *History of Parliament: The House of Commons 1715–54*, ed. R. Sedgwick, London, 1970, Vol. II, pp. 180–81.

37. Touzeau, *Rise and Progress*, pp. 339, 379–380, 404.

38. Touzeau, *Rise and Progress*, pp. 426–27; E. Cruickshanks, 'Richard Gildart', *History of Parliament*, II, p. 63.

39. Touzeau, *Rise and Progress*, pp. 425–27, 435–41.

40. Touzeau, *Rise and Progress*, pp. 421–26, 438–42.

41. Touzeau, *Rise and Progress*, pp. 402–03, 419.

42. Touzeau, *Rise and Progress*, pp. 381, 406–07, 435–42.

43. Touzeau, *Rise and Progress*, pp. 379–83, 418, 444–45, 456.

44. Calculations based on TOWNBOOK.

45. A link was made between a councillor or official in the Town Book and a testator or adult male burial where forename and surname was identical and there was no more than ten years time-lag between the appearance in each source; if an additional identifying tag, such as occupation, was present the time-lag was extended to twenty years. Some 91 links with testators and 220 links with adult male burials were rejected as doubtful.

46. Lewis, 'Demographic and Occupational Structure', pp.144–48.

47. A comparison of the occupation profile with Dr Lewis's more representative profile of the whole population derived from parish registers shows that building, craft, transport and menial workers are under-represented among officers and councillors: Lewis, 'Demographic and Occupational Structure', pp. 59–61.

48. There were 63 distinct occupations in Newcastle in the 1660s: J. Langton, 'Residential patterns in pre-industrial cities', in Barry, ed., *Tudor and Stuart Town*, p. 185.

49. J. Patten, 'Urban occupations in pre-industrial England', *TIBG*, 3, 1977, pp. 296–313. The categories used here are based on those developed by J. Langton and refined by F. Lewis to allow analysis by type of occupation dealing, manufacturing, service or use of material: J. Langton, 'Residential patterns in pre-industrial cities', p. 205; Lewis, 'Demographic and Occupational Structure', pp. 59–61.

50. Some 4 per cent of councillors in Gloucester, 1680–1700, and in Bristol, 1605–1642, were textile workers. Weavers made up 35 per cent of mayors in Norwich between 1680 and 1697: P. Clark, 'The civic leaders of Gloucester 1580–1800', in *The Transformation of English Provincial Towns 1600–1800*, ed. P. Clark, London, 1984, p. 315; D. H. Sacks, 'The corporate town and the English state: Bristol's "little businesses" 1625–1641', in Barry, ed., *Tudor and Stuart Town*, p. 317; P. Corfield, 'A provincial capital in the late seventeenth century: the case of Norwich', in *The Early Modern Town*, ed. P. Clark, London, 1976, p. 245.

51. Sacks, *Widening Gate*, pp. 165–66; Jackson, *Hull*, p. 308; Newton, *Eighteenth-century Exeter*, p. 38; I. Maver, 'Guardianship of the community', in *Glasgow Volume I: Beginnings to 1830*, ed. T. M. Devine and G. Jackson, Manchester, 1995, ch. 7; J. W. Kirby, 'Restoration Leeds and the aldermen of the corporation 1661–1700', *Northern History*, XXII, 1986, p.135.

52. G. Holmes, *Augustan England*, London, 1982, pp. 9–12; P. Borsay, *The English Urban Renaissance*, Oxford, 1989, pp. 225–32.

53. Trade is reconstructed from port books of 1664–65 and 1708–09: PRO E190/1337/16; E190/1375/08; Plantation Registers of 1744–73: Maritime Archives and Library, Merseyside Maritime Museum: D/514/2/1, reproduced on microfilm: M. M. Schofield and D. J. Pope, eds, *The Liverpool Plantation Registers 1744–73 and 1779–84*, Wakefield, 1978. Property is derived from the hearth taxes of 1663, 1664, 1666 and 1673: PRO: E179/250/8; E179/250/11; E179/250/9; E179/132/355; a poor rate assessment of 1708: H. Peet, *Liverpool in the reign of Queen Anne 1705 and 1708*, Liverpool, 1908; a rate assessment of 1743, LplRO 920PT51.

54. PRO: E190/1337/16.

55. PRO: E179/250/8; E179/250/11; E179/250/9; E179/132/355.

56. M. Power, 'Councillors and commerce in Liverpool 1650–1750', *Urban History*, 24, 1997, p. 313.

57. PRO: E190/1375/08.

58. Touzeau, *Rise and Progress*, p. 370. Reluctance to serve, demonstrated by fining to avoid office, was uncommon in Liverpool. Compare Hull: G. Forster, 'Hull in the sixteenth and seventeenth centuries', in *Victoria County History, York: East Riding*, ed. K. J. Allison, Vol. I, London, 1969, pp. 123–24.

59. There were some 365 merchants recorded shipping in and out of Liverpool in 1709, 40 of them accounting for above ten shipments. In Hull in 1702 there were 116 merchants shipping outwards, only 22 of whom accounted for ten or more shipments in the year: Forster, 'Hull ', p. 183.

60. Sacks, *Widening Gate*, pp. 257–65.

61. There were 89 warehouses in the town in 1743: assessment LplRO 920 PT51; for control of the Common: J. Ramsay Muir, *A History of Liverpool*, Liverpool, 1907, pp. 71, 109, 145; for 1708 averages: Power, 'Councillors and commerce', p. 318.

62. Peet, *Liverpool in the reign of Queen Anne*.

63. Entries from 1743 to 1748 were input into a computer file, PLANT, deposited in the Data Archive, Essex. Investment in a ship was usually divided into shares to finance shipbuilding and offset risk: R. Davis, *The Rise of the English Shipping Industry in the Seventeenth and Eighteenth Centuries*, London, 1962, pp. 81–90

64. LplRO 920 PT51; RATE1743, deposited in the Data Archive, Essex.

65. A. C. Wardle, 'Sir Thomas Johnson: his inpecuniosity and death', *THSLC*, 90, 1938, pp. 181–84.

66. The attraction of gentility for the sons of bourgeoisie has attracted particular attention by historians of London: H. Horwitz, 'The mess of the middle class revisited: the case of the big bourgeoisie of Augustan London', *Continuity and Change*, 2, 1987, p. 285; N. Rogers, 'Money, land and lineage: the big bourgeoisie of Hanoverian London', in *The Eighteenth-century Town*, ed. P. Borsay, London, 1990, pp. 282–89.

67. Power, 'Councillors and commerce', pp. 119–20. Merchants in late seventeenth-century London also tended to hold property on major streets, and craftsmen in alleys and lanes: M. Power, 'The social topography of Restoration London', in *London 1500–1700*, ed. A. L. Beier and R. Finlay, London, 1986, pp. 209–12.

68. TOWNBOOK.

69. Jackson, *Hull*, pp. 2, 96; K. Morgan, *Bristol and the Atlantic Trade in the Eighteenth Century*, Cambridge, 1993, pp. 94–98; Sacks, *Widening Gate*, p. 353.

70. Touzeau, *Rise and Progress*, p. 337; Muir and Platt, *Municipal Government in Liverpool*, p. 249.

6
Politics

The effect of the charter of 1695 on Liverpool suggests that politics played an important role in the evolution of the town. This chapter considers its political history and attempts to assess the influence of political agreement or conflict on the progress of the town and port. It assesses the role of the most active players in the context of the overall change in the structure of power discussed in Chapter 5.[1] Several factors are evaluated: how the groups exercising political power in the town competed for position; how national policies affected local ambitions; how cohesive the governing group was; and what political, religious and economic interests cemented alliances or promoted antagonisms.

The study can be set within the recent general analysis of the politics of trade between the Restoration and the reign of George I by Perry Gauci. Setting out to establish the attitudes to, influence of, and associational culture of merchants in the period of the commercial revolution, he explores merchants in London, in the declining port of York, and the burgeoning port of Liverpool to assess the character and position of overseas traders at a time when mercantile input to the state was increasingly recognised by national governments still controlled by landowners. He emphasises the sudden increase in trading activity in Liverpool, quite different in trend from the large-scale established operations of merchants in London or the difficulties of overseas traders in York. He goes on to argue that the Liverpool merchants responsible for the increase in trade made efforts to assimilate into Liverpool society, many marrying local women, buying property, and taking communal and governing responsibilities in the town. Men such as Thomas Johnson and Richard Norris were well aware of the need to work for the town interest and in partnership, not only with other traders but with all townsmen.[2] Gauci describes Liverpool developing a 'supportive environment' for traders. Finally, he recognises the sophistication of Liverpool merchants in using Parliament to push for town improvements, an ability common among merchants in other towns in the period but notable in a comparatively new centre of overseas trade.[3] Liverpool council provided the means by which such political action was channelled and the lack of traditional and competing trading companies or interests in the town was a key factor in fostering united action among town merchants.

The assumption of corporate responsibility has been examined in Chapter 5. In this chapter the extent of political activity and consensus, important concerns in Gauci's work, is explored. The task is complicated by the intricacy of the political process during the century after the English Revolution. The continuation and resolution of national political and religious tensions resulting from the Civil War has been subject to much scrutiny in recent years. The central part played by religious tension in the politics of the Restoration period has been emphasised. Fear of the political danger posed by dissenters provoked a series of religious acts to enforce conformity. A counter policy of toleration pursued by Charles II in the declaration of indulgence, designed in particular to promote Catholics, inflamed Anglican loyalists. The political battle to guarantee succession to his brother, the Catholic Duke of York, exacerbated the problem and provoked the first Whig party, a coalition of those sympathetic to dissent, those opposed to court influence, and some Anglicans concerned about popery and arbitrary government.[4] The uneasy confrontation of those loyal to Anglicanism and the court, and those concerned with some liberty of conscience and wary of the danger of Catholicism and arbitrary government, reached a pitch in the Exclusion Crisis in 1679–81. The fears of the Whig exclusionists seemed realised when James II attempted to promote a Catholic and arbitrary court control, or, from his perspective, a toleration policy after 1685. Though the revolution of 1688–89 solved the problem of Catholic promotion, tensions between Anglicanism and Protestant dissent continued. Throughout the reign of William and Mary, and Queen Anne, the religious issue remained central to political discourse.[5]

Such political and religious tensions were played out at a local level, where local magistrates acted to defend Anglicanism or dissent, and followed or opposed control from the court. The local response in towns was varied. There have been able studies of the experience of London, Bristol and Great Yarmouth, but they do not provide a template for experience elsewhere.[6] What is clear is that the interplay of national and local politics was becoming increasingly important, especially in towns, for it was there that political and religious disaffection created by the English Revolution lingered. The late Stuart regime attempted to ensure compliant magistracies by the Corporation Act and the issuing of new town charters.[7] But political opposition still broke out in periods of crisis, during the struggle over exclusion between 1679 and 1681, or the revolution of 1688–89. Towns continued to foster political conflict in the 'rage of party' in the reigns of William III and Queen Anne. Later, some became centres of opposition to Whig hegemony in the age of Walpole.[8]

The major political changes in this period and the variety of towns make generalisations about national politics and the role of towns difficult. The enterprise becomes even more tricky when assessing the role of a town which, because of its small size, was not typical of the longer-established regional capitals which had for centuries played an important political role. That condition was changing as the increase in population and commercial involvement made Liverpool more significant. Like most towns, Liverpool was subject to increasing royal control, purged of dissenting councillors under the Corporation Act and subject to two new charters, one sought in 1677 and another imposed in 1685. It is difficult to see the town as a significant challenge to royal control and policy during the Restoration period. Dissenters did not reappear on the council after ejection in 1662. The town was, to an extent, controlled by local landowners. Most of its MPs before 1689 were nominees of the Earl of Derby, for example. Moreover, limited in its experience of high politics, the town played a muted part in political national struggles such as exclusion, unlike the lively reaction in Bristol and, of course, London, a centre of agitation.[9] Like many towns Liverpool also kept a low profile during the uncertainties of James II's reign.

After the revolution of 1688–89, and a third charter of 1695 which vested political control in local merchants for the first time, the town corporation acted to develop its institutions and infrastructure. Though political and religious tensions between Whig and Tory in an age of fierce electoral conflict were evident they do not appear to have been as divisive as in towns such as Buckingham, Marlborough, Portsmouth or York, or to have provoked riots as in Southwark or Coventry in 1705.[10] In contrast, a series of protests against local Whig oligarchy broke out in the 1720s and 1730s. Like York, Norwich, Preston and Worcester in the 1720s, and Bristol and Scarborough in the 1730s, opposition stirred, in part populist reaction to the entrenched Whig council, in part a protest against Walpole's stranglehold on power at the centre.[11] It is perhaps significant that the town experienced serious and prolonged political tension only when its population had become large, its trading wealth established, and its oligarchical council entrenched.

This brief introduction highlights some obvious characteristics of Liverpool. The struggle for autonomy in the period up to 1695, the predominant political consensus from 1695 till 1710, and the increasing political tension after 1710 will be examined in more detail. Though Liverpool experienced political and religious tensions it is argued that they were not serious enough to inhibit its rapid growth and that political consensus helped it progress.

Autonomy, 1660–1695

Liverpool in 1660 was smaller and less commercially developed than older ports such as Hull and Bristol. Hull's Society of Merchants and Bristol's Society of Merchant Adventurers, founded in earlier periods of commercial activity and still regulating trade and representing merchants in the seventeenth century, had no counterpart in Liverpool. Lacking such an infrastructure, political control in the town was disputed with several landowners, a process described most fully by Mullett.[12]

The Molyneuxs, local aristocrats who had long leased the fee farm of Liverpool and filled the position of constable of the castle, were the most aggressive. When Caryll, Viscount Molyneux, resumed the lordship of the town and constableship of the castle after the Restoration there began a running dispute which was to last for over a decade. There were two issues in dispute. The first was his demand for £20 of burgage rents from the town as well as the fee farm rent of £14.6s.8d due to the king. Though Mayor Alexander Greene and seven aldermen ordered a deputation on 30 December 1661 to treat with Molyneux to rectify the 'mistake' the town continued the payment of £20 and provided Lord Molyneux with a list of the town's burgage rents on 3 June 1662. Relations between Molyneux, a Catholic, and this group of puritan aldermen (five of the seven were deprived of their office in 1662 under the provisions of the Corporation Act) were strained for historical and religious as well as financial reasons.[13]

A second quarrel increased tension. As lord of the manor, Lord Molyneux laid claim to the Common to the southeast of the town and, to improve access to it, planned a bridge over the Liver Pool. On 23 March 1669 Mr John Sturzaker, deputy mayor, the aldermen and common council claimed that they had 'time out of mind been reputed to have the rightful seigniory of the same Common under his majesty', and ordered any building works to be pulled down, a threat evidently carried out by Edward Marsh and James Whitfield who were sued by Molyneux at the assizes. On 26 April 1671 Mayor Thomas Johnson and four other councillors were empowered to negotiate to conclude the dispute. It was agreed that the bridge could be built on payment of a rent of two pence per annum by Lord Molyneux to the corporation in recognition of their right to the Common. The agreement was a significant victory for the town for it enabled it to benefit from the extensive eighteenth-century building development around the first dock.[14]

The Earls of Derby were a second landowning family to play an active role in the town. Several earls served as mayor: Charles, eighth Earl, in 1666–67, William, ninth Earl, in 1677–78, and James, tenth Earl, in 1707–08 and 1734–35.[15] This did not guarantee amity. The strenuous efforts of the council to obtain a new charter in the eighth Earl's mayoralty were unsuccessful and Derby's lack of effort in promoting it may have been reflected in his compensatory gift of a great silver mace to the town the following year. The earl was sometimes resisted by the corporation. When in November 1669 he demanded possession of houses recently built between his Liverpool house, the Tower, and the River Mersey, the mayor, aldermen and common council replied that the land belonged to the corporation and could not be surrendered.[16] One respect in which the Earls of Derby held consistent influence in the town during this period was in promoting clients, William Banks, Ralph Assheton, Ruisshe Wentworth, or court candidates such as Sir William Bucknall, to serve in Parliament.[17]

The third influential landlord family was the long-established Moore family, owners of Old Hall and Bank Hall, and landlords of much property in the town in the 1660s. Sir Edward Moore, son of Colonel John Moore who had commanded the parliamentary garrison in the town, married into a Northumbrian royalist family and attempted to re-impose the family's political authority in the town. Three times he stood unsuccessfully for office, as parliamentary candidate in April 1660, when he was defeated by Gilbert Ireland whose uncle had served as MP for Liverpool before him, as mayor in October 1669 losing to Thomas Bicksteth, a tradesman, whose part was noisily taken by freemen voters, and as parliamentary candidate in the by-election of December 1670, only to be humiliated by losing to a London brewer and court candidate, Sir William Bucknall, who was supported by Mayor Thomas Johnson.[18] Moore poured out his disappointed ambitions in *The Moore Rental*, a diatribe against many of his tenants who had failed to support him, a record of frustrated political hopes as well as of a landlord and his tenants.[19]

The struggles between the town and these three families demonstrate the position of local landowners in the town but also the determination of mayors and councillors to resist their demands and defend the interests and autonomy of the town. In contrast, the involvement of Liverpool with the crown and national politics demonstrates the limits of corporation power. When the Corporation Act was applied to Liverpool in November 1662, as it was to other towns, six aldermen, seven common councillors and the town clerk were removed from office because they were dissenters. The deprived aldermen read like a roll call of the mayors of the 1650s: Ralph Massam (mayor in 1652), Edward Williamson (1653), Gilbert Formby (1656), Thomas Blackmore (1657), Richard Percival (1658), and Thomas Williamson (1659). They were replaced with more reliable Anglican nominees, though one of the new aldermen, Peter Lurting, proved a troublesome member of the new establishment.[20]

Religious and political tension in the town in the following decades is not easy to interpret because the town record is brief and cryptic. Muir and Mullett try to make sense of faction in the council but with limited success.[21] Conflict broke out in 1672 during the mayoralty of Sylvester Richmond, a physician who had settled in Liverpool ten years before and a firm supporter of the Anglican establishment.[22] A resolution was passed at the council on 28 October 1672 threatening with dismissal any member of council who supported a paper read at the council. The paper does not survive and it is impossible to identify the issues in dispute. At the end of Richmond's year of office there was a riot when he adjourned the election court on 18 October 1673, after Mr James Jerrome was chosen mayor and before the election of bailiffs: 'Richard Lurting, Thomas Stockley, Joshua Cubban, Edward Litherland, in disturbance of the peace and against their freemen oaths, riotously united and refused to let the mayor led by the serjeant at mace leave, three times forcing him to return to his place, not without some violence, keeping him two hours'.[23]

What lay behind the outburst is unclear. Given Richmond's Anglican stance the protestors may have been dissenters but there is no direct evidence of this. Muir sees it as a protest by freemen electors against the mayor's denial of their right to elect bailiffs, but there is no evidence to prove this either.[24] The social character of some of the protestors would support the notion of such a populist outburst. Lurting and those of the 29 followers who can be identified were well below the social and political level of the mayor and councillors they opposed. Richard Lurting was an anchorsmith, Thomas Stockley an innkeeper, William Houghton a porter, Richard Mercer a seaman, William Trueman a draper, Thomas Tyrer perhaps a ship carpenter, Richard Windall a cooper or perhaps a mariner, and William Valentine a gunsmith. Sylvester Richmond, in contrast, was a physician and his successor as mayor, James Jerrome, a merchant.[25] Moreover, the protestors were unused to local power. While some of them had acted in subordinate offices for the corporation, scavengers, aletasters and beadles, only Richard Lurting, the leader, and William Houghton became councillors, and then many years later.[26] The immediate effect of their action was disgrace. The four leaders were deprived of their freedom and their followers were all fined £5.[27]

A second political tussle in 1676–77 involved weightier antagonists. It began on 15 October 1676 with aldermen Thomas Andoe, Thomas Johnson and Peter Lurting admitting new freemen in the last days of the mayoralty of Thomas Chapman. Freemen were normally admitted by the whole council. It censured the irregular admission on 1 November 1676 and instructed Mayor Robert Williamson to seek a renewal of the town charter.[28] Andoe, Johnson and Lurting were aldermen of much experience. Thomas Andoe had served as mayor in 1655 and as the Earl of Derby's deputy in 1667–68; Thomas Johnson had joined the council in 1663 and been mayor in 1670; Peter Lurting had been appointed alderman in 1662 by the Corporation Act commissioners and served as mayor in 1663.[29] Muir suggests that the three men were attempting to boost the number of freemen at the election court as a counter to the Anglican ascendancy achieved by Richmond and Jerrome in 1673.[30] There is no evidence to prove this, though Johnson was later the first Whig mayor of the town in 1695.

Whatever the intentions of the censured aldermen they resigned from the council: Peter Lurting begged to be excused because of his age; Thomas Johnson refused to take his oath as an alderman unless he was elected to a new office; Thomas Andoe simply declared himself discharged.[31] Moreover, there was a quick response to the request for a new charter. Granted in 1677, it established 15 burgesses 'dwelling without that town', local nobility and gentry from the surrounding Lancashire parishes loyal to the court, in an enlarged council of 60, and it removed the right of election of mayor and bailiffs from freemen and vested it in the council. In effect, it sought to guarantee an Anglican and loyal magistracy in the town. The charter was granted following an early flurry of charters issued by Charles II in the 1660s but before the wholesale re-issuing of charters in the 1680s which aimed to purge town magistracies after the Exclusion Crisis. Although it was sought by the council, the weakening of town autonomy so soon after the successful resisting of the Molyneux and Moore pretensions resulted in the development of an anti-court interest in the town.[32]

In spite of this there was little obvious Whig sentiment expressed in the town during the Exclusion Crisis. Unlike Bristol, where Whig and Tory protagonists were very active, Liverpool remained quiet. Parliamentary elections, still controlled by the Earl of Derby, were not hotly contested.[33] No obvious factions emerged in council. It may be that the withdrawal from office of aldermen such as Thomas Johnson and Thomas Andoe in 1676 left the anti-court party bereft of leadership in the town. Local dissenters were not sufficiently well established to provide a supporting lobby for exclusion, as they were in Bristol.[34] Liverpudlians did follow events in London and Oxford, and a loyal address of 3 August 1681 to Charles II made particular reference to the defence of protestantism and liberties, but it is difficult to use this as evidence of partisan Whig or Tory support. In contrast, a visit of the Duke of Monmouth to Liverpool in September 1682 elicited some Whig enthusiasm. He was greeted with musket volleys by the rabble, entertained by alderman John Chorley, and granted the freedom of the town by Mayor Windall, a mariner. That the leader of a 'loyal' council created by the charter of 1677 should fete Monmouth is surprising and Windall might have been caught in a political event he had not the experience or wisdom to control. It is significant that Chorley and he are the only councillors recorded as implicated and they seem to have acted alone.[35]

The episode encouraged the crown to seek further control. On 19 August 1684, Mayor Robert Seacombe and 14 councillors travelled to Bewsay near Warrington, the home of the Tory Sir Richard Atherton, to surrender the charter of 1677 to Lord Chief Justice Jeffries. Its replacement included a clause enabling the king (by the date of issue James II) to remove any mayor, alderman or common councilman at pleasure.[36] Control by local landowners was replaced by control by the crown. James II soon exercised the right on 14 August 1687, removing Mayor Oliver Lyme and alderman Sylvester Richmond after they refused to abandon proceedings against Richard Lathom and his wife, Catholics, who kept a school.[37] Richmond was a loyal Tory, his replacement, alderman John Chorley, a Whig. The episode demonstrates very well the inversion of the traditional alliance between the crown and local magistrates.

The revolution of 1688–89 heralded the most momentous political change in Liverpool. The charter of 1685 was suspended, Richard Savage, Lord Colchester, and Thomas Norris of Speke were returned as Whig MPs in the 1690 election, and Jasper Mauditt, a Whig, became mayor in 1693.[38] The most significant change arose from a parliamentary by-election in December 1694. When Richard Savage, Lord Colchester, was elevated to the Lords as Earl Rivers he persuaded Jasper Mauditt to stand in his place. Mauditt duly won with 400 votes to the 15 of his Tory opponent, Thomas Brotherton. Mayor Alexander Norres, however, returned Brotherton, arguing that Mauditt was ineligible to sit as MP since he was borough coroner.[39] The House of Commons supported Mauditt, and Norres was imprisoned for seven weeks for electoral fraud.

Encouraged by this success the Liverpool Whigs petitioned the privy council for a new charter, provoking a struggle against Norres and his Tory supporters. On 29 March 1695 Norres and 31 councillors agreed to defend the charter of 1677 and became known as 'old charter men'.[40] The Whigs, led by Thomas Johnson senior, returning to active politics for the first time since 1676, Thomas Johnson his son, and Thomas Norris MP, the 'new charter men', continued to press their case. Arguing that the 1677 charter was invalid because the previous charter of 1626 had not been properly surrendered strengthened their case.[41] A new charter, granted in September 1695, named Thomas Johnson the elder as mayor and 40 new councillors. Johnson was sworn in by Thomas Norris and Jasper Mauditt, the town MPs, on 3 October.[42]

The 'new charter party' victory in 1695 led to a revolution in the personnel and character of the council. The day after the new regime was installed Thomas Alanson, Richard Jones and John Crowther refused to take the oaths of common councilmen and were replaced by James Benn, Edmund Livesey and Peter Eaton. The total turnover of councillors was much greater. Some 25 councillors who had supported Alexander Norres on 29 March 1695 had disappeared by the time Thomas Johnson's new council met on 9 October. At this meeting, which voted to cover the costs of obtaining the new charter, were 15 new men, eight of them to become mayors in the succeeding eight years.[43]

Long-serving Tory councillors were replaced by Whig newcomers. Alexander Norres, the disgraced mayor, had served on the council since 1685, Thomas Alanson, an ironmonger, since 1686, Thomas Tyrer, a tailor, since 1685, Robert Seacome since 1672, Richard Windall, mariner, since 1669, and Richard Jones since 1662. The new Whig councillors, except for Thomas Johnson senior, a councillor in 1663, were inexperienced. Thomas Johnson junior had joined the council in 1689. Richard Norris and Levinius Heuston, the new bailiffs, Charles Diggles, John Lady, John Cockshutt, a merchant, Robert Sheilds, a goldsmith, and Joseph Prior, a watchmaker, joined the council for the first time in 1695.[44]

It would be foolish to come to sweeping conclusions about the transfer of power. There were more merchants among the new men, which might fit preconceptions about the mercantile character of Whigs, but some old Tories were merchants too.[45] There is no evidence of religious dissent, another feature of Whiggism, among the new men (nonconformists continued to be excluded from council office, unlike in Bristol or London) though councillors such as Johnson, himself an Anglican, were tolerant of dissent.[46] What is in no doubt is that the Tory group which had controlled the council in the 1680s was destroyed. The new men were to have a profound effect on the town in the following two decades.

Progress, 1695–1710

The local revolution in government in 1695 vested control in the hands of town merchants for the first time. The overwhelming eighteenth-century mercantile predominance of the council remarked in Chapter 5 dates from this time. The assumption of parliamentary representation by townsmen is another symptom of the change. Whereas in the previous thirty years MPs for the town had been court or Derby nominees, town merchants now filled seats at Westminster: Jasper Mauditt in December 1694, William Norris of Speke in November 1695, William Clayton in January 1701, Thomas Johnson in December 1701, Richard Norris of Speke in May 1708, and John Clieveland in October 1710.[47]

The assumption of power coincided with an unprecedented period of improvements in the town. Many towns underwent improvements of course. Liverpool stands out in initiating fundamental changes such as creating a parish for the first time or building the first dock. As early as 17 September 1656 Colonel Birch, once military governor and MP, expressed the ambitions of the town: 'to labour that the town be made a parish of itself, distinct from Walton, in regard it is the only port in Lancaster and has always had all parochial privileges'; and 'to have it made a free and independent port of itself'.[48] Both ambitions were advanced after 1695. Liverpool became a parish and built a second church, St Peter, and planned and built the first commercial wet dock in the country, a facility which helped set the commercial course for the town over the next two centuries. It could be argued that these achievements were due to the political cohesion and energy of the new Whig councillors, or that their unity resulted from such achievements. They were not so united as to avoid party strife altogether but the Whig caucus on the council was able to push through policies despite political differences. Thomas Johnson's letters as MP in London to Richard Norris in Liverpool allow a particularly close view of the developments and political struggles of these years.[49]

The creation of the parish of Liverpool was a longstanding ambition. Since 1399 the church of Our Lady and St Nicholas had been a chapel of the mother church at Walton-on-the-Hill a few miles north of the town. The rector of Walton claimed tithe payments from Liverpool and a voice in the appointment of a minister in Liverpool. On 21 December 1669 the council determined to resist, declaring that the town had enjoyed the right of appointment since the seventh year of Queen Elizabeth. It duly elected Mr Robert Hunter of Macclesfield as minister on 11 July 1670.[50] There was no dispute over their right to appoint in 1688 when Robert Hunter died. William Atherton and Robert Styth were jointly appointed to minister to the growing town.[51]

In December 1697 mayor James Benn took steps to make the town a separate parish and consulted the rector of Walton, Richard Richmond, himself a Liverpool councillor. A crucial step in obtaining his consent was an agreement to compensate Richmond for lost tithes in 1698. Once this was done William Clayton and Sir William Norris, the MPs for the town, were instructed to procure an Act of Parliament to create Liverpool a separate parish. The town produced a printed *Case of the Corporation of Liverpool* to help obtain the Act.[52] The preamble proclaimed Liverpool to have 'become a place of great trade and commerce, and very populous; and although they have had a parochial chapel, yet by reason of increase of people the same is not sufficient for them, and… being an ancient corporation are desirous to be a parish of themselves.' The new church provided for, St Peter, was built on the road which crossed Lord Molyneux's bridge to the Common. Thomas Johnson sent several letters from London in the summer and autumn of 1703 to Richard Norris discussing interior decoration and seating.[53] The careful planning of the venture suggests confidence and sophistication.

The gaining of ownership of the castle, which followed soon after, was symbolic of the corporation's control of the whole town. In November 1701 Lord Molyneux seized the castle to try to ensure his continued control of the constableship after the office had been given to Lord Rivers. For a year from February 1702 Thomas Johnson and William Clayton, the town MPs, attempted to enlist the help of rival patrons, Sir John Leveson Gower, chancellor of the Duchy of Lancaster, and the Earl of Derby, to obtain a grant of the castle. In 1704 the lease was granted.[54] Thomas Johnson began planning in April 1707 what could be done with the ground, so strategically situated on a knoll between the town and the Liver Pool: 'I think a handsome square might be made very well... but to be let to people who would build good houses and make them uniform... I do hope it may be built by merchants or such private families; this would be a mighty ornament to the town.' The experience of London houses and squares was clearly in his mind and gracious development the aim.[55] It was some time, however, before the site was developed. On 4 July 1709 a warrant was issued to the Earl of Derby, lord lieutenant of the county, to take an inventory of the arms and deliver them to Ralph Peters the town clerk. It was not until 1714 that an Act of Parliament was obtained for the building of the third church of the town, St George, on the site, and in June 1726 Thomas Steers and Edward Litherland were engaged to build it.[56]

As stated in Chapter 1, the decision to build the first dock in 1708 was the most momentous improvement of the age. Thomas Johnson was thinking about the idea in January 1707 when he wrote to Richard Norris to report his talking with George Sorocold, 'a very ingenious man', who thought that using stone from the castle to build a dock would save money.[57] It was on 3 November 1708 that the council asked Sir Thomas Johnson and Richard Norris, the two MPs for the town, to treat with a proper person to come to the town and draw a plan of the intended dock. William Bibby, Edward Litherland and Thomas Ackers were local men who had planned the construction of quaysides in the Liver Pool for ships in April 1709, but Thomas Steers of London was engaged to build an enclosed dock where ships could lie unaffected by tides. In October 1709 the MPs were ordered to obtain an Act of Parliament to sanction the dock and raise the estimated £6,000 it would cost. By May 1710 Thomas Steers was in post and the mayor, John Earle, and the aldermen and council made trustees for the work.[58]

The projected cost of the dock was high for a corporation with an annual income of less than £400.[59] As the preamble to the Act stated:

'[it] will cost more than the inhabitants of the said borough and corporation can raise and... the same cannot be effected without the aid and assistance of all trading persons to and from the same'. 'Aid and assistance' meant dock dues, and 'trading persons to and from the same' included any trader landing at any point under the jurisdiction of Liverpool Customs inspectors, that is the entire Mersey estuary. The issue of how the town could benefit from traders who entered the Mersey had been tested exhaustively in a legal dispute with the London cheesemongers in the previous decade. As freemen of London they had claimed exemption from payment of Liverpool dues when they loaded boats at Ince and Frodsham up-river from Liverpool. The town, nevertheless, seized their cheese and was sued by the London company. Despite determined efforts by Jasper Mauditt for the corporation in legal proceedings between 1696 and 1699 the verdict went against the corporation, and Mayor Richard Norris was attempting to cope with the debts incurred in December 1700. Johnson and Norris's dock bill in December 1709 threatened the London cheesemongers again. Both parties printed their case, the Liverpool argument much strengthened by Acts for pier repairs at Dover, Whitby and Yarmouth, duties for which were levied on boats using any part of those harbours. This time, the cheesemongers did not gain exemption from dues and the bill was passed with only minor amendments.[60]

The Act was a major breakthrough for the corporation. The dock was opened in 1715 and Steers was elected dock master on 10 October 1717. With Mr Sylvester Morecroft's new Customs house built in 1722 at the head of the dock Liverpool offered an unrivalled facility. It was the only early eighteenth-century dock built by a town corporation and it gave the town a significant competitive advantage. The dock became a model for later docks in Bristol, Hull, Edinburgh and London. When, on 11 January 1738, Thomas Steers was asked to build a second dock at a cost of £12,000, the tradition of dock building in Liverpool was set.[61]

The dock was the most remarkable evidence of the council's initiative in these early eighteenth-century years but there were other less dramatic initiatives. In June 1707 John Seacome, a councillor and merchant appraiser in 1704 and 1706, presented a paper to the council on a method of leasing corporation property for three lives and 21 years. The council was clearly planning to manage its property on the Common to best advantage and it became a major source of revenue by the late eighteenth century. On 20 August 1707 it appointed a lawyer as town clerk. Mr Ralph Peters, son-in-law of alderman Preeson, immediately improved record keeping, beginning freemen's registers and apprentice books for the first time, another instance of the town catching up with practice long established in other towns. On 9 December 1708, a month after the council instructed Thomas Johnson and Richard

Norris to seek an Act for the dock, they were instructed to obtain a patent for a second market day for the town, on a Wednesday. Helped by the Earl of Derby, a 31-year patent was obtained in February 1709, and with it came the right to collect prisage on wines. Ralph Peters was to collect the duty and account for it to the mayor.[62]

What is noteworthy about the initiatives of the period between 1695 and 1710 is not that they were pioneering, the dock excepted, but that they came in a rush. Liverpool came of age in these two decades, developing a dynamic which was not to slacken for a century and a half. The character and interaction of the political leaders who grasped the opportunity therefore holds a particular interest. The achievements of the period suggest a degree of unanimity among them during a period when political differences might have been a major obstacle to concerted action. From the 1694 Triennial Act there began a 'rage of party' which split urban communities, particularly at election times. Tory and Whig divisions and Anglican and dissenting tensions were sharp realities in many towns. It was a period when a series of occasional conformity bills reflected a determination among Anglicans to push dissenters out of political life, and 'the church in danger' was a slogan much trumpeted between the mid-1690s and the hysteria of the Sacheverell affair. Concern about the frequent wars fought under William III and Queen Anne was another contentious issue.[63]

London is an obvious example of a city where party politics sharply divided society at the time. Whig dissenters were heavily represented in city government and monopolised the Bank of England and the New East India Company. Whigs controlled the city after 1689, becoming the establishment party by the reign of Queen Anne. Tories, represented in the old East India Company and Royal African Company, mobilised around the issue of the defence of Anglicanism and more open government.[64] In some market towns, Buckingham, Camelford, Marlborough and Devizes, party affiliation was so strong that rival Tory and Whig corporations developed, or rival mayors held office. The 1705 and 1710 elections in particular were troubled, the first in the wake of the Tory manoeuvre to tack an occasional conformity bill to a money bill, the second at the time of the Sacheverell furore, and there were riots in Southwark, Coventry and Devizes. Large provincial ports seem to have been less disturbed. Bristol was dominated from 1695 by Whigs, though the town voted Tory in 1710 in the Sacheverell backlash. Hull, too, was thoroughly Whig and chose its MPs on individual merits rather than on party lines.[65]

How did party politics affect Liverpool at this time? It has been argued above that the 1695 charter established a Whig council with an identity distinct from the previous Tory administrations. This does not mean that party divisions did not exist. As Johnson wrote to Richard

Norris on 17 March 1701, 'I am afraid the old temper continues'. One issue which split councillors was tobacco duty. Alderman Richard Houghton, a merchant of Water Street and one of the old charter men of 1695, was clearly at odds with Johnson. Houghton wanted tobaccco imported and exported without casks being opened and repacked. Johnson saw this as a major threat to profitability for it entailed selling tobacco at low prices. On 17 March 1701 he wrote: 'Tobacco sold at a low price will spike our market... Since we have increased in people as we have increased in trade, and take away that the people give too, and then you have done with the new improvements.' Not repacking entailed an abandonment of allowances from the Customs and the loss of even more profit. HM Customs granted allowances on damaged or wet tobacco but were alert to the practice of some importers of deliberately breaking up consignments to fraudulently claim such allowances. Some Liverpool merchants, Clayton and Houghton among them, were for stamping out the practice perhaps because of their association with the court interest which included the Customs service. Thomas Johnson, Levinius Heuston and others saw only financial ruin in abandoning the practice.[66]

Party politics were most obvious at elections, especially at mayoral elections in 1702, 1703 and 1705, but they do not suggest a neat Whig/Tory division. On 9 October 1702 Johnson wrote from Liverpool to Richard Norris about the attempt to put up a suitable mayoral candidate. Joseph Briggs, a merchant of Castle Street, was nominated for the Tory or old charter party when John Clieveland refused to stand, though 'after his usual manner... was drunk two nights together'. For the Whigs or new charter party Johnson supported John Cockshut, a merchant, after Joseph Prior, a watchmaker, had withdrawn through illness.[67] What is interesting about the poll on 18 October 1702 is that Briggs, the Tory candidate, was supported not only by old charter men, Mayor Thomas Bicksteth, Alderman Tyrer and Alderman Windall, but also by Jasper Mauditt and Mr Sharples, new charter men. Party affiliation was clearly fluid. According to an account two days later by Johnson's brother-in-law, Peter Hall, it was when the townsmen, 'no way biassed', saw through the old charter party's game that Cockshut came through strongly and was elected.[68]

In the following year, on 15 October 1703, Thomas Johnson described a second mayoral election which suggests the secondary importance of party. John Clieveland esquire, a tobacco and sugar merchant from Leicestershire royalist stock, and an old charter candidate who had refused to stand the previous year, was nominated by the council and threatened with a fine if he refused. There was more to this pressure on a Tory candidate than determination to stop the avoidance of office, not usually an issue in the town. Clieveland's hand was forced by 37 councillors signing under the corporate seal requiring him to serve as mayor. After Clieveland had been sworn on 19 October a 'great council' was held and the old councillors invited. Mr Alanson, one of the old charter men, made his excuses and did not go.[69]

Party strife in the third contested mayoral election in 1705 is more obvious. Ten Whig councillors supported J. Gibbons, son-in-law of Peter Hall and also related to Johnson. A rival group of five Tory councillors, George Tyrer, Richard Houghton, John Clieveland, Cuthbert Sharples and William Webster, together with Mrs Clayton representing perhaps William Clayton the Tory MP, backed William Webster. Webster won, partly because alderman Houghton rounded up 60 freemen sailors on polling day to sway the vote.[70] The Tory cause was evidently still alive.

The Whig charter of 1695 did not, therefore, create a solidly Whig establishment. Party allegiance existed. However, it did not seem to dominate political life. None of the contested mayoral contests were very intense. Johnson talks about the Tory councillors in indulgent terms. They were opponents to be outsmarted in local elections, if possible, but also fellow councillors with whom he needed to work. Party allegiance could also change. John Clieveland is a good example. He had been an opponent of the 1695 charter but later allied with Johnson and the new charter party. Having been forced to become mayor in 1703 he swung back to the Tory group by 1705 but was never an active party politician. It is significant that he remained on the Lancashire commission of the peace after 1715.[71] The need for Liverpool men to work together and their coincidence of interest in fostering the town was more important than party allegiance.

Parliamentary elections in these years support the evidence of party voting. Tory candidates sometimes defeated Whig opponents. Of the 21 Liverpool MPs between 1690 and 1713, 14 were Whigs and seven Tories. Though Thomas Johnson seemed immovable as a Whig MP from 1701 until 1723, his fellow member in the elections of December 1701, July 1702 and May 1705 was a Tory, William Clayton. The disputed election of 1705 is particularly interesting because Clayton's return was against the trend of national Whig gains. Clayton defeated the Whig Richard Norris partly because of his personal vote.[72] His success in a year of Whig recovery suggests, too, that freemen electors were not bound by party loyalty. Three years later, in 1708, Clayton lost his seat to Richard Norris in the national Whig gains of that year. A second Tory election success occurred in 1710, a year of Tory gains, when John Clieveland defeated Richard Norris to join Thomas Johnson in Parliament. William Clayton succeeded Clieveland in his sixth stint as MP in 1713. Parliamentary elections suggest a politically divided town with significant Tory as well as Whig support. Tory support for

Anglicanism showed itself in 1711 in the contest provoked by the rector, Henry Richmond, considered below. On the other side were a significant number of dissenters in the town by this date, as well as their supporters. Richard Harrison estimates the number of nonconforming freemen in 1718 as 164, 10 per cent of the electorate.[73]

There was, however, no sign that the parties were bitterly divided. There were no election riots in the town. Moreover, Whig and Tory seemed to be able to work together in amity. Thomas Johnson junior and William Clayton, the town MPs who served together from 1701 to 1708, illustrate the point well. Both were from Lancashire families, Johnson from relatively humble origins, the son of a father who became a merchant and mayor of Liverpool, Clayton from a large and more important family near Preston, nephew of a merchant and mayor of Liverpool in 1680. Both were transatlantic merchants dealing in tobacco and sugar, both served as mayor (Clayton in 1689–90, Johnson in 1695–96), and both acted as MP for the town (Clayton from 1698 to 1708 and 1713 to 1715, Johnson from 1701 to 1723).[74] They were, however, politically divided, Johnson a Whig and one of the leaders of the new charter party in 1695, Clayton an opponent of the charter and one of those excluded from the council in 1695. Reconciled by 1698 he was returned unopposed as MP. His staunch lobbying of Liverpool's interests caused Johnson to approve of him, preferring him in 1702 as fellow MP to Richard Norris, a Whig. He described him as 'very sensible... and has a good notion of most business', and effective at Westminster, being 'too apt to speak things with the largest but that I find here is a necessary qualification'.[75] The capacity of both men to work together suggests that the common enterprise was more important than party affiliation.

The innovations of the years 1706–09 may have been due to the determination of a small group of men. Thomas Johnson the younger (Sir Thomas from 1708), first full-term Whig mayor after 1695 and MP from 1701, was one critical player. He was joined at Westminster by a second key player, Richard Norris, in 1708. They were jointly responsible for obtaining the Act for the new dock. Norris had entered the Whig council with Johnson in 1695 and become a close friend. Like Johnson he imported tobacco and sugar. He was from a local gentle family at Speke which was closely involved with commerce in Liverpool. His mother, Katharine, came of a London merchant family. His elder brothers, Thomas and William, served as Liverpool MPs: Thomas helped obtain the charter of 1695; William drafted the Act for the new parish in 1698. A third brother, Edward, married Ann Clieveland, who cannot be traced as related to the Liverpool merchant family. His sister, Ann, married William Squire, another Liverpool merchant. A better example of the intermeshing of gentility and commerce, Whig and Tory in Liverpool would be difficult to find.[76]

A third important figure was Sylvester Morecroft, draper and post-master of Chapel Street. As mayor in 1706–07 he was responsible for the appointment of a new town clerk in 1707. He retained control as deputy-mayor to James, Earl of Derby, in 1707–08 and continued his central role in the following year when the decision to build the dock was made, being named as JP immediately after the mayor, John Seacome. Though not an overseas merchant, Morecroft played a central role in regulating trade, being made a Customs collector by 1707 and the first treasurer of the town in 1716 dealing with the finances of the new dock. He built a new Customs house at the head of the new dock. The combination of his initiative on the council and Johnson and Norris's representation of the town at Westminster may well explain the achievements of these years.[77]

The common enterprise of creating a new and significant port perhaps reduced political tension in Liverpool. Merchants' common interest was too powerful for party allegiance to disrupt. In some respects the situation bears comparison with Exeter, a larger and more socially diverse town. It too benefited from commercial growth in the first decade of the eighteenth century after the Exe navigation was improved in 1701. This common interest, together with the control exercised over politics by Sir Edward Seymour, the formidable recorder of the city, and the stability afforded by long-serving councillors and officers, guaranteed consensus.[78]

The fact of Liverpool's small size and a homogeneous mercantile political elite undoubtedly helped agreement. Unlike the many political and economic fissures in London, a much larger and more complicated commercial centre, merchants in Liverpool maintained a common interest and cohesion. In spite of splits between old and new charter men, most shared the same trade in the same ships. There was no distinct financial interest. Nor did religious differences seem to have been intensely divisive. Johnson, Norris and other leaders would hardly have been able to dominate in the larger arena of the capital as they did in Liverpool.[79]

Hegemony, 1710–50

Long-term dominance in government can lead to discontent and resistance. Just as Walpole's administration was increasingly challenged in the 1730s and early 1740s, local hegemony was subject to challenge. Rogers has argued that opposition to Whig control tended to be based on high church Tory principles in the first two decades of the eighteenth century but changed to a populist resistance to overbearing power by the 1730s. It occurred in London and in several provincial towns: York,

Worcester, Preston and Bristol.[80] The pattern was exemplified by Liverpool. The relative cohesion of the leadership began to fray in the second decade of the eighteenth century with a high church Tory revolt in 1711, and this was followed in the late 1720s and early 1730s by a serious and sustained attack upon the financial and political hegemony of the council.

The Tory revolt of 1711 was provoked by Henry Richmond, joint rector of Liverpool from 1706. The son of Sylvester Richmond, the mayor involved in the election court fracas in 1673, and brother of Richard Richmond, rector of Walton, Henry shared high church anger at the impeachment of Henry Sacheverell in London.[81] He instigated the protest by questioning the validity of the charter of 1695. On 4 April 1711 the council ordered Sir Thomas Johnson, Jasper Mauditt and Alderman Richard Norris to employ solicitors to defend the charter against the challenge of one who had gained his benefice under the same. He was not the only protestor. On 20 May 1711 a resolution admitted that the council was 'greatly divided into parties of High Church and Low', the most direct evidence of the reality of religious divisions in the town. In response to the minister's attempt to have the 1677 charter reinstated, the council instructed Thomas Bootle, a young student of the Temple, to obtain affidavits from ancient freemen that it had been gained 'surreptitiously' and never been accepted by the town.[82]

The affair proved a short-lived but serious political embarrassment. On 29 October 1711 the portmoot grand jury presented Henry Richmond for absence from his ministry with the result that 'vice and debauchery' had increased. He had put himself at the head of a factious party and encouraged tumults. The challenge to the charter was contested in court and, on 5 October 1711, the council ordered Bryan Dawney, the town Customer, to reimburse Johnson, Mauditt and Norris for the cost incurred. Dawney refused and when he was replaced by Nathaniel Smith, on 7 May 1712, Mayor James Townsend attempted to adjourn the council. The minister failed in his challenge to the charter but he obviously commanded significant support. The alarm occasioned by the affair was shown by a council decision to provide a charter chest secured with five locks with keys distributed among five senior aldermen so that no one individual could in future gain access to the charters without general consent.[83] Richmond continued to challenge the council's authority, attempting to collect Easter dues and nominate a new parish clerk to St Peter's church in 1714, contrary to custom. His death in 1721 solved a political and ecclesiastical problem.[84]

There were, however, symptoms of a deeper discontent with the ruling group. In part this resulted from the financial strains of building the dock. On 13 October 1720 the council debated a complaint that a small group had sold the dock to themselves. Mayor Thomas Fillingham, Sir Thomas Johnson, alderman George Tyrer and others (Thomas

Steers was probably involved as bailiff that year) defended themselves, and challenged anyone with a better scheme for paying off the debt to make it known. At about the same time Sylvester Morecroft, the first treasurer of the corporation appointed in 1716 to monitor the financing of the dock, was dismissed for meddling with records and replaced by Peter Hall.[85]

It was the more fundamental issue of how open town politics should be which rocked the stability of government for a decade. For thirty years control had been vested in a small and powerful council, an era dominated by Sir Thomas Johnson and Richard Norris whose deaths in 1728 and 1729 removed a controlling influence.[86] The challenge to the narrow oligarchy was initiated by Sir Thomas Bootle, the lawyer who had acted for the council in the dispute with Henry Richmond in 1711. Bootle, a Lancashire gentleman, London lawyer and opposition Whig, had courted the town for some time. He presented two fire engines to the town in 1718 and was elected MP in April 1724 and mayor in 1726.[87] Once mayor he ceased to call the council and instead summoned an assembly of freemen in common hall. He could cite constitutional justification. The charter of 1695 contained a loosely drafted clause which allowed the mayor and bailiff and any 25 freemen of the borough to 'ordain and perform all things as fully as if all the forty-one councilmen of the aforesaid town were present and assembled in common council'.[88] This was interpreted by the council as fixing a quorum of councillors to transact business. But it could equally be read as empowering the mayor and a bailiff to govern with an alternative group of 25 freemen in common hall.

Bootle's motives for abandoning monthly council meetings are obscure. They might have derived from a wish to stand in a parliamentary election of August 1727, and a concern that the council would not allow him, as mayor, to do this. He took a poll at a common hall on 1 August 1727 to allow him to resign the mayoralty and went on to be elected MP for the town for the second time. In his place as mayor the freemen elected alderman George Tyrer, merchant.[89] Tyrer, mayor in 1710 and colleague of Johnson in managing the dock and its debts, was an experienced and long-serving councillor. He clearly shared Bootle's antipathy to the council for he continued to ignore it. The policy was continued by his successor as mayor, Captain John Hughes, elected on 18 October 1727, another long-serving councillor.[90] To get over the difficulties resulting from the council not meeting he agreed to the setting up of a committee of seven senior aldermen to oversee the financing of the new church of St George, and to prepare corporation leases.[91]

The council could only be summoned by the mayor. Bryan Blundell, merchant, elected mayor on 18 October 1728, finally called a council on 6 November 1728. It censured aldermen Bootle, Tyrer and Hughes.[92] A subsequent meeting on 5 March 1729 elaborated the criticism: Thomas Bootle had declined to hold councils, vacated his office and, 'by his example and advice', Mr George Tyrer and Mr John Hughes had pretended to act as mayors and, 'like enemies to the corporation... perversely refused to assemble or meet in council'. Blundell's mayoralty did not resolve the crisis, however. He, too, was concerned about the council. He failed to attend a council on 2 July 1729. It nevertheless admitted a new freeman, Thomas Vernon. On 3 September 1729 the council ordered that new freemen were to be vetted by an aldermanic committee. This seems to have been an attempt to restore power to the senior aldermen of the council and Mayor Blundell, and aldermen Tyrer, Hughes and Cunliffe, withdrew.[93] Their retreat was temporary. Foster Cunliffe, merchant, elected mayor on 18 October 1729, proceeded to ignore the council again.

The role of the council was one issue in the political struggle. The other was the admission of freemen. The wholesale admission of freeman had long been a sensitive issue because it could afford electoral advantage. It had led to the condemnation of Johnson, Andoe and Lurting in 1676. It became an issue again in the mayoralty of John Scarisbrick in 1723–24 when 167 freemen were admitted. The motives for the mass admission are unclear. Scarisbrick was later bailiff to Mayor Foster Cunliffe in 1735 and it may be this was an early attempt to widen political participation.[94] The council party could also use freemen admissions to ensure votes for a council candidate at mayoral and parliamentary elections. Indeed, in 1729, it was essential if the council was to win back its position.

On 5 November 1729 the council resolved that the senior alderman and a bailiff could admit new freemen, even against the wish of the mayor. Alderman Richard Gildart, son-in-law of Sir Thomas Johnson, promptly nominated 105 freemen. Mayor Cunliffe, aldermen Tyrer, Poole and Hughes, and bailiff Robert Whitfield thereon 'withdrew abruptly, arbitrarily and illegally'.[95] The anti-council group fought back on 6 February 1730 by getting the council to declare that such admissions, without the mayor, were void, and retained their hold on power later that year when George Tyrer was elected mayor again. Gildart and his council colleagues refused to be defeated. On 6 February 1731 the council agreed that the door be locked while a list of new freemen was read. Mayor Tyrer quit his bench but was not allowed to leave the room and this time the freemen were validly admitted. With the electoral advantage of new freemen, Gildart was voted mayor on 18 October 1731, and immediately began to purge the council of populists. Aldermen Josia Poole, bailiff of Mayor Hughes in 1727, alderman William Squire, absent since 1719, alderman Thomas Bootle, absent in London, and Mr Charles Pole, also in London, were discharged on 13 December because they were no longer living in the town.[96]

The 'populist party' might be a misleading title to attach to Bootle and his followers. They certainly depended on freemen support at the mayoral polls between 1726 and 1730. But the number of ringleaders was quite small: to Bootle, Hughes, Blundell, Cunliffe and Tyrer, the anti-council mayors, can be added Robert Whitfield, bailiff under Bootle, and Cunliffe. Even with the other bailiffs who served during the five years of conflict they form a group of only about a dozen. They formed an opposition cabal anxious to break the long control of the town exercised by a closed Whig council. In economic background, however, they look very like their Whig establishment enemies. Bootle, it is true, was a lawyer, but Tyrer was a merchant, and Hughes, Blundell and Cunliffe were also merchants trading alongside Johnson, Mauditt and Gildart.

The 'populist party' enjoyed a last flourish in the years 1733 to 1735. There was a tumult on 18 October 1733 when William Pole was elected mayor. Thomas Brereton, the outgoing Whig mayor, supporting Pole, had some difficulty in keeping order and brought the poll to a premature end. Legal challenges to the election of Pole by the anti-council group were mounted during his year of office but without success.[97] When, however James, Earl of Derby, an independent Whig peer, accepted the mayoral nomination in 1734 a year later, with George Tyrer and John Hughes as bailiffs, the anti-council group was once more in power. Derby died in his year of office, on 1 February 1735, and the deputy mayor, Bryan Blundell reverted to the practice of calling a common hall. On 4 February 1735 Blundell, Tyrer and Hughes proposed that Robert Whitfield, bailiff of Thomas Bootle in 1726 and Foster Cunliffe in 1729, discharged from the council on 6 February 1734 for non-attendance, be restored. Alderman Richard Kelsall organised a written protest among the councillors and the trio abandoned their attempt.[98]

The council was still not meeting and, when Cunliffe was elected mayor and Bryan Blundell bailiff on 18 October 1735, it looked as if the anti-council group had won. During the year, however, Cunliffe and Blundell seemed to lose confidence. On 23 September 1736 a council met to review the 'pretended' common hall called by Hughes and Tyrer on 4 February 1735 and the attempted reinstatement of Whitfield. Hughes and Tyrer were discharged from the council because they had acted 'in breach of trust reposed in them as council men'. Though given an opportunity to plead their case at a council, on 3 November 1736, they claimed only that they were illegally dismissed. John Hughes later repented in October 1740 and was restored to the council.[99]

It is significant that Richard Gildart was elected as mayor in succession to Cunliffe in October 1736 to impose council control, just as he had in 1731. The survival of the council in these decades was due to the presence of stubborn senior Whig aldermen, such as Gildart and Kelsall, who resisted Bootle and his followers. Thomas Brereton of

Chester, a client of Sir Richard Grosvenor and staunch Walpole Whig, was a third. He became a councillor in Liverpool in 1724, was mayor in succession to Gildart in 1732–33, and kept order during the tumultuous election of William Pole in 1733.[100]

The struggle against the council was reflected in representation at Westminster. In the elections of 1715 and 1722, Sir Thomas Johnson protected the Liverpool Whig interest in Parliament. Thomas Bootle, an opposition Whig elected as MP for Liverpool in April 1724, was balanced in November that year by Thomas Brereton, a court Whig, and they served together until May 1729. When Brereton was defeated as MP by the populist candidate, Sir Thomas Aston, in May 1729 two opposition Whigs, Bootle and Aston, represented Liverpool in Parliament at the same time that anti-council mayors, Bryan Blundell, Foster Cunliffe and George Tyrer ran the town. For a period the opposition party seemed all powerful. Just as Richard Gildart won back the mayoralty for the council party in 1731, parliamentary representation was won back by court Whigs in the election of May 1734, when Thomas Brereton and Richard Gildart defeated Thomas Bootle and Foster Cunliffe.[101] For the rest of the period court Whigs retained power at Westminster. The challenge to Whig power in the town was over, apart from a fierce but brief complaint by alderman Joseph Glegg in 1750 when the council applied for a new charter to reinforce its position and prevent a repetition of the years from 1726 to 1736.[102]

The failure of the populist challenge was due to a combination of factors: the small number of populist rebels compared with the large Whig majority on the council; the determination of Whig councillors such as Richard Gildart to recover power; and the great difficulty that a mayor and bailiffs had in running a fast-growing town without the advice and authority of a council. The council traditionally made decisions about policy and expenditure, issued leases, and admitted freemen. A mayor could prevent a council from meeting but could not make policy or control expenditure without its backing.

Conclusion

Though much remains unclear about the political development of Liverpool during the period, because the town record is too often cryptic or patchy, the broad picture is clear enough. In 1660 the town was under-developed in many ways. Though it was chartered and possessed a proper urban system of government it had no merchant or craft guilds, no independent parish and was subject to landlord interference. Its leaders were taken up with local affairs and kept a low profile in the national political crises of 1679–81 and 1688–89. The determination with which it stood up to Lord Molyneux in the dispute over ownership of the Common was an early sign of an emerging corporate self-confidence, and the vesting of control in a closed council dominated by town merchants in 1695 was a formal endorsement of a new autonomy of the town. The merchants who developed transatlantic trade and town property in the late seventeenth century turned their attention to improving the town with dramatic effect once they had power. The creation of a parish, the plans to develop the medieval castle site, and, above all the decision to build the first dock, were achievements accomplished within fifteen years of 1695. Moreover, they occurred in a period when political conflict often disrupted towns.

There are particular reasons to explain why Liverpool improvements were not interrupted by political instability. Intolerance of Anglicans and dissenters does not seem to have been as intense in Liverpool as in many other towns. The lack of a strong Anglican clerical presence in the town may have muted the animus against dissenters. Their exclusion from the council in 1662 and low political profile thereafter no doubt helped toleration. Also important was the common interest of men of different religious persuasions in working together in overseas trade. Liverpool trade with Ireland, Virginia and the West Indies was open to all. Merchants were not separated into companies with particular limits and privileges but shared the same ships, travelled to the same destinations and dealt in the same commodities. Political or religious conflict between men who traded daily together on the quayside would have been difficult and economically counter-productive, though clearly the consensus broke down in the 1720s and 1730s. Freedom to trade within the town resulted, perhaps, in a certain toleration of religious difference. Craftsmen and mariners agreed on the necessity of fostering trade, for they, too, depended on the ready transport of raw materials into the town and export of their products. It would be surprising if Whig or Tory principles, Anglican or dissenting passions, had been strong enough to overcome the common economic interest which bound them together.

The close oligarchy imposed in 1695 created cohesion. The 41 councillors comprised merchants who had worked together but been excluded from town government. Suddenly they were given control and could provide solutions to their common commercial needs. The novel experience of government and the obvious needs of a growing port fostered co-operation. The resulting political elite of the town was small, economically selective, and politically self-perpetuating. Three decades of such control stimulated a populist reaction against closed government in the mid-1720s. When it did, the council proved able to resist the challenge. Their policy of building docks for a growing port met too many needs to be challenged for long. The political consensus constructed during the fifteen years after 1695 was durable enough to last until municipal reform in 1835.

Notes

1. Using the evidence of Liverpool Town Books: LplRO 352 MIN/COU 3–10.

2. For clarification of multiple references to these and other individuals and families in Chapters 3–6, see the index.

3. Perry Gauci, *The Politics of Trade: The Overseas Merchant in State and Society, 1660– 1720*, Oxford, 2001, pp. 55–57, 101–05, 150–53.

4. G. Holmes, *British Politics in the Reign of Anne*, London, 1967; H. Horwitz, *Parliament Policy and Politics in the Reign of William III*, Manchester, 1977; T. Harris, P. Seaward and M. Goldie, eds, *The Politics of Religion in Restoration England*, Oxford, 1990; T. Harris, *Politics under the Later Stuarts: Party Conflict in a Divided Society 1660–1715*, London, 1993, especially pp. 9–13, 62–75.

5. E. Cruickshanks, 'Religion and royal succession: the rage of party', in *Britain in the First Age of Party 1680–1750*, ed. C. Jones, London, 1987, pp. 22–24; Harris, *Politics under the Later Stuarts*, pp.119–28, 152–56, 180–81.

6. G.de Krey, *A Fractured Society: The Politics of London in the First Age of Party 1688–1715*, Oxford, 1985; J. Barry, 'The politics of religion in Restoration Bristol', in Harris et al., eds, *Politics of Religion*, pp. 163–189; P. Gauci, *Politics and Society in Great Yarmouth 1660–1722*, Oxford, 1996.

7. J. Miller, 'The crown and the borough charters in the reign of Charles II', *EHR*, 100, 1985, pp. 55–56.

8. Harris, *Politics under the Later Stuarts*, pp. 104–08, 120–28, 176–77, 187–96; N. Rogers, 'The urban opposition to Whig oligarchy 1720–60', in *The Origins of Anglo-American Radicalism*, ed. M. and J. Jacob, London, 1984, pp. 133–39.

9. Barry, 'Politics of religion in Restoration Bristol', pp. 172–78; G. de Krey, 'London radicals and revolutionary politics 1675–83', in Harris et al., eds, *Politics of Religion*, pp. 141–47.

10. Harris, *Politics under the Later Stuarts*, pp. 187–91; J. V. Beckett, 'Introduction: stability in politics and society 1680–1750' in Jones, ed., *Britain in the First Age of Party*, p. 5.

11. Rogers, 'Urban opposition to Whig oligarchy', pp. 137–39; H. Dickinson, *The Politics of the People in Eighteenth-century Britain*, New York, 1995, p. 108.

12. G. Forster, 'Hull in the sixteenth and seventeenth centuries', in *Victoria County History York: East Riding: vol. I*, ed. K. J. Allison, London, 1969, p. 145; D. H. Sacks, *The Widening Gate: Bristol and the Atlantic Economy 1450–1700*, Berkeley, 1991, pp. 119–26, 197–218; M. Mullett, 'The politics of Liverpool 1660–1688', *THSLC*, 124, 1972, pp. 31–56.

13. J. Ramsay Muir, *History of Liverpool*, Liverpool, 1907, pp. 62, 71, 109, 128, 144–46; James Touzeau, *The Rise and Progress of Liverpool from 1551 to 1835*, Liverpool, 1910, p. 261; LplRO 352 MIN/COU 1/3, pp. 724–22, 739.

14. LplRO 352 MIN/COU 1/3, pp. 887, 888, 927, 938; Muir, *History of Liverpool*, pp.144–45.

15. Mayoral years began on 18 October.

16. Touzeau, *Rise and Progress*, pp. 270–71; Mullett, 'Politics of Liverpool', p. 45; LplRO 352 MIN/COU 1/3, p. 905.

17. See B. D. Henning, ed., *History of Parliament. The House of Commons 1660–90*, vol. I, London, 1983, pp. 288–90.

18. Muir, *History of Liverpool*, pp. 124, 128, 141–44; Mullett, 'Politics of Liverpool', pp. 32–44.

19. T. Heywood, ed., *The Moore Rental*, CS, 10, Manchester, 1847; Muir, *History of Liverpool*, p. 143; C. W. Chalklin, 'Estate development in Bristol, Birmingham and Liverpool 1660–1720', in *Town and Countryside*, eds C. W. Chalklin and J. R. Wordie, London, 1989, pp. 111–13; R. D. Watts, 'The Moore family of Bank Hall, Liverpool, 1606–1730', unpublished PhD thesis, University of Wales Bangor, 2004.

20. J. R. Jones, *Country and Court: England 1658–1714*, London, 1978, p. 37; LplRO MIN/COU 1/3, pp. 139–41; J. Ramsay Muir and E. M. Platt, *History of Municipal Government in Liverpool to 1835*, Liverpool, 1906, p. 101.

21. Muir, *History of Liverpool*, chapter 10; Mullett, 'Politics of Liverpool'.

22. Muir and Platt, *Municipal Government in Liverpool*, p. 102.

23. Touzeau, *Rise and Progress*, p. 287; transcripts from Town Books by T. N. Morton: LplRO 352 CLE/TRA 2/6 pp. 19–21; Muir and Platt, *Municipal Government in Liverpool*, p. 103.

24. Muir and Platt, *Municipal Government in Liverpool*, p. 103.

25. The occupations of only eight of the 30 participants were traced by nominal linkage with parish register burials and Liverpool testators.

26. TOWNBOOK.

27. LplRO 352 CLE/TRA 2/6, ff. 20, 21.

28. LplRO 352 CLE/TRA 2/6, ff. 32–35.

29. TOWNBOOK.

30. Muir and Platt, *Municipal Government in Liverpool*, p. 104.

31. LplRO 352 CLE/TRA 2/6 ff. 37–38.

32. Muir and Platt, *Municipal Government in Liverpool*, pp. 105, 191–203; Miller, 'Crown and borough charters', pp. 57–79; Harris, *Politics under the Later Stuarts*, p. 61.

33. Henning, *History of Parliament*, I, pp. 288–90.

34. Dissenters were not re-admitted to the council after 1662. Compare Bristol: Sacks, *Widening Gate*, pp. 320–28; and London where in 1688 dissenters made up 15 per cent of the common council: De Krey, *Fractured Society*, pp. 20–21.

35. Mullett, 'Politics of Liverpool', p. 49, 51; Touzeau, *Rise and Progress*, p. 304.

36. Touzeau, *Rise and Progress*, p. 310; Mullett, 'Politics of Liverpool', pp. 47–48; Muir and Platt, *Municipal Government in Liverpool*, pp. 107, 204–05, 108, 230.

37. Touzeau, *Rise and Progress*, p. 319; Muir and Platt, *Municipal Government in Liverpool*, p. 108.

38. Information from History of Parliament Trust unpublished paper, 'Liverpool elections 1690–1715'. Grateful acknowledgement is made to Richard Harrison and the copyright of the History of Parliament; Mauditt's mayoralty from TOWNBOOK; Muir and Platt, *Municipal Government in Liverpool*, p. 109.

39. LplRO 352 CLE/TRA 2/6 f. 158; History of Parliament unpublished biography of Thomas Brotherton; Muir and Platt, *Municipal Government in Liverpool*, p. 109.

40. History of Parliament unpublished paper, 'Liverpool elections 1690–1715'; Muir and Platt, *Municipal Government in Liverpool*, p. 110.

41. T. Heywood, ed., *The Norris Papers*, CS, 9, Manchester, 1846, pp. 25–29.

42. LplRO 352 CLE/TRA 2/6 f. 159; Touzeau, *Rise and Progress*, p. 339; Muir and Platt, *Municipal Government in Liverpool*, p. 249.

43. LplRO 352 CLE/TRA 2/6, pp. 156–57, 160; TOWNBOOK.

44. TOWNBOOK, with occupations derived from linkage with parish registers and wills.

45. Notably John Clieveland who accounted for 57 overseas shipments in the port book of 1708–09, not far short of Sir Thomas Johnson's 74: PRO: E190/1375/08.

46. H. Horwitz, 'Party in a civic context: London from the exclusion crisis to the fall of Walpole', in *Britain in the First Age of Party, 1680–1750*, ed. C. Jones, London, 1987, p. 173; de Krey, *Fractured Society*, pp. 20–21; Heywood, *Norris Papers*, pp. 79–82.

47. Henning, *History of Parliament*, I, pp. 288–90; information on MPs after 1695 is from History of Parliament unpublished paper, 'Liverpool Elections 1690–1715'.

48. LplRO 352 MIN/COU 1/3 p. 627.

49. Some are printed in Heywood, *Norris Papers*; more are in LplRO 920 NOR 1 & 2.

50. LplRO 352 MIN/COU 1/3 pp. 908, 919.

51. Touzeau, *Rise and Progress*, p. 322.

52. Touzeau, *Rise and Progress*, p. 342; S. Handley, 'Local legislative initiatives for economic and social development in Lancashire, 1689–1731', *Parliamentary History*, 9, 1990, pp. 19–20.

53. Heywood, *Norris Papers*, pp. 128–30.

54. Heywood, *Norris Papers*, pp. 69, 71, 78, 194, 116, 119, 121, 126; Muir and Platt, *Municipal Government in Liverpool*, pp. 118–19.

55. Muir, *History of Liverpool*, p. 175; Heywood, *Norris Papers*, p. 159; M. Power, 'East and west in early-modern London', in *Wealth and Power in Tudor England: Essays Presented to S. T. Bindoff*, ed. E. Ives, R. J. Knecht and J. J. Scarisbrick, London, 1978, p. 180.

56. Muir, *History of Liverpool*, p. 175; Touzeau, *Rise and Progress*, pp. 355–56, 418.

57. Heywood, *Norris Papers*, p.165.

58. Touzeau, *Rise and Progress*, pp. 379–80, 385; J. Longmore, 'Liverpool Corporation as landowners and dock builders 1709–1835', in Chalklin and Wordie, eds, *Town and Countryside*, pp. 116–22.

59. Muir and Platt, *Municipal Government in Liverpool*, p. 118.

60. Touzeau, *Rise and Progress*, pp. 331–33; Handley, 'Local legislative initiatives', pp. 34–36.

61. Touzeau, *Rise and Progress*, pp. 444–45; Longmore, 'Liverpool corporation', pp. 120–22, 139–42; H. J. Dyos and D. H. Aldcroft, *British Transport: An Economic Survey from the Seventeenth Century to the Twentieth*, Leicester, 1969, p. 59; Touzeau, *Rise and Progress*, pp. 444–45.

62. Touzeau, *Rise and Progress*, pp. 374–75, 446, 453, 384, 386.

63. Harris, *Politics under the Later Stuarts*, pp. 152–58, 176–96.

64. Horwitz, 'Party in a civic contest', pp. 181–87; De Krey, *Fractured Society*, pp. 14–32.

65. Harris, *Politics under the Later Stuarts*, pp. 190–91, 195; Jackson, *Hull in the Eighteenth Century*, pp. 300–01.

66. Heywood, *Norris Papers*, pp. 79–82, 110–01, 114–15, 119–20, 161–64, for additional letters on the tobacco duty struggle.

67. Details on Clieveland from unpublished History of Parliament biography; derived from TOWNBOOK; for Briggs and an account of the election see Heywood, *Norris Papers*, p. 95.

68. For Bickesteth, see Heywood, *Norris Papers*, pp. 83–84; details on Mauditt from TOWNBOOK and unpublished History of Parliament biography; details of Sharples, Windall, Hurst and new charter and old charter signatories from TOWNBOOK; for the election, see Heywood, *Norris Papers*, pp. 99–100.

69. Heywood, *Norris Papers*, pp. 131, 133; Touzeau, *Rise and Progress*, p. 370.

70. Heywood, *Norris Papers*, pp. 143–45.

71. Information from unpublished History of Parliament biography.

72. Harris, *Politics under the Later Stuarts*, pp. 189–91.

73. History of Parliament unpublished paper, 'Liverpool Elections 1690–1715'.

74. TOWNBOOK.

75. History of Parliament biography and paper, 'Liverpool elections 1690–1715'; Heywood, *Norris Papers*, pp. 89–91.

76. Heywood, *Norris Papers*, vii–xxi; History of Parliament unpublished biographies of Thomas, William and Richard Norris; for Clieveland family see Figure 4.1; for links between land and commerce in London see H. Horwitz, 'The mess of the middle class revisited: the case of the big bourgeoisie of Augustan London', *Continuity and Change*, 2, 1987, pp. 263–96.

77. TOWNBOOK; Touzeau, *Rise and Progress*, pp. 375, 377, 402, 419; Heywood, *Norris Papers*, p. 166.

78. R. Newton, *Eighteenth-century Exeter*, Exeter, 1984, pp. 21–22, 34–37, 46–48, 52–55.

79. De Krey, *Fractured Society*, pp. 20–21, 23–32, 40–44; Horwitz, 'Mess of the middle class revisited', pp. 268–69, and 'Party in a civic context', pp. 173–88; N. Rogers, 'Money, land and lineage: the big bourgeoisie of Hanoverian London', in *The Eighteenth-century Town*, ed. P. Borsay, Harlow, 1990, pp. 270–75.

80. Rogers, 'Urban opposition to Whig oligarchy', pp. 135–39.

81. H. Fishwick, *History of Garstang*, CS, 105, Manchester, 1879, p. 186; W. A. Speck, *Stability and Strife: England 1714–1760*, London, 1977, p. 93.

82. LplRO 352 CLE/TRA 2/8 ff. 138–44.

83. LplRO 352 CLE/TRA 2/6 ff. 145, 157, 152; Touzeau, *Rise and Progress*, p. 395.

84. LplRO 352 CLE/TRA 2/8, pp. 167, 170, 211.

85. Touzeau, *Rise and Progress*, pp. 382, 403.

86. TOWNBOOK.

87. Thomas Bootle was son of Robert Bootle of Maghull, a chancery lawyer and opposition Whig attached to Pultney, the Earl of Derby and the Duke of Somerset: R. Sedgwick, ed., *History of Parliament I: The House of Commons 1715–54*, London, 1970, pp. 473–74. For fire engines, see Touzeau, *Rise and Progress*, p. 405.

88. Muir and Platt, *Municipal Government in Liverpool*, pp. 111–12.

89. LplRO 352 CLE/TRA 2/8, ff. 240–45.

90. TOWNBOOK; Touzeau, *Rise and Progress*, pp. 382, 421.

91. LplRO 352 CLE/TRA 2/8, ff. 28.

92. TOWNBOOK; Touzeau, *Rise and Progress*, pp. 381, 406–07.

93. LplRO 352 CLE/TRA 2/8, ff. 37–44. Touzeau, *Rise and Progress*, p. 425.

94. Touzeau, *Rise and Progress*, p. 415.

95. Touzeau, *Rise and Progress*, pp. 425–26; LplRO 352 CLE/TRA 2/8, ff. 45–46.

96. LplRO 352 CLE/TRA 2/8, ff. 47–54.

97. Touzeau, *Rise and Progress*, pp. 433–44; Bootle took action against the corruption of 600 new freemen, Customs and Excise men and salt officers, in the parliamentary election of May 1734, when he was defeated: Sedgwick, *House of Commons*, pp. 270–72.

98. Touzeau, *Rise and Progress*, p. 435. James, 10th Earl of Derby, was an opposition Whig, and, with Richard, 5th Viscount Molyneux, George Booth, 2nd Earl of Warrington, and Lord Barrymore, supported Thomas Bootle: Sedgwick, *House of Commons*, pp. 270–71.

99. Touzeau, *Rise and Progress*, pp. 439, 441–42.

100. Sedgwick, *House of Commons*, pp. 484–85.

101. Sedgwick, *House of Commons*, pp. 270–72.

102. Muir, *History of Liverpool*, p. 170.

Conclusion

The aim of this book has been to seek a clearer understanding of Liverpool's growth from relative obscurity into the major provincial port of eighteenth-century England. To this end new approaches have been used to examine aspects of the society of early modern Liverpool and thus to augment previous historical investigations of the development of one of the most remarkable towns in modern Britain. Those earlier works were limited, focusing principally on the constitutional development of the town and the growth of its trade. This book provides new insights into the character of Liverpool which help an understanding of the challenges and achievements of Liverpudlians in the first century of the town's rapid growth.

The instability of life in a growing port town is the prevailing impression from the demographic study. That mariners faced dangers on a voyage of shipwreck, disease and accident is obvious enough. For mariners' families there were knock-on effects, all too evident in the high infant and young child mortality figures revealed by family reconstitution. The strains of single parenting for months at a time, the lack of a regular income and the dangers of infection brought to the port by large numbers of visitors and goods were all possible contributing factors.

In addition to the individual tragedies of poverty, neglect and death which mariners' families routinely experienced, there was the instability of a rapidly growing population new to the town. Social cohesion, fostered by familiarity and the passing on of family knowledge and assets over generations, had to be established by other means. Liverpool was, of course, a small town in which it would have been easy to get to know others, but constant inmigration of newcomers made this an unending task. The statistic that 96 per cent of partners married in the town after 1717 are not traceable in the baptism registers is very striking. The town was dominated by newcomers intent on making their fortunes, at the level of the entrepreneurial trader as well as lower down the social scale. Nor was there a set of traditional institutions, such as fraternities or guilds, which newcomers could join to ease their entry into the mysteries of trade and manufacture. The immigrant was unduly dependent on the qualities of wit or personality, or for a young person, the individual social contacts which a parent might have been able to establish. The placing of a young man as apprentice to an established and successful merchant, mariner or craftsman was perhaps crucial if he was to succeed and make his fortune.

What compounded the mobile character of the population was the tendency of many who had migrated into the town to retain strong links with their roots in southwest Lancashire or further afield. The discovery from family reconstitution that a large majority of those married in Liverpool were not buried in the town is a striking testimony to the transient character of the population, albeit only ninety years are in focus and seafaring losses and poor law resettlement must be acknowledged. Nonetheless, the port was, for many, a place of work and career rather than a permanent home. They appear to be residents 'in' rather than 'of' Liverpool.

The significance of mariners in the labour force is hardly surprising in a town that was developing into a major port. But the dominant size of the sector is striking. Any occupation which accounts for between 20 and 30 per cent of a workforce is remarkable and says much about the degree of specialisation in the town. This character is compounded when port-related occupations of shipbuilding and fitting, and dock administration and Customs are also included. The claim that between a third and a half of the town economy relied directly on the manning and monitoring of trading vessels suggests that the town was unusually specialised. A majority of the working population was involved: merchants and dealers, dock workers and suppliers of services to mariners and ships. Something approaching two-thirds of the working population might be a conservative estimate.

Such economic specialisation might have encouraged whole families to enter the same craft or trade. Though most families were new and would not have a traditional occupation to follow there are numerous Liverpool examples of occupational traditions developing in families over time, whether in merchanting, the novel sugar baking, or among crafts and businesses, such as the butchery, shipwrighting and building instanced above. Whether this was any more pronounced in Liverpool than in any other town is impossible to say, though it might be supposed that the passing on of business experience or the sharing of capital and custom within families was important in a town which lacked formal guilds, the other normal conduit of economic co-operation. To demonstrate a tendency towards occupational tradition within families requires further analysis in empirical terms. However, from such study it may be possible to claim this as mechanism whereby people in Liverpool exerted control over an uncertain working environment.

Some of the strategies used by townspeople for coping with and even benefiting from the unstable character of life in the fast-growing town have been demonstrated. Marriage played as important a role in building up fortunes in this commercial environment as in others, and as it is always assumed to have done among landowning families. The passing on of assets to spouses, children and other family members had a particular importance in a town where life was uncertain, and profits unpredictable. Seagoing men, because they faced the uncertainty of a voyage, were among those most inclined to make wills to provide for their families or acknowledge their creditors. The preponderance of seafarers in the will-making cohort biases statistical analysis and explains some differences between Liverpool and other towns in patterns of bequest. Such patterns were found to conform by and large to gender differences, with women's tendency to bequeath more widely to lateral kin contrasting with men's lineal ties and the descent of property. Degrees of sophistication in financial dealings and property distribution varied according to social strata rather than over time. Certainly the strategies adopted by the upper echelons in Liverpool within the first decades of its expansion belie any impression of the place as a frontier town.

The innovative application of multi-source record linkage provided a context for testamentary evidence. This not only compensated for the acknowledged limitation of will-based data but also facilitated a clearer understanding of the unique personal situations behind the broad patterns of bequest. Such contextualisation clearly revealed that the economic role of women in the town was important and was not confined to being marriage partners to consolidate wealth and influence. Women were active in several other ways. In a male-dominated port environment, women clearly played prominent roles in providing board, food and drink, and serving in shops and markets. As important was the pivotal role they played in the ownership and transmission of family assets. Women were notable owners of property and capital. Even a cursory reading of the rate of 1708 reveals their importance as controllers of real estate in a town where 13 per cent of properties belonged to women. It is no longer possible to ignore women's formal contribution to the economy of the town to set beside their informal and largely undiscoverable domestic role.

In the light of the uncertainty of life in Liverpool a study of the role of government in the town assumes great importance. The existence of a long-standing tradition of officers in the town and 'ancient laws and laudable customs' provided a set of everyday rules which long-term residents and in-migrants were expected to live by and these must have helped to maintain order and stability. At the same time, the growth of late seventeenth-century overseas trade provided unprecedented opportunities for a new group of entrepreneurs to wrest political control from the great landlords whose traditional role had been temporarily strengthened by the Restoration. The seizure of power in 1695 proved a turning point for the town. The new merchant establishment committed the town to a tradition of dock building which went a long way to guaranteeing the success of their trading ventures. At the same time the dock development provided spin-off employment for seamen, craftsmen and unskilled labourers, and at once the new merchant-councillors became the employers and the political masters of the town. The combination proved to be potent and, supported by a constitution which gave them control of entry to the council, the new political elite controlled the town for almost a century and a half.

It is difficult to imagine so radical a coup in any developed port in the late seventeenth century, where an earlier generation of merchants already controlled local politics and overseas trade. The Liverpool merchants of 1695 were new men, in trade and politics. They shared the same commercial interests, and, in the absence of a previous entrenched generation, could work together without challenge. It explains, perhaps, the ability of councillors to co-operate without serious political or religious tensions in the decades around 1700 and push through developments such as the parish and the first dock. Their success in government and in trade made them appear the natural leaders of the fast-developing society of the town. The formidable assets that they came to control in these years, commodity trades, real estate and experience in government, gave them a stance as natural leaders which made their position difficult to challenge. The failure in 1736 of a major revolt against them confirmed their political command of the town and their commercial direction of trade.

Liverpool was a town in transition. After relatively quiet centuries, demographic, economic, social and political change was under way and the port which emerged was one of the most remarkable developments on the map of eighteenth-century Britain. Some of the characteristics of the society associated with the changes were a response to economic opportunity. Inmigrants, for example, were lured to the town by the employment opportunities created. However, the new townsmen created their own economic opportunity. The energy and initiative of those who made the town, the mariners and merchants who provided labour and capital, the men and women who passed on assets to the next generation, and the councillors who gambled on an experiment in dock building were all instrumental in generating activity and wealth. The result was a dynamic town of opportunity and challenge.

The instigators of initiatives and activity are recorded in the main sources of this study. But what of those who fall beyond the recorded materials of Liverpool's eighteenth-century past or have not been the focus of this text? The orphaned, the elderly, the crippled and the poor merit further study, as do the mechanisms and institutions which cared for them.

Nineteenth-century Liverpool has offered the historian great opportunity to study public health issues. Indeed the town was notorious. But were the conditions in eighteenth-century Liverpool so different? Claims have been made that the town in the earlier period was healthy and invigorating, but did this optimistic gloss merely hide the beginnings of later trends? Material accumulated in the course of this study may provide important evidence for those who wish to explore these themes.

A further problem of the eighteenth-century town was its perceived lack of culture. The concentration on trade and money may have provided the means for art and education, but the extent to which these were taken up by the townsfolk of eighteenth-century Liverpool is difficult to gauge. Certainly the following generations, drawing upon both new and inherited wealth, built a city abundant with the symbols of culture. For the earlier generation a number of the database files gathered for this book could be put to good use in the study of literacy, education and philanthropy.

The priority for historians of eighteenth-century Liverpool, however, remains a more detailed analysis of the overseas and coastal trade of the town. There is a need for port books and other trade data to be systematically analysed further. When this is done, a much more detailed picture will emerge of the commodities and traders during the first century of significant commercial growth. When collated with further enquiry into the events and personalities mentioned in the Town Books a thoroughly informed view of the early history of Liverpool will be possible. The investigations in this book are a first contribution to a much-needed rewriting of the history of the town, and are intended to foster renewed interest in the study of a remarkable place.

Appendix 1
Sources and methods

Study of early eighteenth-century Liverpool is facilitated by a diverse array of information. The nature of this data is summarised in Figure 1. Essentially, sources fall within one of three categories: longitudinal sources which extend over considerable time periods, for example, the parish registers, cross-sectional sources which document information at one fixed point in time such as tax assessments, and textual sources which offer descriptive or personal information.

The foundation materials for this study are the Liverpool Parish Registers, a corpus of surviving wills and associated documents, and the Liverpool Town Books. The other sources are various fiscal, civil, ecclesiastical and personal sources. Most important among these are four Hearth Tax listings, and assessments in 1705, 1708 and 1743. Aspects of the economic activity of the mercantile sector are found in the Port Books, and shipowning in the Plantation Registers. In addition, Apprentice Books, Freemen's Rolls and details of Parliamentary elections have been consulted. Other records include Civil War reparations claims, expressions of loyalty such as the Present Monies of 1661 and the Association Oath Rolls of 1696, and subscription lists from the latter years of the period in 1745 and 1748. Liverpool Vestry minutes are utilised, as are Anglican registers of other parishes principally within Lancashire and Cheshire, and marriage licences and bonds for the diocese of Chester. Non-Anglican registration is limited to fragmentary Quaker, Presbyterian, and Roman Catholic records and registers of papists' estates. Published personal papers have been used as well as Alumni listings of the Universities of Oxford and Cambridge and the Dictionary of National Biography.

Sources are dispersed in various repositories, and are available as original manuscript, microfilm copy or in published form. The probate records and other county material are in Lancashire County Record Office. More immediately local sources, such as the Parish Registers of Liverpool churches and Liverpool Town Books, are held at the Liverpool Record Office. National records were consulted at the British Library, and the Public Record Office (now National Archive). Material was also utilised in the Cheshire County Record Office, Warrington Reference Library, the Archive Department of Manchester Central Library, St Helens Local History and Archives Library, Merseyside Maritime Museum, and the University of Liverpool special collections.

Testamentary Records

The probate material for Liverpudlian testators requires description in terms of the ecclesiastical court origins; the selection criteria; the survival of wills and ancillary items; the accession procedure and its consequences; and any characteristics of the corpus which may be significant.

The rubric on probate jurisdiction of the ecclesiastical Prerogative Courts was apparently honoured as much, if not more, in the breach than the observance.[1] Thus the Chester Diocesan courts are found to have granted probate on estates in more than one diocese, and on wills of those dying both at sea and 'beyond the seas'. In fact between 1660 and 1760 probate was granted from Chester on the wills of Liverpudlians with property in every part of the British Isles and in both the West Indies and North America. The testators also died on both land and sea in remote locations.

There was consequently a wider and more inclusive representation of testators in the records of local courts than could have been anticipated. Therefore concentration upon surviving probate material from archdeaconry and diocesan courts was justified.[2] The Chester diocesan probate records have been divided into county holdings which place Liverpool in Lancashire. The method of indexing, and thus accession, at Lancashire County Record Office suggested the constituents of 'Liverpool Wills 1660–1760'.[3] Such items are the wills of all testators self-designated as 'of Liverpool' and whose year of probate was between 1660 and 1760. Thus among testators 'of Liverpool' may be included mariners of foreign origin and unspecified association with Liverpool, and local people all of whose real estate was in adjoining townships and who appear to be the individuals described in parish burial registers as 'of' that same place. Excluded are an indeterminate number of business and professional men who participated in the social and economic life of Liverpool but invested their money and moved their abode to estates elsewhere, thus being lost to the ranks of Liverpool testators. As general social zoning by movement to suburbs was not established during this period there should be minimal loss due to that factor. From 1699 the new parish and the borough of Liverpool were coterminous. Prior to that date testators using a parochial definition would describe themselves as 'of the parish of Walton-on-the-hill'. However, it would seem

Appendix 1: *Sources*

Static Sources:

	1660	1670	1680	1690	1700	1710	1720	1730	1740	1750
Hearth Taxes	x1663									
	x1664									
	x1666									
	x1673									
Local landlord Rental										
Moore Rental	x1667/8									
Rate/Tax Assessments					x1705				x1743	
					x1708					

Longitudinal Sources:

	1660	1670	1680	1690	1700	1710	1720	1730	1740	1750
Liverpool Parish Registers Bapt., Bur., Mge.	<----------------------------------- - - - - - - - - -- - - - - --------->									
Walton Parish Registers (former mother church to Lpl) Mge.	<-->									
Liverpool Roman Catholic Bapt.									<-------->	
Liverpool Independent Bpt.				<- - - - - - - - - - ---------------------->						
Liverpool Wills	<- ---------------------------->									
Liverpool Town Books	<-->									
Lancashire Marriage registers, licences /bonds (Liverpool spouses only)	<- - - - - - - - - - - - - - - - - ---------------------------------->									
Port Books (sample years)	<--->x<--------------------------->x<-------------------------------->									
Plantation Registers								<------------>		
Liverpool Apprenticeship Records				<- - - - - - - - -- ---------------------->						

Textual sources:
Angier Non-conformist diaries 1661–1685
Diary of Nicholas Blundell 1702–1728
Diary of Henry Prescott 1704–171 1

that most testators living in the burgeoning port between 1660 and 1699 considered themselves Liverpudlian.

Adopting a periodisation based on the date of the first grant of probate results in the inclusion of testators making wills, and possibly dying, before 1660, and the exclusion of those dying before 1760 but with probate delayed. However, date of probate is the only date in the cataloguing regime of the record office.

The survival of inventories, executors' accounts, or anything else filed with a will is impossible to assess before the testator's material is issued in the record office, since the format of the index subsumes all other items under the will entry. This created some minor difficulties for the methodological development. It transpired that with 1,769 wills from 1660–1760 some 331 inventories survived but only five executors' accounts.

The content and form of Liverpool wills have been found to vary greatly as could be expected in a collection of some 1800 items spanning a century and drawn by, or for, testators as disparate as barely literate dying seamen and scions of the landed gentry making detailed provisions obviously considered over time. Legal restrictions on testation meant that only free adult males and *unmarried* women 'of sound mind' could make wills. The former were legally restricted until 1693 by *legitim* in the Northern Province (Archdiocese of York). This gave freedom of testation over only a third of their estates (one-third each must go to wife and children). Catholic recusants suffered various additional restrictions during the period. Married women lost proprietorial control to their husbands and could make a will only by prior agreement under pre-marriage settlement. Liverpool's port function seems the reason for a wider variation in the wealth and status of testators than might be expected elsewhere. Valuations of less than £5 indicate the inclusion of significantly poorer individuals in the ranks of testators than could be expected if probate requirements had been observed. This must counter somewhat the anticipated wealth bias.

The uses of the material are twofold: first to address social and economic questions concerning a burgeoning eighteenth-century port town by means of core testamentary evidence; secondly to ask questions of a wider accumulation of material concerning the same community. Thus the inquiry necessitates essentially distinct but overlapping methodologies; initially to create and internally analyse, in statistical terms, a database of the testamentary evidence; ultimately to use nominal record linkage techniques for prosopographical purposes, and to explore the possibility of reconstructing networks of kinship and association within what was a rapidly growing and apparently fluid population. The relational database of some 36,500 records, from the wills of 1,769 testators, has 25,500 nominal records of which only the testators' file is unique to individuals. Other files may contain multiple mentions of an individual who, for example, benefited under more than one will.

The construction of a detailed biography involves the identification of an individual within a number of sources and thence the linking together of pertinent information. The assessment of the greater significance of that individual's life then involves further linkage, principally through the reconstruction of extended family connections but also through the identification of economic and social relationships. Complex chains and webs of linked records are therefore constructed. The process of compilation has to overcome problems commonplace within nominal record linkage such as mis-identification through common or shared names, assessment of the probability that a linkage is correctly made, and due weighting to all possible linkages.[4] Computer-aided multi-source record linkage constitutes arguably a new methodology for the appraisal of a large urban society.

The technique employed in this study builds upon the linkage strategy used in reconstitution but draws upon a far greater and more flexible record base than parish registers alone, and might be termed a variant of total reconstitution.[5] To commence the linkage process a foundation or base must be selected. The source that captures the central period is the 1708 Rate assessment and this has formed the pivotal point for record linkage both backwards and forwards within the entire range of the database.

The networks reconstructed to date number some 280, incorporating over 7,500 individuals. There is no significance in a count of 'family trees' because these can be very different in form, varying in complexity from the most basic which is no more than the names of the testator and his wife and the date of probate from a single will, to the other extreme of connections which comprise vast interlocking genealogies: one spreads over 17 linked networks, spanning six generations, includes 60 testators, and identifies some 750 individuals, not all of whom registered vital events in Liverpool. Networks of kinship and association have been analysed for aspects of wealth tracing, occupational dynasties, migration and residential proximity of kin, nonconformity, and political activity.

Vital Event Registration: Parish Registers[6]

The surviving registers for Liverpool commence in 1660 with those of the parochial chapel of Our Lady and St Nicholas, a chapel of ease to St Mary's Church, Walton-on-the-Hill. These registers continued through the change of 1699 when Liverpool became a 'parish of itself' which was co-extensive with the borough until 1835. The existing chapel was augmented by a second church, St Peter, which was consecrated in

1704. The growing town required two more Anglican places of worship before mid-century: St George consecrated in 1734 and St Thomas in 1750. The parish was not divided into ecclesiastical districts, therefore theoretically all registers must be consulted to ensure the presence or absence of individuals.[7]

The parish register database consists of three main files containing baptisms, approximately 23,000 records; burials, approximately 22,000 records; and marriages, approximately 6,500 records. When entering information from the parish registers an 'all-inclusive' approach was adopted, thus files contain information not only on date and principal names of those registering events, but also place of residence and occupation where included. The inclusion of such information was not compulsory and varied greatly over time. This variation is particularly obvious when attempting to construct occupational profiles or analyse migrational behaviour through assessment of place of origin.[8] On occasion other snippets of information were noted in the registers and in order to provide the most comprehensive picture of Liverpool vital event registration in this period, this too was recorded in the basic computer files.

Records in the parish register database were used in a number of ways: first, for family reconstitution where baptism, burial and marriage records were linked systemically into family units and then various demographic parameters analysed; secondly, in the study of occupation; and thirdly, by comparison with that in other sources to reinforce links for named individuals and family networks. By merging and combining basic baptism, burial and marriage files and by introducing other basic source files, such as willmakers, hearth tax residents etc., it became possible to present a huge array of information on named individuals. To maintain this data in a reasonably manageable form a second 'tier' of files was added to the parish register database. Each individual was assigned a unique number that was carried through wherever they appeared in the basic files and file combinations. In this way, information pertinent to an individual could be gathered together from any number of sources.

Entries for individual Liverpudlians have been sought in all the volumes and microfiches published by the Lancashire Parish Register Society. Listings of marriage licences and bonds have also been consulted.[9] Where necessary further inquiry has been made of original records for both Lancashire and Cheshire on microfilm.[10]

Vital Event Registration: Quakers' Records

Records do not survive for the Liverpool Meeting which was established in Hackins Hey from 1706 and where the first burial was in

1711. Therefore data have been abstracted from records of the Monthly meeting at Hardshaw, St Helens, and are random recoveries. Not all records fully identify individuals and it would be dangerous to assume linkage, where there is no detail of address, because of the small surname pool in southwest Lancashire. Nominal records pertaining to Friends from Liverpool can be culled from the Accounts of Sufferings 1660–1734 in which Liverpool seems synonymous with Knowsley; Minutes of Hardshaw Meetings 1678–1786; Quaker Registers: Births, Marriages, Burials 1650–1837; and 'Bickerstaffe Burial Ground', a list of interments for the seventeenth and eighteenth centuries covering Friends from a wide area of southwest Lancashire.[11]

Vital Event Registration: Independent Records

The Presbyterian/Independent Key Street Chapel kept a baptismal register from 1709 giving the name of father and child with occasional recording of father's occupation and residence.[12] The standard of each separate entry is good but general record-keeping suffered somewhat from the ill-health of the minister, and the consequent delay in transcription.

Vital Event Registration: Roman Catholic Records

The baptismal register of St Mary's Catholic chapel commenced in 1741.[13] Unfortunately it has suffered much damage and deterioration which reduces its use for identifying individuals. There was a hiatus in registration from May 1746 to February 1747. Nominal details, if decipherable, are recorded for the child, father, mother, *and* male and female godparents. Many surnames are Irish, and residence is sometimes given as 'of' or 'formerly from Ireland', but seldom detailed in Liverpool. There is no record of fathers' occupations but very occasional record of the father's status as 'Mr' or 'Captain'.

Liverpool Town Books

The Town Books are the main municipal record for the town of Liverpool and are extant from 1550 to 1835. The original records are at Liverpool Record Office, and are edited and published for the period between 1550 and 1671.[14] They contain a record of elections of officers, of council meetings and councillors attending, of portmoot or quarter sessions courts, admissions of new freemen and much other occasional information about the town and its government.

For the purposes of this book the officers and councillors recorded each year between 1650 and 1750 were transcribed into a computer file, TOWNBOOK.[15] The mayor, bailiffs and some other officers were chosen at the election court held every year on 18 October; the remaining officers were chosen at the first portmoot court soon after. Lists of councillors were recorded either at the election court, or at the end of the record of council or assembly meetings, sometimes with signatures, sometimes as a list of names.

The resulting file contains 6,953 records, individuals appearing repeatedly each year they served in an office or on the council. For purposes of identification these names were manually studied and reduced to a file of 1,587 individuals. The Town Books do not usually give information about officers and councillors other than their offices and the dates served; addresses and occupations are seldom given, for example, but usually titles of respect are accorded, Mr, esquire and gentleman for example, and aldermen are identified. In order to analyse the personnel of government in Chapter 5, the names of officers and councillors were manually linked with names in Dr Ascott's testators file and Dr Lewis's adult male burials file. These provided information about occupation for 588 more individuals to add to the 251 ascribed an occupation in the Town Books, as well as occasional details about place of residence and family relationships. Rules for linking names in the different sources were observed: the surname and forename were to be identical and there was to be no more than a ten years' lag between the appearance of identical names for a link to be made. The result was that about 57 per cent of officers and councillors had attached to them additional information about occupation or status. Though very far from being complete, this allowed cautious generalisations about the character of the groups in government to be made.

A second set of data was systematically derived from Town Books, the names of newly admitted freemen from 1650 to 1708. These were input into a file, FREEMEN, to allow the entry of townsmen into active economic and political activity in the town to be established. For the period after 1708 an Apprentice Register can be used for a similar purpose, albeit at an earlier stage of individuals' engagement in the town.

A third set of data was extracted from Town Books, the decisions of Liverpool councillors and their political activity. This information was manually transcribed onto record cards from the most complete published extracts of the Town Books by James Touzeau.[16] All significant episodes and decisions were followed up in the original Town Books, or in the extracts from the Town Books carefully compiled in 13 volumes by T. N. Morton, town clerk to the corporation from 1880 to 1898.[17] This information was of particular use in reconstructing the politics of Liverpool in Chapter 6.

Fiscal Records: Hearth Taxes

The Hearth Tax returns for England and Wales should be nominal list-ings detailing heads of household and the number of hearths for which they were liable to pay 1s. each every Michaelmas and Lady Day for 27 years from 1662. Hasty preparation of the original Act was perhaps the reason for many subsequent amendments: to distinguish property owners from occupiers, to provide exemptions for the poor, and to stip-ulate the inclusion of both exempt and liable households.[18]

The surviving hearth tax returns for Liverpool (one each from 1663, 1664, 1666 and 1673) fall within the period 1662 to 1674. It is in fact from the periods of local government involvement, 1662 to 1666, and 1669 to 1674, that the bulk of all detailed hearth tax listings survive. In general most counties produced eight assessments during those nine years. Liverpool listings, of three assessments and one collectors' account (1666), were recorded under West Derby hundred in Lancashire returns, and are available as microfilm copies.[19]

The Liverpool hearth tax lists include an assessment for Lady Day 1664. Such lists incorporate both chargeable and exempt hearths and are considered the most comprehensive because produced under local government auspices. Nonetheless, local officials might have been more susceptible to blandishments, and evasion of this unpopular tax is unde-niable.[20] The details of extant Liverpool lists substantiate this. There were 254 householders for 1663, 283 for 1664, 228 for 1666, 252 for 1673: 1,017 records in total which have been rationalised to 505 indi-viduals.[21] The variation in the number of households over the ten years seems to bear no relation to an increasing population as reflected in Town Book records of the increment in Inspectors of Inmates.[22] The omission of an individual from, for example, the assessment of 1673 when he is known to persist in the same house from 1663 to death in 1690 points up the deficiencies of the source.[23] Only the assessment for 1663 was listed satisfactorily by street in Liverpool; the apparently similar 1666 listing has no note of Water Street so that inhabitants of a major thoroughfare cannot be distinguished.

Fiscal Records: The Moore Rental, 1667

This source was edited and published some 150 years ago, albeit in partial form; that is to say including only property in Liverpool.[24] The stated *raison d'être* of the Moore Rental was the instruction and guidance of the son of its compiler, Edward Moore, of Bank Hall near Liverpool.

Moore described his Liverpool property in detail street by street. He recounted its immediate history, and suggested potential for both development and radical rent revision. Tenants and, where appropriate, sub-tenants were named, often with a character sketch, or more usually, a character assassination. Tenancy was normally for three lives plus 21 years and those names still in each lease were also recorded, together with their relationship, if any, to the tenant. The nominal roll numbers 260, covering 105 tenancies, which were held by 91 individuals, of whom seven held two properties each, and three held three or more. There are other duplicated entries when individuals were named in more than one lease.

The source is somewhat irregular in format, inconsistent in data, and partial in its coverage of the population and the extent of Liverpool. However it is invaluable specifically in providing evidence that substantial numbers of citizens 'escaped' the Hearth Tax net, and revealing that people adjudged by Moore to be poor were *included* in Hearth Tax listings while some, of whom he made no such comment, were *excluded*. The genealogical information afforded by Moore's detail of 'lives' in leases is especially useful because the Rental source is dated so close to the Interregnum gap in the parish registers.

Moore also used 'addresses' which do not feature in the topographical Hearth Tax listings. It must be presumed that certain alleys and lanes were customarily subsumed, for assessment purposes, within the thoroughfares off which they branched. Likewise, although property fronted specific streets, there is evidence of a less clearly defined concept of address in examples of property mentioned under the street onto which it backed.

Fiscal Records: 1705 and 1708 Assessments

These sources have been edited and published.[25] The assessments of Liverpool for 1705 and 1708 were made respectively for 'granting an aid to Her Majesty by a Land Tax...',[26] and for a rate for the relief of the poor. Only the latter, the rate of 1708, provides a virtual street directory, because, unfortunately, from the assessment of 1705 the details of the North Side (of a line drawn down Dale Street / Water Street) have not survived.

The population is represented in the assessments by property owners and tenants, or, more accurately, by ratepayers and their tenants, who may in fact have been 'under-tenants'. The listing was by street and Townfield, rather than by name. Therefore multiple entries for any individual may be scattered throughout the listings and may occur, in some instances, as both ratepayer and tenant. The entries can be rationalised: for example, to individuals distinguished according to whether they occur in one or both assessments. The tax and rate were levied on property, stock in trade and money at interest. Hence the rating of tenants who were being assessed for their stock. Nominal details were supplemented by status ascription and, very occasionally, by occupational designation, more of which were added by the editor from parish register entries. However, these all required checking with parish registers and testamentary evidence because certain editorial annotation can be recognised as inaccurate.

Fiscal Records: 1743 Assessment

The assessment of 1743 contains a list of property owners and tenants in the town. It seems to provide a view of real estate in the town similar to that provided by the better-known poor rate assessment of 1708. Unfortunately the manuscript assessment book in Liverpool Record Office is not clearly identified. It does not have a descriptive heading and is identifiable only by an archivist's pencilled note, 'Rate assessment c1743'.[27] No reference to a poor rate levied in the town has been found in the Town Books in 1742 or 1743 but Vestry minutes of 26 April 1743 appoint assessors to make a survey. Its format and content are similar to a rate of 1756 explicitly headed 'Assessment on houses, land and personal estate towards the relief of the poor pursuant to a vestry order, Tuesday 20 April 1756', and it is possible that the 1743 document was compiled for the same purpose.[28] The information was input into a computer file, RATE1743, deposited at the Essex Data Archive.

The rate consists of 2,676 names responsible for property in the town, mostly dwellings, and 270 more names responsible for land and enclosures. Using a crude multiplier of five persons per house this suggests a population of 13,400 or more, perhaps three-quarters of the number we might expect in the town at this date.[29] Insofar as it includes most of the streets in the town in the mid-eighteenth century it does seem to be geographically comprehensive.

Though of limited use for estimating population the rate has been of use. Despite difficulties in linking names with other sources because one-third of the names in the rate are recorded only by surname and status description, it was possible to identify prominent town councillors and officers among the ratepayers of 1743 and to establish the property they lived in or owned. When set beside their investment in transatlantic ships indicated by plantation registers this allowed an estimate of their comparative investment in shipping and real estate in Chapter 5.

Fiscal Records: Port Books

The Port Books were instituted in the late sixteenth century in order to tighten Customs administration. Distinct records were to be kept of coastal and overseas trade; the latter included the colonies, the Channel Islands, Ireland, Scotland (to 1707), and the Isle of Man (to 1765). The arrangements were not rescinded until 1799 but lax management had rendered the system ineffective in some ports many years previously: for example, the last overseas book for Liverpool is for 1725–26.

Blank books were issued annually to officers in each port: the Customer, collecting the duty; the comptroller, checking the Customer; the searcher, checking the cargo.[30] As full series do not survive it is preferable, if sampling, to select records which were compiled by one official. Even so it is salutary to be reminded that 'Port Books are seducers. They have an air of plausibility which they may not merit.'[31] Nonetheless their reliability has been assessed, and much work has been based on them.[32]

The existing microfilms of Liverpool Port Books are unusable. Therefore the original documents were consulted in the Public Record Office.[33] The books utilised in this study were from the 1660s and 1700s: 'coastal' compiled by Customer and Controller for Christmas 1665–Christmas 1666;[34] 'overseas' compiled by the Customer for Christmas 1664–Christmas 1665, and Christmas 1708–Christmas 1709. The coastal book for 1665–66 is short (6 folios) but a third of it is in poor condition. The 'overseas' book for 1664–65 has some non-crucial damage, 'spotting' throughout, and an almost illegible cover page. There are no problems with the book for 1708–09, other than those common to all Port Books which stem from a ship's cargo often being split into innumerable items. This makes the books time-consuming and difficult to work with until input to a computer database for rationalisation. After that it is possible, for example, to group all entries for one ship/voyage and to evaluate the shipments of each merchant within a total cargo. The Liverpool project benefited greatly from the computing expertise of the Port Books Programme at the University of Wolverhampton, which was generously passed on by Dr Graeme Milne.[35] The computer files of the two projects are thus compatible and comparable.

Fiscal Records: Plantation Registers

The Plantation Registers result from the seventeenth-century Navigation Acts and subsequent legislation designed to augment them. The regulations were protectionist in nature in that trade between Britain and transatlantic plantations was reserved to vessels built, owned, mastered and largely manned by British subjects. Registration was required under the original Act of 1660.[36] However by 1696 further legislation was enacted, 'for a more effectual prevention of frauds', whereby the owners of British or plantation-built ships had to swear on oath that their ships complied with the requirements of the Act before the ships could be employed in the plantation trade.[37] The oath was to be sworn before, and registered by, the Collector and Controller of Customs in the port of ownership or, if the vessel was owned in the plantations or the Channel Islands, the oath was taken before the Governor and the Crown's principal revenue officer. Certificates and duplication into a general registry are not extant, nor are most local registers. However, four volumes survive for Liverpool between 1744–84 and include 3,800 entries of vessels giving details of ship's name, port, master, ship's type, tonnage, building and ownership.[38] The partnerships revealed in ownership of Liverpool ships are of particular interest. The registration of 251 ships for the years 1744–48 listed a total of 747 owners, of whom many recurred in different partnerships.[39]

Subsidiary Sources

The nominal records in the Apprentice Books 1707–57 are neither consistently detailed nor comprehensive, but may include names of apprentices, their sponsors and their masters.[40] Other lists of townsfolk were generated during the period for different purposes: Civil War reparations were claimed by 357 Liverpudlians; 200 subscribed to the Present Monies of 1661; 500 signed the Association Oath Rolls of 1696; there were 121 subscribers to the Infirmary in 1745; and 139 to 'Plans of Harbours' in 1748.[41] Supplementary enquiry has been made of published sources including the Liverpool Vestry Books;[42] registers of Catholic recusant fines and their estates;[43] details of Liverpool Parliamentary elections;[44] the Alumni listings for the Universities of Oxford and Cambridge;[45] and the Dictionary of National Biography.[46] Contemporary diaries and items of correspondence have been perused also.[47]

Notes

1. For the probate jurisdiction of Prerogative Courts see D. E. Ascott, 'Wealth and Community: Liverpool 1660–1760', unpublished PhD thesis, University of Liverpool, 1996, pp. 41–42.

2. A survey of accessible indices of prerogative holdings revealed no Liverpool testators listed at York and only 21 Liverpudlian wills proved in the

Prerogative Court of Canterbury between 1657 and1700, many of which duplicate diocesan holdings.

3. Listing at LRO WCW is by name, place, occupation/status and year of probate. For detail see Appendix 2.

4. For detail of multi-source record linkage see Ascott, 'Wealth and Community', for methodology, pp. 92–101, 111–21; for application, pp. 383–451.

5. See P. Sharpe, 'The total reconstitution method: a tool for class specific study?', *LPS*, 44, 1990, pp. 41–51.

6. For detail of the development of parish registration see W. E. Tate, *The Parish Chest. A Study of the Records of Parochial Administration in England*, 3rd edn, Cambridge, 1969, pp. 43–83. As local practice did not necessarily follow national regulation, see also R. A. P. Finlay, 'Parish Registers. An Introduction', *Historical Geography Research Series*, 7, Norwich, 1981. For discussion of the rubric and results see J. C. Cox, *The Parish Registers of England*, London, 1910.

7. St Nicholas: H. Peet, ed., *The Earliest Registers of the Parish of Liverpool (St. Nicholas Church)*, LPRS, 35, Rochdale, 1909; R. E. Dickinson, ed., *The Registers of Our Lady and St .Nicholas, 1705–1725*, LPRS, 101, Preston, 1963; LplRO 283 NIC 1/4; St Peter: LplRO 283 PET 1/1,1/2,1/3, 7/1; St George: LplRO 283 GEO 1/1.

8. For a detailed discussion of the form, quality and typicality of the Liverpool parish registers see F. Lewis, 'The Demographic and Occupational Structure of Liverpool: a study of the parish registers, 1660–1750', unpublished PhD thesis, University of Liverpool, 1993, Chapters 4 and 5.

9. W. Irvine, ed., *Marriage Licences Granted within the Archdeaconry of Chester in the Diocese of Chester*, RSLC, *1661–67*, 65, 1912; *1667–80*, 69, 1914; *1680–1691*, 73, 1918; *1691–1700*, 77, 1923; W. A. Tonge, ed., *Marriage Bonds of the Ancient Archdeaconry of Chester, now Preserved at Chester*, RSLC, *1700–06/07*, 82, 1933; *1707–11*, 85, 1935; *1711–15*, 97, 1942; *1715–19*, 101, 1946.

10. The principal inquiry was of the mother church. A. Smith, ed., *The Registers of the Parish Church of Walton-on-the-Hill*, LPRS, 5, Wigan, 1900; R. E. Dickinson, ed., *The Registers of the Parish Church of Walton-on-the-Hill*, LPRS, 91, Preston, 1950; LplRO 283 SMW 1/3, 1/5. Unpublished material for parishes now within the boundaries of Liverpool was consulted at Liverpool Record Office; other parishes were researched at the respective County Record Offices of Lancashire and Cheshire.

11. St Helens Local History and Archives Library: the first two items are available on microfilm of LRO MFI/51 and M/PO/122; the Register is a rather selective transcript M/PO/125 which concentrates on the St Helens area; J. T. Haines, Bickerstaffe Burial Ground, 1978, ref: A 97.3.

12. LplRO Hq. 929.3 PAR.

13. LplRO 282 HIG 1/1.

14. LplRO 352 MIN/COU 1–16. Published volumes are: J. A. Twemlow, ed., *Liverpool Town Books, I, 1550–1571*, and *II, 1572–1603*, Liverpool, 1918–

1935; for the period 1603–1625, G. Chandler, *Liverpool under James I*, Liverpool, 1960; for the period from 1625 to 1649, G. Chandler, *Liverpool under Charles I*, Liverpool, 1965; *Liverpool Town Books 1649–1671*, ed. M. Power, RSLC, 136, 1999.

15. This file and FREEMEN are deposited at the Essex Data Archive.

16. J. Touzeau, *The Rise and Progress of Liverpool from 1551 to 1835*, Liverpool, 1910.

17. LplRO 352/CLE/TRA 2/ 1–13.

18. See T. Arkell, 'Printed instructions for administering the Hearth tax', in *Surveying the People*, ed. K. Schurer and T. Arkell, Oxford, 1992, pp. 38–64.

19. PRO: E179/250/8; E179/250/11; E179/250/9; E179/132/355.

20. See T. Unwin, 'Late seventeenth century taxation and population: the Nottinghamshire Hearth Taxes and Compton Census', *Historical Geography Research Series*, 16, 1985, pp. 11–12.

21. Computer listings are deposited in the Essex Data Archive as HEARTH63, HEARTH64, HEARTH66, HEARTH73.

22. Touzeau, *Rise and Progress*, p. 297.

23. Edward Tarleton, mariner, probate 1690.

24. T. Heywood, ed., *The Moore Rental*, CS, 10, Manchester, 1847.

25. H. Peet, ed., *Liverpool in the Reign of Queen Anne, 1705 and 1708*, Liverpool, 1908. Computer listing of the 1708 poor rate is deposited in the Essex Data Archive as RATE1708.

26. 3 & 4 Anne, c. 1.

27. LplRO 920 PLU PT51.

28. LplRO 920 PLU PT52.

29. See Chapter 2.

30. A lucid account of the intention, coverage and format of Port Books is given in D. Woodward, 'The Port Books of England and Wales', *Sources for Maritime History*, III, 1973, pp. 147–65.

31. R. W. K. Hinton, *The Port Books of Boston, 1601–40*, Lincoln Record Society, 50, Hereford, 1956, p. xxxii.

32. S-E. Åström, 'The Reliability of the English Port Books', *Scandinavian Economic History Review*, XVI, No. 2, 1968, pp. 125–36. Possibly the best-known works based on Port Books are T. S. Willan, *The English Coasting Trade, 1600–1750*, Manchester, 1938; T. C. Smout, *Scottish Trade on the Eve of Union, 1660–1707*, Edinburgh, 1963. Computer-assisted study from the University of Wolverhampton is available on CDROM: N. C. Cox, D. P. Hussey and G. J. Milne, eds, *The Gloucester Coastal Port Books, 1575–1765, on CDROM*, Marlborough, 1998.

33. PRO: E190/1338/1; E190/1337/16; E190/1375/8.

34. The Books covering Christmas 1707–midsummer 1708, midsummer 1708–Christmas 1708 could not be addressed in the time available.

35. See Cox, Hussey and Milne, *Gloucester Coastal Port Books*.

36. 12 Charles II, c. 18.

L

37. 7 & 8 William III, c. 22. For an account of the illegal trade, the complaints it drew from English merchants, and remedies thereto see M. M. Schofield and D. J. Pope, Introduction to *The Liverpool Plantation Registers 1744–1773 and 1779–1784*, Wakefield, 1978. Discussion of plantation registers *per se* is included in R. S. Craig and R. C. Jarvis, *Liverpool Registry of Merchant Ships*, CS, 3rd series,15, Manchester, 1967.

38. The volumes have been consulted on good microfilm. Originals are held in the Maritime Archives and Library, Merseyside Maritime Museum: D/514/2/1.

39. The entries from 1744 to 1748 were put into a computer file, PLANT, deposited in the Data Archive, Essex.

40. LplRO 352 CLE/REG/4.

41. R. Stewart-Brown, *The Inhabitants of Liverpool from the 14th to the 18th Century*, Liverpool, 1930; W. Gandy, ed., *Lancashire Association Oath Rolls. A.D. 1696*, London, 1921; T. H. Bickerton, *A Medical History of Liverpool from the Earliest Days to the Year 1920*, London, 1936, Appendix III; Stewart-Brown, *Inhabitants*.

42. Peet, *Liverpool Vestry Books*.

43. W. E. Gregson, ed., 'Recusant Rolls for West Derby Hundred, 1641', *THSLC*, 50, 1898, pp. 231–47; A. J. Mitchinson, ed., *The Return of the Papists for the Diocese of Chester*, 1705, Wigan, North West Catholic History Society, 1986; E. E. Estcourt and J. O. Payne, eds, *The English Catholic Nonjurors of 1715*, London, 1900; R. S. France, ed., *Lancashire Papists' Estates, 1717–1788*, vol. I, RSLC, 98, 1945; vol. II, RSLC, 108, 1977.

44. J. Rose, ed., *Lancashire and Cheshire historical and genealogical notes*, vols 1 & 2 Leigh, printed at the 'Chronicle' office, 1879–81.

45. J. Foster, *Alumni Oxonienses*, Oxford, 1891; J. Venn and J. A. Venn, *Alumni Cantabrigiensis*, Pt. 1, vol. 1, Cambridge, 1922.

46. L. Stephen and S. Lee, eds, *Dictionary of National Biography*, London, 1885–1900

47. E. Axon, ed., *Oliver Heywood's Life of John Angier of Denton together with Angier's Diary... also Samuel Angier's Diary*, CS, 97, Manchester, 1937; J. D. Marshall, ed., *The Autobiography of William Stout of Lancaster 1665–1752*, CS, 3rd series, 14, Manchester, 1967; R. Trappes-Lomax, ed., *The Diary and Letter Book of the Rev. Thomas Brockbank 1671–1709*, CS, 89, Manchester, 1930; J. J. Bagley and F. Tyrer, eds, *The Great Diurnal of Nicholas Blundell of Little Crosby, Lancashire*, vol. 1: 1702–1711; vol. 2: 1712–1719; vol. 3: 1720–1728, RSLC, 110, 1968; 112, 1970; 114, 1972; J. Addy and P. McNiven, eds, *The Diary of Henry Prescott, LL.B., Deputy Registrar of Chester Diocese*, vol. 1: 1704–1711; vol. 2: 1711–1719, RSLC, 127, 1987; 132, 1994; M. Blundell, ed., *Cavalier: Letters of William Blundell to his Friends 1620–1698*, London, 1933; T. Heywood, ed., *The Norris Papers*, CS, 9, Manchester, 1846; F. Nicholson and E. Axon, ed., *Memorials of the Family of Nicholson of Blackshaw, Dumfriesshire, Liverpool and Manchester*, private printing, 1928.

Appendix 2
Probate listing

The catalogue for Liverpool testamentary material at Lancashire Record Office (LRO) is the appropriate volume of the Record Society of Lancashire and Cheshire: J. P. Earwaker, ed., *Index to the Wills and Inventories now Preserved in the Court of Probate at Chester,* vol. 15 (1887) 1660–1680; vol. 18 (1888) 1681–1700; vol. 20 (1889) 1701–1720; vol. 22 (1890) 1721–1740; vol. 25 (1892) 1741–1760. These date from the late nineteenth century, thus constituting an archival item in their own right. They contain anomalous spelling of names and may lack occupational/status data even when they are clearly stated in the will preamble. Prior to the adoption of the New Style (Gregorian) calendar in 1752 they date items by year beginning 25 March. The format for accession is by class (WCW) name, place, occupation/status and year of probate, e.g. WCW Alcock, Jane, of Liverpool, widow, 1667. The following list omits the class and place (always Liverpool). It includes additional information where the index is deficient or wrong, and when probate is far from the dating in the text, as in: Carter, Hannah, widow, 1717 [will 1709].

Alcock, Edward, mercer, 1665
Alcock, Jane, widow, 1667
Arrowsmith, Jeremiah, tailor, 1725
Ashbrooke, Robert, mariner, 1692
Baldwin, Thomas, clerk, rector, 1753
Bamber, John, yeoman, 1710
Barrow, Robert, merchant, 1715
Beckett, William, merchant, 1746
Bibby, William, bricklayer, 1732
Birchall, Daniel, gentleman, 1734
Blundell, Bryan, merchant, 1756
Boulton, Richard [mariner], 1731
Briggs, Joseph [merchant], 1707
Brooke, Roger, merchant, 1753
Bushell, Anne [widow], 1686

Bushell, William [mariner], 1676
Carter, Hannah, widow, 1717 [will 1709]
Carter, Thomas, gentleman, 1696
Catterall, Elizabeth, widow, 1711
Clayton, Elizabeth, widow, 1745
Clayton, William, merchant, 1715
Cleavland, Richard [sugar baker], 1683
Cleavland, Suzanna [widow], 1685
Cleiveland, Ann, widow, 1735
Cleiveland, John, merchant, 1716
Cook, Zachariah, merchant, 1699
Cooke, Cicely [wife/bread baker], 1755
Danvers, Daniel, sugar baker, 1710
Danvers, Sarah, widow, 1733
Danvers, Samuel, sugar baker, 1720
Dewhurst, Lawrence, mariner, 1756
Dutton, John, yeoman, 1745
Farrington, Mary, spinster, 1741
Finney, Thomas, shoemaker, 1750
Fleetwood, Mary, widow, 1732
Formby, Margery [widow], 1684
Galaspy, George, mariner, 1701
Galaspy, Margaret, widow 1709
Gallaway, Richard, shipwright, 1747
Gandy, William, yeoman, 1711
Gildus, John, chirugeon, 1717
Grayson, Joseph [labourer], 1746
Greson, David, tobacco pipemaker, 1736
Hamilton, Maxwell, gentleman, 1755
Harper, Jane, widow, 1736
Heald, Margaret, widow, 1669
Heaward [Howard], Jane [widow], 1679
Henshaw, John, mariner, 1741
Houghton, Richard, merchant, 1712
Houghton, Richard, merchant, 1755
Howard, Joan, widow, 1757
Huddleston, Mary, widow, 1747
Huddleston, Robert, shipwright, 1713
James, Edward, shipwright, 1747
James, John, merchant, 1740
James, Robert, ship carpenter, 1699
James, Roger [shipwright], 1701
Jones, Alice, widow, 1665
Jones, Roger, pewterer, 1661

Kelsall, Richard, gentleman, 1751
Kirks, Moorcroft, gentleman, 1749
Lewis, George, mariner, 1699
Ligoe, James, butcher, 1747
Livesley, Jonathan, mariner, 1720
Lyon, Edward, pipemaker, 1721
Mackmullen, John, mariner, 1701
Mackmullen, Margery, 1706
Martindale, John, yeoman, 1756
Matthews, Thomas [tailor], 1691
Mauditt, Jasper, merchant, 1714
Mercer, James, butcher, 1749
Mercer, Thomas, mariner, 1710
Moone, Robert [mariner], 1703
Moorcroft, Richard, butcher, 1693
Morecroft, Gother, butcher, 1737 [will 1697]
Nicholls, John, merchant, 1748
Parker, George, cabinet maker, 1759 [will 1747]
Patten, Hugh, merchant, 1736
Pemberton, John, formerly apothecary, 1705
Pemberton, John, merchant, 1744 [will1737]
Phelps, Ann, widow, 1709
Powell, Samuel, merchant, 1745
Pryor, William, cordwainer, 1715
Richmond, Silvester, merchant [doctor], 1692
Rimmer, Richard [mariner], 1697
Robinson, Daniel, shipwright , 1736
Robinson, Esther, widow, 1752 [will 1743]
Robinson, John, joiner, 1743
Roby, Thomas, gentleman, 1719
Roderick, Anthony [Antonio Roredrigu], mariner, 1751
Roney, Henry, mariner, 1749
Rymer, Anne, widow, 1709
Scaresbrick, John, mariner, 1712
Scaresbrick, Joyce, widow, 1719
Seacome, Robert, [yeoman], 1704
Sheilds, Elizabeth [silversmith], 1723
Sheilds, Robert, goldsmith, 1710
Short, Edward, butcher, 1735
Stringer, James [Jacob] parish clerk, 1752
Summerset, Elizabeth, widow, 1740
Tarleton, Ann, widow, 1709
Tarlton, Edward, senior [mariner], 1690
Valentine, William [gunsmith], 1689

Walsh, Catherine, widow [wife], 1706
Watkinson, Cuthbert, gunsmith, 1701
Webster, Sarah, widow, 1731 [will 1718]
Williamson, Anne, widow, 1750 [will 1745]
Williamson, Margaret, widow, 1711
Williamson, Robert [mariner], 1684
Wills [Willis], Thomas [gentleman], 1695
Winfield, Phoebe, widow, 1708
Woods, Allen [yeoman], 1705
Wright, Hannah [widow], 1734
Yewdale, Anne, widow, 1719 [will 1710]
Yewdall, Jeremiah, merchant, 1706

Appendix 3
Overall sample sizes, including blank entries

	Adult male burial	Adult male marriage	Child baptism-burial before adjustment	Child baptism-burial after adjustment
1665	20	14	95	95
1675	6	22	83	76
1685	33	34	177	162
1695	17	17	97	90
1705	85	32	318	288
1715	84	40	447	402
1725	131	78	598	535
1735	104	74	840	735
1745	193	159	912	840

Bibliography

Manuscripts and original sources

Wills 'of Liverpool' 1660–1760
   Lancashire RO (LRO) WCW

Anglican Parish Registers
St Nicholas, Liverpool   Liverpool RO (LplRO) 283 NIC 1/4
St Peter, Liverpool   LplRO 283 PET 1/1, 1/2, 1/3, 7/1
St George, Liverpool   LplRO 283 GEO 1/1
St Thomas, Liverpool   LplRO 283 THO 1/1
St Mary, Walton-on-the-Hill   LplRO 283 SMW 1/3,1/5

Quaker registration
Hardshaw Meeting   LRO MFI/51
   St Helens Local History and Archives Library: M/PO/122,M/PO/125,A 97.3

Independent Registers
Paradise St chapel, Liverpool   LplRO Hq. 929.3 PAR

Roman Catholic Registers
St Mary, Liverpool   LplRO 282 HIG 1/1

Liverpool Port Books
Customer & Controller 'Coastal' 1665–1666   PRO E190/1338/1
Customer 'Overseas' 1664–1665   PRO E190/1337/16
Customer 'Overseas' 1708–1709   PRO E190/1375/8

Liverpool Plantation Registers
Maritime Archives and Library, Merseyside Maritime Museum D/514/2/1

Liverpool Hearth Tax, 1663   Public Record Office (PRO) E179/250/8

Liverpool Hearth Tax, 1664   PRO E179/250/11
Liverpool Hearth Tax, 1666   PRO E179/250/9
Liverpool Hearth Tax, 1673   PRO E179/132/355

Liverpool assessment, 1743   LplRO 920PT51

Liverpool Apprentice Books   LplRO 352 CLE/REG/4
Liverpool Freemen Rolls   LplRO 352 CLE/REG/4/1
Liverpool Town Books   LplRO 352 MIN/COU 3–10.
Liverpool town clerk transcripts   LplRO 352 CLE/TRA 2/6, 2/8.

Secondary and printed primary sources

A General Description of all Trades digested in Alphabetical order, printed for T. Waller, London, 1747.

A Short View of the dispute between the Merchants of London, Bristol and Liverpool and the advocates of a new joint-stock Company concerning the regulation of the African Trade, 1750.

Addy, J. and P. McNiven, eds, *The Diary of Henry Prescott, LL.B., Deputy Registrar of Chester Diocese*, vol. 1: 1704–1711; vol. 2: 1711–1719, RSLC, Vol. 127, 1987; Vol. 132, 1994.

Akerman, S., 'An evaluation of the family reconstitution technique', *Scandinavian Economic History Review*, Vol. 25, 1977, pp. 160–70.

Allison, K. J., ed., *Victoria County History, York: East Riding*, vol. I, London, Oxford UP, 1969.

Amussen, S. D., *An Ordered Society: Gender and Class in Early Modern England*, Oxford, Blackwell, 1988.

Anderson, B. L., 'Provincial Aspects of the Financial Revolution of the Eighteenth Century', *Business History*, Vol. 11, 1969, pp. 11–22.

Archer, I, *The Pursuit of stability: Social Relations in Elizabethan London*, Cambridge, Cambridge UP, 1991.

Arkell, T., 'Printed instructions for administering the Hearth tax', in *Surveying the People: The Interpretation and Use of Document Sources for the Study of Population in the Later Seventeenth Century*, ed. K. Schürer and T. Arkell, Oxford, Leopard's Head Press, 1992, pp. 38–64.

Arkell, T., N. Evans, and N. Goose, eds, *When Death Do Us Part: Understanding and Interpreting the Probate Records of Early Modern England*, Oxford, Leopard's Head Press, 2000.

Ascott, D. E. and F. Lewis, 'Motives to Move: reconstructing individual migration histories in early-eighteenth century Liverpool', in *Migration, Mobility and Modernization in Europe*, ed. D. Siddle, Liverpool, Liverpool UP, 2000, pp. 90–118.

Ascott, D. E., 'Wealth and Community: Liverpool, 1660–1760', unpublished PhD thesis, University of Liverpool, 1996.

Ashton, T. S., *An Economic History of England: The 18th Century*, London, Methuen, 1955.

Åström, S.-E., 'The Reliability of the English Port Books', *Scandinavian Economic History Review*, Vol. XVI, No. 2, 1968, pp. 125–36.

Axon, E., ed., *Oliver Heywood's Life of John Angier of Denton together with Angier's Diary... also Samuel Angier's Diary*, Chetham Society, Vol. 97, Manchester, 1937.

Ayers, P., *The Liverpool Docklands: Life and work in Athol Street*, Liverpool, n.d.

Bagley, J. J. and F. Tyrer, eds, *The Great Diurnal of Nicholas Blundell of Little Crosby, Lancashire*, Vol. 1: *1702–1711*, Vol. 2: *1712–1719*, Vol. 3: *1720–1728*, Record Society of Lancashire and Cheshire, Vol. 110, 1968; 112, 1970; 114, 1972, Manchester.

Baigent, E., 'Bristol Society in the Later Eighteenth Century with special reference to the handling of fragmentary historical sources', unpublished DPhil thesis, University of Oxford, 1985.

Bailey, F. A., 'The minutes of the trustees of the turnpike roads from Liverpool to Prescot, St. Helens, Warrington and Ashton-in-Makerfield, 1726–89', *Transactions of the Historic Society of Lancashire and Cheshire*, Vol. 88, 1936, pp. 159–200.

Bailey, N., *Dictionarium Britannicum*, London, T. Cox, 1730.

Baines, E., *History, Directory, and Gazetteer of the county Palatine of Lancaster*, vol. I, Liverpool, William Wales & Co., 1824.

Baines, T., *History of the commerce and town of Liverpool, and of the rise of manufacturing industry in the adjoining counties*, London, Longmans, 1852.

Barker, T. C. and J. R. Harris, 'The Early Coal Magnates: the Cases of Huyton and Sarah Clayton of Liverpool, 1757–1762', in *A Merseyside Town in the Industrial Revolution*, ed. T. C. Barker and J. R. Harris, Liverpool, Liverpool UP, 1954, pp. 24–30.

Barker, T. C., 'Lancashire coal, Cheshire salt and the rise of Liverpool', *Transactions of the Historic Society of Lancashire and Cheshire*, Vol. 103, 1951, pp. 83–101.

Barrie Rose, R. 'A Liverpool's sailors' strike in the eighteenth century', *Transactions of the Lancashire and Cheshire Antiquarian Society*, Vol. 68, 1959, pp. 85–92.

Barry J., 'Introduction', in *The Tudor and Stuart Town: A Reader in English Urban History 1530–1688*, ed. J. Barry, London, Longmans, 1990, pp. 1–34.

Barry, J., 'The politics of religion in Restoration Bristol', in *The Politics of Religion in Restoration England*, ed. T. Harris, P. Seaward and M. Goldie, Oxford, Blackwell, 1990, pp. 163–89.

Bebb, E. D., *Nonconformity and Social and Economic Life 1660–1800*, London, Epworth Press, 1935.

Beckett, J. V., 'Introduction: stability in politics and society 1680–1750', in *Britain in the First Age of Party 1680–1750: Essays Presented to Geoffrey Holmes*, ed. C. Jones, London, Hambledon, 1987, pp. 1–18.

Beier, A. L., 'Engine of manufacture: the trades of London', in *London 1500–1700: The Making of the Metropolis*, ed. A. L. Beier and R. Finlay, London, Longmans, 1986, pp. 141–67.

Ben-Amos, I. K., 'Women apprentices in the trades and crafts of early modern Bristol', *Continuity and Change*, Vol. 6, no. 2, 1991, pp. 227–52.

Berg, M., 'Women's Property and the Industrial Revolution', *Journal of Interdisciplinary History*, Vol. 24, no. 2, 1993, pp. 233–50.

Bickerton T. H., *A Medical History of Liverpool from the Earliest Days to the Year 1920*, London, Murray, 1936.

Blease, W. L., 'The Poor Law in Liverpool, 1681–1834', *Transactions of the Historic Society of Lancashire and Cheshire*, Vol. 61, 1909, pp. 97–182.

Blome, R., *Britannia*, 1673.

Blundell, M., ed., *Cavalier: Letters of William Blundell to his Friends 1620–1698*, London, 1933.

Bonfield, L., R. M. Smith and K. Wrightson, *The World We Have Gained: Histories of Population and Social Structure*, Oxford, Oxford UP, 1986.

Bongaarts, J., 'Intermediate fertility variables and marital fertility', *Population Studies*, Vol. 30, 1976, pp. 227–41.

Borsay, P., 'The English urban renaissance: the development of provincial urban culture *c*.1680–*c*.1760', in *The Eighteenth-Century Town: A Reader in Urban History, 1688–1820*, ed. P. Borsay, Harlow, Longmans, 1990, pp. 159–87.

Borsay, P., *The English Urban Renaissance: Culture and Society in the Provincial Town 1660–1770*, Oxford, Clarendon Press, 1989.

Boult, J., ed., 'A Littoral Survey of the Port of Liverpool', *Transactions of the Historic Society of Lancashire and Cheshire*, Vol. 22, 1870, pp. 171–246.

Boulton, J., *Neighbourhood and Society: A London Suburb in the Seventeenth Century*, Cambridge, Cambridge UP, 1987.

Braudel, F., *Capitalism and Material Life, 1400–1800*, London, Weidenfeld & Nicolson, 1973.

Brewer, J. and R. Porter, eds, *Consumption and the World of Goods*, London, Routledge, 1993.

Brierley, A., ed., *The Registers of the Church of St. Thomas the Martyr, Upholland in the County of Lancaster*, Lancashire Parish Register Society, Vol. 23, Rochdale, 1905.

Brodsky, V., 'Widows in Late Elizabethan London: Remarriage, Economic Opportunity and Family Orientations', in *The World We Have Gained: Histories of Population and Social Structure*, ed. L.

Bonfield, R. M. Smith and K. Wrightson, Oxford, Oxford UP, 1986, pp. 122–54.

Brown, R. L., 'The Rise and Fall of the Fleet Marriages', in *Marriage and Society: Studies in the Social History of Marriage*, ed. R. B. Outhwaite, London, Europa, 1981, pp. 117–37.

Buckatzsch, E. J., 'Occupations in the Parish Registers of Sheffield, 1655–1719', *Economic History Review*, 2nd series, Vol. 1, 1948–49, pp. 303–06.

Camp, A. J., *Wills and their Whereabouts*, London, 1974.

Carr, L. G. and L. S. Walsh, 'Inventories and the Analysis of Wealth and Consumption Patterns in St. Mary's County, Maryland, 1658–1777', *Historical Methods*, Vol. 13, no. 2, 1980, pp. 81–103.

Carr, L. G., 'Inheritance in the Colonial Chesapeake', in *Women in the Age of the American Revolution*, ed. R. Hoffman and P. J. Albert, Charlottesville, VA, Virginia UP, 1989, pp. 155–208.

Chalklin, C., *The Rise of the English Town, 1650–1850*, Cambridge, Cambridge UP, 2001.

Chalklin, C. W., 'The greater urban estates: Bath, Birmingham, Manchester and Liverpool', in *The Provincial Towns of Georgian England: A Study of the Building Process, 1740–1820*, ed. C. W. Chalklin, London, Arnold, 1974, pp. 73–112.

Chalklin, C. W., 'Estate development in Bristol, Birmingham and Liverpool 1660–1720', in *Town and Countryside: The English Landowner in the National Economy 1660–1860*, ed. C. W. Chalklin and J. R. Wordie, London, Unwin Hyman, 1989, pp. 102–15.

Chalklin, C. W., *The Provincial Towns of Georgian England: A Study of the Building Process, 1740–1820*, London, Arnold, 1974.

Chandler, G. and E. Saxton, *Liverpool under James I*, Liverpool, Brown, Picton and Hornby Libraries, 1960.

Chandler, G. and E. K. Wilson, *Liverpool under Charles I*, Liverpool, Brown, Picton and Hornby Libraries, 1965.

Chandler, G., *Four Centuries of Banking: As Illustrated by the Bankers, Customers and Staff associated with the Constituent Banks of Martins Bank Limited*, vol. 1, London, Batsford, 1964.

Chaytor, M., 'Household and kinship: Ryton in the late 16th and early 17th centuries', *History Workshop Journal*, Vol. 10, 1980, pp. 25–60.

Checkland, S., 'Business attitudes in Liverpool 1793–1807', *Economic History Review*, Vol. V, 1952, pp. 58–75.

Clark, A., *Working Life of Women in the Seventeenth Century*, ed. A. L. Erickson, London, Routledge, 1992.

Clark, P., 'Migrants in the city: the process of social adaptation in English towns 1500–1800', in *Migration and Society in Early Modern England*, ed. P. Clark and D. C. Souden, London, Hutchinson, 1987, pp. 267–91.

Clark, P., ed., *The Cambridge Urban History of Britain, Vol. II, 1540–1840*, Cambridge, Cambridge UP, 2000.

Clark, P., 'The civic leaders of Gloucester 1580–1800', in *The Transformation of English Provincial Towns 1600–1800*, ed. P. Clark, London, Hutchinson, 1984, pp. 311–45.

Clark, P., *The English Alehouse: A Social History 1200–1830*, London, Longmans, 1983.

Clarke, M., 'Thomas Steers', in *Dock Engineers and Dock Engineering: Papers Presented at a Research Day School 13.2.1993 NMGM*, Liverpool, 1993, pp. 5–17.

Clemens, P., 'The rise of Liverpool 1665–1750', *Economic History Review*, Vol. 29, 1976, pp. 211–25.

Coale, A. J. and P. Demeny, *Regional Model Life Tables and Stable Populations*, Princeton, NJ, Princeton UP, 1966.

Collins, Greenville, *Great Britain's Coasting-Pilot. The first part. Being a new and exact survey of the sea-coast of England, from the... Thames to the westward, with the islands of Scilly, and thence to Carlile...*, London, 1693.

Corfield, P. J., 'A provincial capital in the late seventeenth century: the case of Norwich', in *The Early Modern Town: A Reader*, ed. P. Clark, London, Longmans, 1976, pp. 233–72.

Corfield, P. J., 'Defining urban work', in *Work in Towns 850–1850 AD*, ed. P. J. Corfield and D. Keene, Leicester, Leicester UP, 1990, pp. 213–20.

Corfield, P. J., *The Impact of English Towns 1700–1800*, Oxford, Oxford UP, 1982.

Cox, J. and N. Cox, 'Probate 1500–1800: a system in transition', in *When Death Do Us Part: Understanding and Interpreting the Probate Records of Early Modern England*, ed. T. Arkell, N. Evans and N. Goose, Oxford, Leopard's Head Press, 2000, pp. 14–37.

Cox, J. C., *The Parish Registers of England*, London, Methuen, 1910.

Cox, N. C., D. P. Hussey and G. J. Milne, eds, *The Gloucester Coastal Port Books, 1575–1765, on CDROM*, Marlborough, Adam Matthew Publications, 1998.

Craig, R. S. and R. C. Jarvis, *Liverpool Registry of Merchant Ships*, Chetham Society, 3rd series, Vol. 15, Manchester, 1967.

Cressy, D., 'Kinship and kinship interaction in early modern England', *Past and Present*, Vol. 113, 1986, pp. 38–69.

Cruickshanks, E., 'Religion and royal succession: the rage of party', in *Britain in the First Age of Party 1680–1750: Essays Presented to Geoffrey Holmes*, ed. C. Jones, London, Hambledon, 1987, pp. 19–44.

Cullen, L. M., *Anglo-Irish Trade, 1660–1800*, Manchester, Manchester UP, 1968.

Davidoff, L. and C. Hall, *Family Fortunes: Men and Women of the English Middle Class, 1780–1950*, London, Hutchinson, 1987.

Davis, R., 'Seamen's sixpences: an index of commercial activity 1697–1828', *Economica*, Vol. 23, 1956, pp. 328–43.

Davis, R., *The Rise of the English Shipping Industry in the Seventeenth and Eighteenth Centuries*, London, Macmillan, 1962.

D'Cruze, S., 'The Middling Sort in Eighteenth-Century Colchester: Independence, Social Relations and the Community Broker', in *The Middling Sort of People: Culture, Society and Politics in England, 1550–1800*, ed. J. Barry and C. Brooks, London, Macmillan, 1994, pp. 181–207.

De Krey, G., *A Fractured Society: The Politics of London in the First Age of Party 1688–1715*, Oxford, Clarendon Press, 1985.

De Krey, G., 'London radicals and revolutionary politics 1675–83', in *The Politics of Religion in Restoration England*, ed. T. Harris, P. Seaward and M. Goldie, Oxford, Blackwells, 1990, pp. 13–62.

De Vries, J., *European Urbanisation 1500–1800*, London, Methuen, 1984.

Defoe, D., *A Tour through the Whole Island of Great Britain*, ed. G. D. H. Cole, London, Davies, 1927.

Derrick, S., *Letters written from Leverpoole, Chester, Corke, the Lake of Killarney, Dublin, Tunbridge-Wells, Bath*, London, 1767.

Devine, T. M., 'The golden age of tobacco', in *Glasgow, Volume I: Beginnings to 1830*, ed. T. M. Devine and G. Jackson, Manchester, Manchester UP, 1995, pp. 139–83.

Devine, T. M. and G. Jackson, *Glasgow, Volume 1: Beginnings to 1830*, Manchester, Manchester UP, 1995.

Dickinson, H., *The Politics of the People in Eighteenth-century Britain*, New York, St Martin's Press, 1995.

Dickinson, R. E., ed., *The Registers of the Parish Church of Walton-on-the-Hill*, Lancashire Parish Register Society, Vol. 91, Preston, 1950.

Dickinson, R. E., ed., *The Registers of Our Lady and St. Nicholas, Liverpool, 1705–1725*, Lancashire Parish Register Society, Vol. 101, Preston, 1963.

Dyos, H. J., and D. H. Aldcroft, *British Transport: An Economic Survey from the Seventeenth Century to the Twentieth*, Leicester, Leicester UP, 1969.

Earle, P., 'The female labour market in London in the late seventeenth and early eighteenth centuries', *Economic History Review*, 2nd series, Vol. XLII, no. 3, 1989, pp. 328–53.

Earle, P., *The Making of the English Middle Class: Business, Society and Family Life in London, 1660–1730*, London, Methuen, 1989.

Earwaker, J. P., ed., *Index to the Wills and Inventories now Preserved in the Court of Probate at Chester*, Record Society of Lancashire and Cheshire, vol. 15 (1887) 1660–1680; vol. 18 (1888) 1681–1700; vol. 20 (1889) 1701–1720; vol. 22 (1890) 1721–1740; vol. 25 (1892) 1741–1760.

Ellis, J. M., 'A dynamic society: social relations in Newcastle-upon-Tyne 1660–1760', in *The Transformation of English Provincial Towns 1600–1800*, ed. P. Clark, London, Hutchinson, 1984, pp. 190–227.

Ellis, J. M., *The Georgian Town 1680–1840*, Basingstoke, Palgrave, 2001.

Enfield, W., *An Essay towards the History of Leverpool*, Warrington, 1773.

Erickson, A. L., *Women and Property in Early Modern England*, London, Routledge, 1993.

Estcourt, E. E. and J. O. Payne, eds, *The English Catholic Nonjurors of 1715: being a Summary of the Register of their Estates with Genealogical and other Notes*, London, Thos. Baker, 1900.

Evans, N., 'Inheritance, Women, Religion and Education in Early Modern Society as revealed by Wills', in *Probate Records and the Local Community*, ed. P. Riden, Gloucester, Sutton, 1985, pp. 53–70.

Fearon, S., and J. Eyes, *A description of the sea coast of England and Wales, from Black-Comb in Cumberland to the point of Linus in Anglesea... with proper directions to avoid all dangers, and sail into any harbour... as also many prospects of the same... according to an actual survey, etc.*, Liverpool, 1738.

Finlay, R. A. P., 'Parish Registers. An Introduction', *Historical Geography Research Series*, Vol. 7, Norwich, 1981.

Finlay, R. A. P., *Population and Metropolis: The Demography of London 1580–1650*, Cambridge, Cambridge UP, 1981.

Fishwick, H., *History of Garstang*, II, Chetham Society, Vol. 105, Manchester, 1879.

Forster, G. C. F., 'Hull in the sixteenth and seventeenth centuries', in *Victoria County History, York: East Riding: Kingston upon Hull*, vol. 1, ed. K. J. Allison, London, Oxford UP, 1969.

Foster, C. F., *Seven Households: Life in Cheshire and Lancashire, 1582–1774*, Arley Hall Press, 2002.

Foster, J., *Alumni Oxonienses: the members of the University of Oxford: their parentage, birthplace, and year of birth, with a record of their degrees: being the matriculation register of the university. 1500–1714 early series, 1715–1886: later series*, Oxford, Parker, 1891.

France, R. S., ed., *Lancashire Papists' Estates, 1717–1788*, vol. I, Record Society of Lancashire and Cheshire, Vol. 98, 1945; vol. II, RSLC, Vol. 108, 1977.

Friedrichs, C., *The Early Modern City 1450–1750*, London, Longmans, 1995.

Gandy, W., ed., *Lancashire Association Oath Rolls. A.D. 1696*, London, private printing, 1921.

Gauci, P., *Politics and Society in Great Yarmouth 1660–1722*, Oxford, Clarendon Press, 1996.

Gauci, P., *The Politics of Trade: The Overseas Merchant in State and Society, 1660–1720*, Oxford, Oxford UP, 2001.

Gautier, E. and L. Henry, *La population de Crulai*, Paris, Presses Universitaires de France, 1958.

Glass, D. V., 'Two Papers on Gregory King', in *Population in History*, ed. D. V. Glass and D. E. C. Eversley, London, Arnold, 1965, pp. 159–220.

Goody, J., J.Thirsk, and E. P. Thompson, eds, *Family and Inheritance: Rural Society in Western Europe, 1200–1800*, Cambridge, Cambridge UP, 1976.

Gore, J., *Gore's Directory for Liverpool and its environs*, Liverpool, 1805.

Grassby, R., 'Social Mobility and Business Enterprise in Seventeenth Century England', in *Puritans and Revolutionaries*, ed. D. Pennington and K. Thomas, Oxford, Clarendon Press, 1978, pp. 355–81.

Gregson, M., *Portfolio of Fragments relative to the History and Antiquities, Topography and Genealogies of the County Palatine and Duchy of Lancaster*, 3rd edition, London, George Routledge and Sons, 1869.

Gregson, W. E., ed., 'Recusant Rolls for West Derby Hundred, 1641', *Transactions of the Historic Society of Lancashire and Cheshire*, Vol. 50, 1898, pp. 231–47.

Haggerty, S. 'Trade and trading communities in the eighteenth-century Atlantic: Liverpool and Philadelphia', unpublished PhD thesis, University of Liverpool, 2002.

Hall, C., 'Strains in the "firm of Wife, Children and Friends"? Middle-class women and employment in early nineteenth-century England', in *Women's Work and the Family Economy in Historical Perspective*, ed. P. Hudson and W. R. Lee, Manchester, Manchester UP, 1990, pp. 106–31.

Hall, P. D., 'Family Structure and Economic Organization: Massachusetts Merchants, 1700–1850', in *Family and Kin in Urban Communities, 1700–1930*, ed. T. K. Hareven, New York, New Viewpoints, 1977, pp. 38–61.

Handley, S., 'Local legislative initiatives for economic and social development in Lancashire, 1689–1731', *Parliamentary History*, Vol. 9, 1990, pp. 14–37.

Harris, T., *Politics under the Later Stuarts: Party Conflict in a Divided Society 1660–1715*, London, Longmans, 1993.

Harris,T., P. Seaward and M. Goldie, eds, *The Politics of Religion in Restoration England*, Oxford, Blackwells, 1990.

Henning, B. D., ed., *History of Parliament. The House of Commons 1660–90*, vol. I, London, Secker and Warburg, 1983.

Henry, L., *Manuel de démographie historique*, Geneva, Droz, 1967.

Hey, D., *The Fiery Blades of Hallamshire: Sheffield and its Neighbourhood, 1660–1740*, Leicester, Leicester UP, 1991.

Hey, D., *The Rural Metalworkers of the Sheffield Region: A Study of Rural Industry before the Industrial Revolution*, Leicester, Leicester UP, 1972.

Heywood, T., ed., *The Moore Rental*, Chetham Society, Vol. 10, Manchester, 1847.

Heywood, T., ed., *The Norris Papers*, Chetham Society, Vol. 9, Manchester, 1846.

Hibberd, D. J., 'Urban inequalities: social geography and demography in seventeenth century York', unpublished PhD thesis, University of Liverpool, 1981.

Hinton, R. W. K., *The Port Books of Boston, 1601–40*, Lincoln Record Society, Vol. 50, Hereford, 1956.

History of Parliament Trust unpublished paper, 'Liverpool elections 1690–1715', and unpublished biographies of Clieveland, Mauditt, Clayton and Thomas, William and Richard Norris. Acknowledgement is made to the copyright of the History of Parliament.

Hodson, T. H., *Cheshire, 1660–1780: Restoration to Industrial Revolution*, Chester, Cheshire Community Council, 1978.

Hoffman, R. and P. J. Albert, eds, *Women in the Age of the American Revolution*, Charlottesville, VA, Virginia UP, 1989.

Holderness, B. A., 'Credit in a rural community, 1660–1800: some neglected aspects of probate inventories', *Midland History*, Vol. 3, no. 3, 1976, pp. 94–115.

Holderness, B. A., 'Widows in pre-industrial society: an essay upon their economic functions', in *Land, Kinship and Life-Cycle*, ed. R. M. Smith, Cambridge, Cambridge UP, 1984, pp. 423–42.

Holdsworth, W. S., *A History of English Law*, vols i, iii, iv, vi, London, Methuen, 1937–1956.

Hollingsworth, T. H., *Historical Demography*, London, Hodder and Stoughton, 1969.

Hollinshead, J. E., 'The people of South-West Lancashire during the second half of the sixteenth century', unpublished PhD thesis, University of Liverpool, 1986.

Holmes, G., *Augustan England: Professions, State and Society, 1680–1730*, London, Allen and Unwin, 1982.

Holmes, G., *British Politics in the Reign of Anne*, London, Macmillan, 1967.

Horwitz, H., *Parliament Policy and Politics in the Reign of William III*, Manchester, Manchester UP, 1977.

Horwitz, H., 'Party in a civic context: London from the exclusion crisis to the fall of Walpole', in *Britain in the First Age of Party 1680–1750: Essays Presented to Geoffrey Holmes*, ed. C. Jones, London, Hambledon, 1987, pp. 173–94.

Horwitz, H., 'The mess of the middle class revisited: the case of the big bourgeoisie of Augustan London', *Continuity and Change*, Vol. 2, 1987, pp. 263–96.

Houlbrooke, R. A., *The English Family 1450–1700*, London, Longmans, 1984.

Hughes, E., *North Country Life in the Eighteenth Century: The North East 1700–1750*, London, Oxford UP, 1952.

Hughes, J. R., 'A sketch of the origin and early history of the Liverpool Bluecoat Hospital', *Transactions of the Historic Society of Lancashire and Cheshire*, Vol. 2, 1859, pp. 163–86.

Hussey, D., 'Re-investigating the coastal trade: the ports of the Bristol channel and the Severn estuary c1695–c1704', unpublished PhD thesis, University of Wolverhampton, 1995.

Hyde, F. E., *Liverpool and the Mersey: The Development of a Port 1700–1970*, Newton Abbot, David and Charles, 1971.

Irvine, W. F., ed., *Marriage Licences Granted within the Archdeaconry of Chester in the Diocese of Chester, 1661–67*, Record Society of Lancashire and Cheshire, Vol. 65, 1912; *1667–80*, Vol. 69, 1914; *1680–1691*, Vol. 73, 1918; *1691–1700*, Vol. 77, 1923.

Irvine, W. F., ed., *A collection of Lancashire and Cheshire Wills not now found in any Probate Registry 1301–1752*, Record Society of Lancashire and Cheshire, Vol. 30, London, 1896.

Jackson, G., 'Glasgow in transition, c.1660–c.1740', in *Glasgow, Volume I: Beginnings to 1830*, ed. T. M. Devine and G. Jackson, Manchester, Manchester UP, 1995, pp. 63–105.

Jackson, G., *Hull in the Eighteenth Century: A Study in Economic and Social History*, London, Oxford UP, 1972.

Jarvis, A., *Liverpool Central Docks 1799–1905*, Gloucester, Sutton, 1991.

Jarvis, R. C., *Customs Letter-Books of the Port of Liverpool 1711–1813*, Chetham Society, 3rd series, Vol. 6, Manchester, 1954.

Jarvis, R. C., 'Illicit trade with the Isle of Man, 1671–1765', *Transactions of the Lancashire and Cheshire Antiquarian Society*, Vol. 58, 1945–6, pp. 245–67.

Jarvis, R. C., 'The Head Port of Chester and Liverpool, its creek and member', *Transactions of the Historic Society of Lancashire and Cheshire*, Vol. 102, 1950, pp. 69–84.

Johnston, J. A., 'The Probate Inventories and Wills of a Worcestershire Parish, 1676–1775', *Midland History*, Vol. 1, 1971, pp. 20–33.

Jones, J. R., *Country and Court: England 1658–1714*, London, Arnold, 1978.

Kermode, J. I., *Medieval Merchants: York, Beverley and Hull in the Later Middle Ages*, Cambridge, Cambridge UP, 1998.

Kirby, J. W., 'Restoration Leeds and the aldermen of the corporation 1661–1700', *Northern History*, Vol. XXII, 1986, pp. 123–74.

Knodel, J. and H. Kintner, 'The impact of breast feeding patterns on the bio-metric analysis of infant mortality', *Demography*, Vol. 14, 1977, pp. 391–409.

Krause, J.T., 'The changing adequacy of English Registration, 1690–1837', in *Population in History: Essays in Historical Demography*, ed.

D. V. Glass and D. E. C. Eversley, London, Arnold, 1965, pp. 379–93.

Lane, P., 'Women, property and inheritance: wealth creation and income generation in small English towns, 1750–1835', in *Urban Fortunes: Property and Inheritance in the Town, 1700–1900*, ed. J. Stobart and A. Owens, Aldershot, Ashgate, 2000, pp. 172–94.

Langton, J. and P. Laxton, 'Parish registers and urban structure: the example of late-eighteenth century Liverpool', *Urban History Yearbook*, 1978, pp. 74–84.

Langton, J., 'Industry and Towns 1500–1730', in *An Historical Geography of England and Wales*, ed. R. A. Dodgshon and R. A. Butlin, London, Academic Press, 1978, pp. 173–98.

Langton, J., 'Liverpool and its hinterland in the late-eighteenth century', in *Commerce Industry and Transport: Studies in Economic Change on Merseyside*, ed. B. Anderson and P. Stoney, Liverpool, Liverpool UP, 1983, pp. 1–25.

Langton, J., 'Residential patterns in pre-industrial cities: some case studies from seventeenth-century Britain', in *The Tudor and Stuart Town: A Reader in English Urban History 1530–1688*, ed. J. Barry, London, Longmans, 1990, pp. 1–27.

Laslett, P., 'Mean household size in England since the sixteenth century', in *Household and Family in Past Time*, ed. P. Laslett and R. Wall, Cambridge, Cambridge UP, 1972, pp. 125–58.

Lewis, F., 'Studying Urban Mobility: the possibilities for family reconstitution', *Local Population Studies*, Vol. 55, 1995, pp. 62–65.

Lewis, F., 'The Demographic and Occupational Structure of Liverpool: a study of the Parish Registers, 1660–1750', unpublished PhD thesis, University of Liverpool, 1993.

Lindert, P. H., 'English Occupations, 1670–1811', *Journal of Economic History*, Vol. 40, no. 4, 1980, pp. 685–712.

Longmore, J., 'Liverpool Corporation as landowners and dock builders 1709–1835', in *Town and Countryside: The English Landowner in the National Economy 1660–1860*, ed. C. W. Chalklin and J. Wordie, London, Unwin Hyman, 1989, pp. 116–46.

Macfarlane, A. D. J., *The Family Life of Ralph Josselin, a Seventeenth-Century Clergyman: An Essay in Historical Anthropology*, Cambridge, Cambridge UP, 1970.

Manual of the International Statistical Classification of Disease, Injuries, and Causes of Death, vol. 1, Geneva, WHO, 1977.

Marriner, S., *The Economic and Social Development of Merseyside*, London, Croom Helm, 1982.

Marshall, J. D., ed., *The Autobiography of William Stout of Lancaster 1665–1752*, Chetham Society, 3rd series, Vol. 14, Manchester, 1967.

Mathias, P., 'Capital, credit and enterprise in the Industrial Revolution', in *The Transformation of England: Essays in the Economic and Social History of England in the Eighteenth Century*, ed. P. Mathias, London, Methuen, 1979, pp. 88–115.

Maver, I., 'The guardianship of the community: civic authority before 1833' in *Glasgow, Volume I: Beginnings to 1830*, ed. T. M. Devine and G. Jackson, Manchester, Manchester UP, 1995, pp. 239–77.

Mayer, J., *History of the Art of Pottery in Liverpool*, Liverpool, 1871.

McCrum, A., 'Inheritance and the family: The Scottish urban experience in the 1820s', in *Urban Fortunes: Property and Inheritance in the Town, 1700–1900*, ed. J. Stobart and A. Owens, Aldershot, Ashgate, 2000, pp. 149–71.

Meldrum, T., *Domestic Service and Gender, 1660–1750: Life and Work in the London Household*, Harlow, Pearson Education, 2000.

Merson, A. L., 'A calendar of Southampton Apprenticeship Registers, 1699–1740', *Southampton Record Series*, Vol. 12, 1968.

Middlebrook, S., *Newcastle upon Tyne, its Growth and Achievement*, Newcastle upon Tyne, Newcastle Chronicle and Journal, 1950.

Millard, J., 'A new approach to the study of marriage horizons', *Local Population Studies*, Vol. 28, 1982, pp. 10–31.

Miller J., 'The crown and the borough charters in the reign of Charles II', *English Historical Review*, Vol. 100, 1985, pp. 53–84.

Milne, G. J., *Trade and traders in mid-Victorian Liverpool: mercantile business and the making of a world port*, Liverpool, Liverpool UP, 2000.

Minchinton, W. E., 'The Merchants in England in the Eighteenth Century', *Explorations in Entrepreneurial History*, Vol. 10, 1957–58, pp. 62–71.

Morgan K., *Bristol and the Atlantic Trade in the Eighteenth Century*, Cambridge, Cambridge UP, 1993.

Morris, C., ed., *The Journeys of Celia Fiennes 1685–c1712*, London, Cresset Press, 1947.

Moss, William, *The Liverpool Guide: including a sketch of the environs*, Liverpool, 1796.

Mott, A. J., 'On books published in Liverpool', *Transactions of the Historic Society of Lancashire and Cheshire*, Vol. 13, 1861, pp. 103–66.

Mullett, M., 'The politics of Liverpool 1660–1688', *Transactions of the Historic Society of Lancashire and Cheshire*, Vol. 124, 1972, pp. 31–56.

Narrett, D. S., 'Men's Wills and Women's Property Rights in Colonial New York', in *Women in the Age of the American Revolution*, ed. R. Hoffman and P. J. Albert, Charlottesville, VA, Virginia UP, 1989, pp. 91–133.

Newton, R., *Eighteenth-century Exeter*, Exeter, University of Exeter, 1984.

Nicholson, F. and E. Axon, eds, *Memorials of the Family of Nicholson of Blackshaw, Dumfriesshire, Liverpool and Manchester*, private printing, 1928.

Nicholson, S. M., *The Changing Face of Liverpool, 1207–1727*, Liverpool, Archaeological Survey of Merseyside, 1981.

O'Brien, P., *Warrington Academy 1757–86: Its Predecessors and Successors*, Wigan, Owl Books, 1989.

Oxley, G. W., 'The administration of the old Poor Law in the West Derby Hundred of Lancashire, 1601–1837', unpublished MA dissertation, University of Liverpool, 1966.

Pain, A. J. and M. T. Smith, 'Do Marriage Horizons accurately measure migration? A test case from Stanhope Parish, County Durham', *Local Population Studies*, Vol. 33, 1984, pp. 44–48.

Parkinson, C. N., *The Rise of the Port of Liverpool*, Liverpool, Liverpool UP, 1952.

Patten, J., 'Urban occupations in pre-industrial England', *Transactions of the Institute of British Geographers*, new series, Vol. 2, 1977, pp. 296–313.

Patten, J., *English Towns 1500–1700*, Folkestone, Dawson, 1978.

Pearl, V., 'Change and stability in seventeenth-century London', in *The Tudor and Stuart Town: A Reader in English Urban History 1530–1688*, ed. J. Barry, London, Longmans, 1990, pp. 139–65.

Peet, H., 'Abstracts of deeds relating to the sale of pews in St Nicholas's Church, Liverpool', *Transactions of the Historic Society of Lancashire and Cheshire*, Vol. 73, 1921, pp. 213–24.

Peet, H., ed., *Liverpool in the Reign of Queen Anne, 1705 and 1708, from a rate assessment book of the town and parish*, Liverpool, Young, 1908.

Peet, H., ed., *Liverpool Vestry Books, 1681–1834*, vol. 1, 1681–1799, Liverpool, Liverpool UP, 1912.

Peet, H., ed., *The earliest Registers of the Parish of Liverpool (St. Nicholas Church): Christenings, Marriages and Burials, 1660–1704, with some of the earlier episcopal transcripts commencing in 1604*, Lancashire Parish Register Society, Vol. 35, Rochdale, 1909.

Peet, H., 'Thomas Steers: the engineer of Liverpool's first dock: a memoir', *Transactions of the Historic Society of Lancashire and Cheshire*, Vol. 82, 1930, pp. 163–242.

Petchey, W., 'The Borough of Maldon, Essex 1500–1688', unpublished PhD thesis, University of Leicester, 1972.

Philpott, R. A., *Historic Towns of the Merseyside Area: A Survey of Urban Settlement to 1800*, Liverpool, National Museums and Galleries on Merseyside, 1988.

Picton, J. A., *Memorials of Liverpool*, London, Longmans, Green & Co, 1873.

Picton, J. A., *Municipal archives and records from 1700 to 1835*, Liverpool, Liverpool City Corporation, 1881.

Platt, E. M., 'Liverpool during the Civil War', *Transactions of the Historic Society of Lancashire and Cheshire*, Vol. 61, 1910, pp. 183–202.

Poole, B., 'Liverpool's trade in the reign of Queen Anne', unpublished MA dissertation, University of Liverpool, 1961.

Pooley, C., 'The residential segregation of migrant communities in mid-Victorian Liverpool', *Transactions of the Institute of British Geographers*, Vol. 2, 1977, pp. 364–82.

Power, M. J., 'Creating a port: Liverpool 1695–1715', *Transactions of the Historic Society of Lancashire and Cheshire*, Vol. 149, 2000, pp. 51–71.

Power, M. J., 'Politics and progress in Liverpool', *Northern History*, Vol. 35, 1999, pp. 119–38.

Power, M. J., 'Councillors and commerce in Liverpool 1650–1750', *Urban History*, Vol. 24, 1997, pp. 301–23.

Power, M. J., 'East and west in early-modern London', in *Wealth and Power in Tudor England: Essays Presented to S. T. Bindoff*, ed. E. Ives, R. J. Knecht, J. J. Scarisbrick, London, Athlone, 1978, pp. 167–85.

Power, M. J., ed., *Liverpool Town Books 1649–1671*, Record Society of Lancashire and Cheshire, Vol. 136, 1999.

Power, M. J., 'The growth of Liverpool', in *Popular Politics, Riot and Labour: Essays in Liverpool History 1790–1940*, ed. J. C. Belchem, Liverpool, Liverpool UP, 1992, pp. 21–37.

Power, M. J., 'The East London working community in the seventeenth century', in *Work in Towns 850–1850*, ed. P. J. Corfield and D. Keene, Leicester, Leicester UP, 1990, pp. 103–20.

Prior, M., 'Women and the urban economy: Oxford 1500–1800', in *Women in English Society 1500–1800*, ed. M. Prior, London, Methuen, 1985, pp. 93–117.

Rabuzzi, D. A., 'Women as merchants in eighteenth-century northern Germany: the case of Stralsund, 1750–1830', *Central European History*, Vol. 28, No. 4, 1995, pp. 435–56.

Ramsay Muir, J. and Platt E. M., *A History of Municipal Government in Liverpool from the Earliest Times to the Municipal Reform Act of 1835*, Liverpool, UP of Liverpool, 1906.

Ramsay Muir, J., *A History of Liverpool*, Liverpool, Liverpool UP, 1907.

Rappaport, S., *Worlds within Worlds: Structures of Life in Sixteenth-century London*, Cambridge, Cambridge UP, 1989.

Rawling, A. J., 'The Rise of Liverpool and Demographic Change in part of South West Lancashire, 1660–1760', unpublished PhD thesis, University of Liverpool, 1986.

Rediker, M., *Between the Devil and the Deep Blue Sea*, Cambridge, Cambridge UP, 1987.

Reed, M., 'Ipswich in the seventeenth century', unpublished PhD thesis, University of Leicester, 1973.

Rideout, E. H., *The Custom House, Liverpool*, Liverpool, Elly, 1928.

Ritchie-Noakes, N., *Liverpool's Historic Waterfront*, London, HMSO, 1984.

Rogers, N., 'Money, land and lineage: the big bourgeoisie of Hanoverian London', in *The Eighteenth-century Town: A Reader in English*

Urban History 1688–1820, ed. P. Borsay, Harlow, Longmans, 1990, pp. 268–91.

Rogers, N., 'The urban opposition to whig oligarchy 1720–60', in *The Origins of Anglo-American Radicalism*, ed. M. and J. Jacob, London, Allen and Unwin, 1984, pp. 132–48.

Rose, J., ed., *Lancashire and Cheshire historical and genealogical notes*, vols 1 & 2, Leigh, printed at the 'Chronicle' office, 1879–81.

Ruggles, S., 'Migration, Marriage, and Mortality: Correcting Sources of Bias in English Family Reconstitutions', *Population Studies*, Vol. 46, 1992, pp. 507–22.

Sacks, D. H., 'The corporate town and the English state: Bristol's "little businesses" 1625–1641', in *The Tudor and Stuart Town: A Reader in English Urban History 1530–1688*, ed. J. Barry, London, Longmans, 1990, pp. 297–333.

Sacks, D. H., *The Widening Gate: Bristol and the Atlantic Economy 1450–1700*, Berkeley, California UP, 1991.

Schofield, M. M. and D. J. Pope, *The Liverpool Plantation Registers 1744–73 and 1779–84*, Wakefield, EP Microform 1978.

Schofield, M. M., 'Shoes and ships and sealing wax; eighteenth century Lancashire exports to the colonies', *Transactions of the Historic Society of Lancashire and Cheshire*, Vol. 135, 1986, pp. 61–82.

Schofield, R. S. and E. A. Wrigley, 'Infant and child mortality in England in the late Tudor and early Stuart period', in *Health, Medicine and Mortality in the Sixteenth Century*, ed. C. Webster, Cambridge, Cambridge UP, 1979, pp. 61–95.

Schofield, R. S., 'Did the Mothers Really Die? Three Centuries of Maternal Mortality in "The World We Have Lost"', in *The World We Have Gained: Histories of Population and Social Structure*, ed. L. Bonfield, R. M. Smith and K. Wrightson, Oxford, Blackwell, 1986, pp. 231–60.

Schofield, R. S., 'Traffic in Corpses: some evidence from Barming, Kent 1788–1812', *Local Population Studies*, Vol. 33, 1984, pp. 49–53.

Schwarz, S. M., 'Population, economy and society in North-East Lancashire, circa. 1660–1760', unpublished PhD thesis, University of Liverpool, 1989.

Sedgwick, R., ed. *History of Parliament I: The House of Commons 1715–54*, London, H.M.S.O., 1970.

Shammas, C., 'Early American Women and Control over Capital', in *Women in the Age of the American Revolution*, ed. R. Hoffman and P. J. Albert, Charlottesville, VA, Virginia UP, 1989, pp. 134–54.

Smith, A., ed., *The Registers of the Parish Church of Walton-on-the-Hill*, LPRS, Vol. 5, Wigan, 1900.

Smith, R. M., ed., *Land, Kinship and Life-Cycle*, Cambridge, Cambridge UP, 1984.

Smout, T. C., *Scottish Trade on the Eve of Union, 1660–1707*, Edinburgh, Oliver and Boyd, 1963.

Snell, K. D. M., 'Parish Registration and the study of labour mobility', *Local Population Studies*, Vol. 33, 1984, pp. 29–43.

Sogner, S. and H. Sandvik, 'Minors in law, partners in work, equals in worth? Women in the Norwegian economy in the 16th to the 18th centuries', *La donna nell'economia. Secoli XIII–XVIII*, Prato, 1990, pp. 633–53.

Souden, D., 'Migrants and the population structure of later seventeenth-century provincial cities and market towns', in *The Transformation of English Provincial Towns, 1600–1800*, ed. P. Clark, London, Hutchinson, 1984, pp. 133–68.

Souden, D., 'Movers and Stayers in Family Reconstitution Populations', *Local Population Studies*, Vol. 33, 1984, pp. 11–28.

Speck, W. A., *Stability and Strife: England 1714–1760*, London, Arnold, 1977.

Spufford, M., *Contrasting Communities: English Villagers in the Sixteenth and Seventeenth Centuries*, Cambridge, Cambridge UP, 1974.

Spufford, M., *The Great Reclothing of Rural England: Petty Chapmen and their Wares in the Seventeenth Century*, London, Hambledon, 1984.

Staves, S., *Married Women's Separate Property in England, 1660–1833*, Cambridge, MA, Harvard UP, 1990.

Stephen, L. and S. Lee, eds, *Dictionary of National Biography*, London, Smith and Elder, 1885–1900.

Stewart-Brown, R., *The Inhabitants of Liverpool from the 14th to the 18th Century*, Liverpool, private printing, 1930.

Stewart-Brown, R., *Liverpool Ships in the Eighteenth Century*, London, Liverpool UP, 1932.

Stobart, J. and A. Owens, eds, *Urban Fortunes: Property and Inheritance in the Town, 1700–1900*, Aldershot, Ashgate, 2000.

Stobart, J., 'Social and geographical contexts of property transmission in the eighteenth century', in *Urban Fortunes: Property and Inheritance in the Town, 1700–1900*, ed. J. Stobart and A. Owens, Aldershot, Ashgate, 2000, pp. 108–48.

Sweet, R., *The English Town, 1680–1840: Government, Society and Culture*, Harlow, Pearson Education, 1999.

Swinburne, H., *A Briefe Treatise of Testaments and Last Willes*, 1590.

Tate, W. E., *The Parish Chest. A Study of the Records of Parochial Administration in England*, 3rd edn, Cambridge, Cambridge UP, 1969.

Tawney, A. J. and R. H. Tawney, 'An occupational census of the seventeenth century', *Economic History Review*, Vol. 5, 1934, pp. 25–64.

Taylor, I. C., 'The court and cellar dwelling: the eighteenth-century origin of the Liverpool slum', *Transactions of the Historic Society of Lancashire and Cheshire*, Vol. 122, 1971, pp. 68–90.

The Liverpool Memorandum-Book or Gentleman's Merchant's and Tradesman's Daily Pocket-Journal for the year MDCCLIII, printed for R. Williamson.

Thirsk, J., 'Seventeenth-Century Agriculture and Social Change', in *Land, Church, and People*, ed. J. Thirsk, Reading, British Agricultural History Society, 1970, pp. 148–77.

Thirsk, J., *Economic Policy and Projects: The Development of a Consumer Society in Early Modern England*, Oxford, Clarendon Press, 1978.

Thompson, E. P., 'The grid of inheritance: a comment', in *Family and Inheritance: Rural Society in Western Europe, 1200–1800*, ed. J.Goody, J. Thirsk and E. P. Thompson, Cambridge, Cambridge UP, 1976, pp. 328–60.

Thompson, R., 'Seventeenth century English and colonial sex ratios: a postscript', *Population Studies*, Vol. 28, 1974, pp. 153–65.

Todd, B., 'Freebench and free enterprise: widows and their property in two Berkshire villages', in *English Rural Society 1500–1800*, ed. J. Chartres and D. G. Hey, Cambridge, Cambridge UP, 1990, pp. 175–200.

Tonge, W. A., ed., *Marriage Bonds of the Ancient Archdeaconry of Chester, now Preserved at Chester*, RSLC, 1700–06/07, Vol. 82, 1933; 1707–11, Vol. 85, 1935; 1711–15, Vol. 97, 1942; 1715–19, Vol. 101, 1946.

Touzeau, J., *The Rise and Progress of Liverpool from 1551 to 1835*, Liverpool, Liverpool Booksellers, 1910.

Trappes-Lomax, R., ed., *The Diary and Letter Book of the Rev. Thomas Brockbank 1671–1709*, Chetham Society, Vol. 89, Manchester, 1930.

Twemlow, J. A., ed., *Liverpool Town Books, I, 1550–1571*, and *II, 1572–1603*, Liverpool, Liverpool UP, 1918–1935.

Tyler, J. W., 'Foster Cunliffe and Sons: Liverpool Merchants in the Maryland Tobacco Trade, 1738–1765', *Maryland Historical Magazine*, Vol. 73, no. 3, 1978, pp. 246–79.

Unwin, T., 'Late seventeenth century taxation and population: the Nottinghamshire Hearth Taxes and Compton Census', *Historical Geography Research Series*, Vol. 16, 1985.

Vann, R. T., 'Wills and the family in an English town: Banbury, 1550–1800', *Journal of Family History*, Vol. 4, 1979, pp. 346–67.

Venn, J. and J. A. Venn, *Alumni Cantabrigiensis: a biographical list of all known students graduates and holders of office at the University of Cambridge, from the earliest times to 1900*, Pt. 1, vol. 1, Cambridge, Cambridge UP, 1922.

Vickery, A., *The Gentleman's Daughter: Women's Lives in Georgian England*, New Haven, CT, London, Yale UP, 1998.

Wallace, J., *A General and Descriptive History of the Ancient and Present State of the town of Liverpool... Together with a circumstantial account of the true causes of its extensive African trade, etc.*, Liverpool, 1795.

Wardle, A. C., 'The early Liverpool Privateers', *Transactions of the Historic Society of Lancashire and Cheshire*, Vol. 93, 1941, pp. 69–97.

Wardle, A. C., 'Sir Thomas Johnson: his impecuniosity and death', *Transactions of the Historic Society of Lancashire and Cheshire*, Vol. 90, 1938, pp. 181–95.

Watts, R. D., 'The Moore Family of Bank Hall, Liverpool, 1606–1730', unpublished PhD thesis, University of Wales Bangor, 2004.

Weatherill, L., *Consumer Behaviour and Material Culture in Britain 1660–1760*, London, Methuen, 1988.

Webb, S. and B., *English Local Government from the Revolution to the Municipal Corporations Act: The Manor and the Borough*, London, Longmans, 1908.

Whyte, I. D., *Migration and Society in Britain 1550–1830*, Basingstoke, Macmillan, 2000.

Willan, T. S., *The English Coasting Trade, 1660–1750*, Manchester, Manchester UP, 1938.

Williams, G., *History of the Liverpool privateers and letters of marque, with an account of the Liverpool slave trade*, London, 1897, repr. Liverpool, Liverpool UP, 2004.

Wilson, C., 'The proximate determinants of marital fertility in England, 1600–1799', in *The World We Have Gained: Histories of Population and Social Structure*, ed. L. Bonfield, R. M. Smith and K. Wrightson, Oxford, Blackwell, 1986, pp. 203–30.

Wilson, R. G., *Gentlemen Merchants: The Merchant Community in Leeds, 1700–1830*, Manchester, Manchester UP, 1971.

Woodward, D., 'The Port Books of England and Wales', *Sources for Maritime History*, Vol. III, 1973, pp. 147–65.

Wrightson, K. and D. Levine, *Poverty and Piety in an English Village: Terling 1525–1700*, New York, Academic Press, 1979.

Wrightson, K., 'Kinship in an English Village: Terling, Essex 1500–1700', in *Land, Kinship and Life-Cycle*, ed. R. M. Smith, Cambridge, Cambridge UP, 1984, pp. 313–32.

Wrigley, E. A. and R. S. Schofield, 'English Population History from Family Reconstitution: Summary Results 1600–1799', *Population Studies*, Vol. 37, 1983, pp. 157–84.

Wrigley, E. A. and R. S. Schofield, *The Population History of England 1541–1871: A Reconstruction*, London, Arnold, 1981.

Wrigley, E. A., 'Family limitation in pre-industrial England', *Economic History Review*, 2nd series, Vol. 19, 1966, pp. 82–109.

Wrigley, E. A., 'Mortality in pre-industrial England: the example of Colyton, Devon, over three centuries', in *Population and Social Change*, ed. D. V. Glass and R. Revelle, London, Arnold, 1972, pp. 243–73.

Wrigley, E. A., 'The changing occupational structure of Colyton over two centuries', *Local Population Studies*, Vol. 18, 1977, pp. 9–22.

Wrigley, E. A., 'Urban growth and agricultural change: England and the continent in the early modern period', in *The Eighteenth-century Town: A Reader in English Urban History 1688–1820*, ed. P. Borsay, Harlow, Longmans, 1990, pp. 39–82.

Wrigley, E. A., R. S. Davies, J. E. Oeppen and R. S. Schofield, *English Population History from Family Reconstitution 1580–1837*, Cambridge, Cambridge UP, 1997.

Wyatt, G., 'Migration in South West Lancashire', *Local Population Studies*, Vol. 27, 1981, pp. 62–64.

Sources in electronic form

The Data Archive, University of Essex: 'The Liverpool Community 1660–1750' (deposited 1998) contains several Liverpool sources in electronic form:

Freemen admissions 1649–1708: FREEMEN

Hearth taxes: HEARTH63; and 64, 66 and 73

Plantation register 1744–48: PLANTN

Port book 1664–65: PBGLC65; OGDSI_65; OGDSO_65

Port book 1708–09: PBGLC09; OGDSI_09; OGDS0_O9

Rate assessment 1708: RATE1708

Rate assessment 1743: RATE1743

Town councillors and officers 1649–1750: TOWNBOOK

Vestry officials: VESTRY

Index

Accars, William 152
Ackers, Thomas 172
Africa 26
Aigburth Hall 95, 120
Alanson, Thomas 169–70, 176
Alcock, Edward 91
Alcock, Jane 91, 108
Allerton 156
America 15, 56–57, 110–11
Andoe, Thomas 152, 167–68, 181
Angola 26
apprenticeship 120–21
Arrowsmith, Jeremiah 125
Ashbrooke, Robert 113
Ashurst, Thomas 141, 156
Assheton, Ralph 166
Aston, Sir Thomas 183
Atherton, Sir Richard 169
Atherton, William 171
Atlantic 1, 15–17, 19–21, 24, 57, 151
Aughton 91

Baldwin, Thomas 121, 156
Baltic 19
Bamber, John 97
Banbury 112
Bank Hall 166
Banks, William 166
Barbados 16, 20, 153
Barlow, William 156
Barrow, Robert 92, 156
Bassnett, William 94, 130

Beckett, William 108
Belfast 21, 153
Benn, James 170, 171
bequests
    context of 122–32
    patterns of 113–19
Bewsay, nr Warrington 169
Bibby, Charles 100
Bibby, William 100, 172
Bicksteth, Thomas 152, 154, 166,
    175
Bills of Mortality 40, 47
Birch, Colonel 171
Birch, Thomas 152
Birchall, Daniel 95
Birkenhead 129
Birmingham 111–12
birth intervals 49–51
Blackburne, John 95
Blackmore, Thomas 166
Bluecoat Hospital/School 14, 119,
    146
Blundell, Bryan 110, 118, 141, 146,
    149, 180–83
Blundell, John 156
Blundell, Nicholas 97
Bootle, Thomas 179–83
Boulton, Hannah 98–99
Boulton, Richard 98–99
breastfeeding 45, 51
Brereton, Owen 156
Brereton, Thomas 182–83

Bridge Alley 33, 99
Briggs, Joseph 175
Bright, Thomas 95
Bristol 9, 15, 18–22, 25–26, 78, 94,
    139, 149, 153, 156, 163–65,
    168,170, 174, 179
Britain 9, 56, 190, 193
Brooke, Roger 95
Brotherton, Thomas 169
Buckingham 164, 174
Bucknall, Sir William 166
Bushell, Anne 90, 112
Bushell, William 90

Cameroon, 26
canals
    Bridgewater 22
    Leeds–Liverpool 22
    Sankey Brook Navigation 22
    Trent and Mersey 22
Cardwell, Edward 95
Carribean 26
Carrickfergus 152
Carrington, Nathan 98–99
Carter, Hannah 125
Carter, Thomas 125
Case, Thomas 92
Castle Hey 92
Castle Street 34, 175
Catterall, Elizabeth 89
Catterall, John 89
Catterall, William 89
Chapel Street 99, 125, 152, 178
Chapel Yard 124
Chapman, Thomas 167
charters 138, 144–45, 162–64,
    167–70, 176–77, 179–80
Chesapeake 26
Cheshire 21–22, 52, 56–57, 95, 111,
    120
Chester 8–9, 24, 111, 131, 139, 183
Chorley, Ann 143
Chorley, John 168–69
Chorley, William 142

Civil War 16, 112, 163
Clayton Square 92
Clayton, Elizabeth 91, 118, 121, 127,
    176
Clayton, Sarah 91–92
Clayton, William 91, 95, 121, 154,
    170–72, 175–77
Clieveland, Alice 92, 126, 129
Clieveland, Ann (wife of John) 92,
    126,
Clieveland, Ann (wife of Edward
    Norris) 177
Clieveland family 126–27, 129
Clieveland, John 126, 129, 153, 156,
    170, 175–76
Clieveland, Richard 126–127, 129,
    131
Clieveland, Suzanna 126–127
Clieveland, William 126, 129
Clinton, Peter 153
Cockshutt, John 156, 170, 175
Colchester, Viscount, Thomas 141
Common 14, 129, 140, 153–55, 165,
    172–73, 183
Cook, Zachariah 94
Cooke, Cicely 88, 90
Coore, Thomas 156
Cork 21
Corporation 14, 90, 92, 153
Cottingham, Katherine 89
Council
    composition and size 144–46
    oligarchy 147–51, *see also*
        merchants
    relationship with local landowners
        165–66
councillors
    constituents of wealth 151–56
    occupation and status of 152–53
    profile of 144–46
Covent Garden 154
Coventry 164, 174
Crosby 91
Croston 54

Crowther, John 169
Cuba 26
Cubban, Joshua 167
Cunliffe, Foster, Alderman 97, 120, 141, 146, 153–54, 156, 181–83
Cunningham, John 153
Customs 8–9, 21, 87, 95, 173, 175, 177, 191
Customs House 18, 25–26, 97, 173

Dale Street 14, 34, 61, 152, 154, 155
Danvers, Daniel 126–28, 130–31
Danvers family 128
Danvers, Samuel 97, 128
Dawney, Bryan 179
Derby Square 62
Derby, Earls of 1, 164, 168, 172
    Charles, eighth 141, 156, 165–67
    William, ninth 165
    James, tenth 141, 156, 165, 173, 178, 182
Devizes 174
Dewhurst, Lawrence 122
Dewhurst, Mary 122
Dewhurst, Roger 122
Diggles, Charles 170
Dissenters 151, 164–65, 168, 184
docks 14, 24–26, see also Old Dock, Dry Dock
Dominica 26
Dover 173
Drogheda 21, 152
Dry Dock 92
Dublin 21, 152–53
Duke Street 155
Dundalk 152
Dungeon Point 92, 129
Dutch War 16
Dutton, John 120

Earle, John 156, 172
Eaton, Anne 90
Eaton, Joseph 90, 156

Eaton, Peter 170
Eccleston, John 91
Eccleston, William 152
Edmund Street 92
English Channel 20
Entwistle, Bertil 141, 156
Entwistle, John 141, 145, 156
Everton 14
Europe 9, 16, 18, 20, 151
Exchange 14
Exclusion crisis 1679–81 144, 163, 168
executors, appointment of 110–12
Exeter 139–40, 144, 149, 156, 178

Fall Well 47
family reconstitution 38
Farrington, Mary 89
Fazakerley, Samuel 143, 152, 156
Fells, John 154
Fenwick Alley 33, 99
Fenwick Street 33, 99
fertility 48–51
Fillingham, Thomas 179
Finney, Thomas 109
Fleetwood, James, junior 100
Fleetwood, James, senior 100
Fleetwood, Mary 100
Formby, Gilbert 166
Formby, Margery 90
Foster, Benjamin 95
Frodsham 22, 173

Galaspy, Margaret 89
Gallaway, Richard 97
Gandy, William 97, 120
Gardner, William 152
Garstang 54, 120, 124
Gibbons, J. 176
Gildart, James 154
Gildart, Richard 141, 146, 154–56, 181–83
Gildus, Esther 89
Glasgow 9, 19–20, 25, 149

Glegg, Joseph 183
Gloucestershire 22
Gold Coast 26
Goodrick, Francis 156
Gower, Sir John Leveson 172
Grayson, Joseph 127
Great Yarmouth 163
Greene, Alexander 165
Greenock 25
Grenada 26
Greson, David 127
Grosvenor, Sir Richard 183

Hall, Peter 153, 175, 176, 180
Hall, Ralph 152
Halsall, Edward 144
Hamilton, Maxwell 95
Hanover Street 14
Hardman, John 154
Harper, Jane 90
Harper, Richard 90
Harrison, Elizabeth 96, 99
Harrison, Richard 177
Haydock 22
Heald, Margaret 89
Henshaw, Esther 98–99
Henshaw, John 98–99
Hereford 22
Heuston, Levinius 170, 174
Heywood, Arthur 132, 154
Heywood, Benjamin 132
High Street 152
Hinkley 109, 111
Houghton, Henry 124
Houghton, Richard, junior 124
Houghton, Richard, senior 124, 154,
    175–76
Houghton, William 167
household size 34–35
Howard, Joan 89, 92
Howland wet dock 24–25
Hoyle Lake 24–25
Huddleston, Mary 92
Hughes, John 146, 180–82

Hull 9, 15, 18, 22, 25, 139, 149,
    156, 165, 174
Hunter, Benjamin 153
Hunter, Robert 171

Ince 173
Independent Chapel 55
Infirmary 14, 35, 119
inland communications 22–24
Interregnum 16
Ireland 1, 8, 15, 18, 20–21, 24,
    55–57, 129, 151–53, 184
Ireland, Gilbert 166
Irish Sea 22
Isle of Man 18, 21, 153

Jamaica 26, 87, 97, 153
James, Edward 100
James, John 100
James, Robert 99
James, Roger, junior 99
James, Roger, senior 99, 100
Jeffries, Lord Chief Justice 169
Jerrome, James 167, 168
Johnson, Thomas, junior (Sir
    Thomas) 145, 149, 152–56,
    162, 169, 170–83
Johnson, Thomas, senior 145, 152,
    155, 165–70
Jones, Alice 90
Jones, Richard 169–70
Jones, Roger 90
Josselin, Ralph 119
Juggler Street 97

Kaye, Elizabeth 90
Kelsall, Richard 108, 182
Kirks, Moorcroft 87

Lady, John 170
Lancashire 8, 20–23, 37–38, 52, 56–
    57, 71, 91, 95, 111, 120, 129,
    132, 168, 176–77, 180, 191
Lancaster 54, 170

Lathom, Richard 169
Leeds 149
Lewis, Alexander 125
Lewis, Edward 125
Lewis, George 123
life expectancy 43–47
Litherland, Edward 167, 172
Little Crosby Hall 100
Liver Pool 24, 47, 153, 165, 172
Livesey, Edmund 170
Livesley, Jonathan 122
London 14, 16, 19, 24–26, 41,
    45–46, 57, 88, 91, 109, 127,
    139–40, 144, 146, 162–64,
    166, 168, 170, 172–73, 178–81
Londonderry 153
Lord Street 92
Lurting, Peter 145, 166–68, 181
Lurting, Richard 167
Lygoe, James 96, 99
Lyme, Oliver 169
Lyon, Edward 90

Mackmullen, Margery 89
Manchester 22
Marlborough 164, 174
mariners 23, 35, 40, 45–47, 50, 60,
    63, 78, 81–87, 89, 94–95,
    99, 108–9, 111–13, 120, 141,
    148–49
maritime sector 27, 147
    occupations, 81–87
marriage, characteristics of 50–58
marriage settlements 119–21
Marsh, Edward 165
Martindale, John 95
Maryland 16, 26, 110
Massam, Ralph 166
Matthews, Thomas 94
Mauditt, Jasper 94, 169–70, 173,
    175, 179, 182
Mercer, Henry 96, 99
Mercer, James 90, 96, 99
Mercer, Mary 90, 96

Mercer, Richard 167
Mercer, Thomas 121
merchants, 14–21, 26, 62, 80–81, 87,
    93–95, 97, 100, 129, 131–32,
    141, 148, 151–53, 156, 162–
    63, 165, 170, 178, 184
    oligarchy, profile of 147–51
Midlands 23
migration 52–58
Milnes, 'daughter' [Bridget] 130–32
mobility 58–62
Molyneux, Caryll, Viscount 165
Molyneux, Lord 1, 153, 172, 184
Monmouth 22
Montserrat 16
Moone, Anne 123–24
Moone, Robert 123
Moor Street 33
Moorcroft, Mary 96, 99
Moore, Colonel John 166
Moore family 1, 166
Moore, Sir Edward 33, 99, 127, 166
Morecroft, Sylvester 146, 156, 173,
    178, 180
mortality 39–48
Mulliney, William 152

Nantwich 22
Netherlands 19
networks
    of accumulation 124–25, 127–32
    of occupation 97–100
Newcastle 9, 15, 78
New East India Company 174
Newry 21
Nicholls, John 119
nonconformity, see also Dissenters 38,
    55, 131–32
Norres, Alexander 169–70
Norris, Ann 177
Norris, Dr 94
Norris, Edward 177
Norris, Richard 146, 156, 162, 170,
    172–74, 176–80

Norris, Thomas 169, 177
Norris, William 170–71, 177
North America 18, 26
North Wales 52, 56–57
Northwich 22
Norton Priory 95
Norwich 140, 144, 164

occupation
   by-employment, 94, 97
   dynasties 97–100
   methodology 69–77
   mobility 93–95
   profile 73–81
   see also councillors, urban officials,
     mariners
Ogden, 'daughter'[Sarah] 130–32
Old Dock 14, 146, 154, 172–74
Old Hall 166
Ormskirk 54
Our Lady and St Nicholas 37, 171
overseers, appointment of 112
Over Whitley 97
Oxford 168

Pardoe, James 154
Parish
   area of 199–200
   creation of 171–72
Park Lane 14
Parker, George 121
Parr, Lancashire 22, 91, 92
party politics 174–78, 182–83
Patten, Hugh 123
[Patten], Sarah 123
Pemberton family 130
Pemberton, John, junior 110, 130–32
Pemberton, John, senior 94, 110,
   130–32
Pennsylvania 110
Percival, John 153
Percival, Richard 152, 166
Peters, Ralph 143, 156, 172–74
Phelps, Ann 109

Pleasington, nr Blackburn 92
Pole, Charles 181
Pole, William 182–83
Poole, Josia 181
Poorhouses 35
population 9, 32–37
population, mariners 23–24, 35
Portmoot 143
Portsmouth 24, 164
Portugal 19
Potteries 23
Powell, Samuel 95
Preeson, Alderman 173
Prescot 22–24
Preston 9, 164, 177, 179
Price, Francis 129
Prior, Joseph 170, 175
privateering 19–21
processing industries 23
Pryor, William 121

Quaker Meeting House 55

Rainford 127
Rainford, Alderman 92
Redcross Street 99
Restoration 8, 18, 89, 144, 163, 165,
   193
Revolution of 1688–89 18, 139, 169
Richmond, Henry 120, 177, 179–80
Richmond, Richard 120, 171, 179
Richmond, Silvester 120, 124, 145,
   167–9, 179
Rimmer, Anne 89
Rimmer, Richard 89
rivers
   Aire and Calder 22
   Avon 22, 25
   Dee 8
   Don 22
   Douglas 22
   Frome 25
   Hull 25
   Irwell 22

Mersey 8, 22, 24, 25, 35, 47, 166, 172
Ribble 22
Severn 22, 23
Thames 46
Trent 22
Weaver 22
Robinson, Anne 122
Robinson, Daniel 98–99
Robinson, James 122
Robinson, Margaret 122
Robinson, Mary 143
Robinson, Richard 143
Roby 127
Roby, Thomas 120
Roderick, Anthony [Antonio Rored-rigu] 88
Roney, Henry 88
Rotherhithe 24
Royal Africa Company 19, 174
Royal Navy 8, 24, 86
Royle, Richard 95

Sacheverell, Henry 174, 179
Sailors' Sixpenny Hospital 14
Sandiford, John 143, 150, 152, 154
Sandiford, Thomas 143, 150
Savage, Richard, Lord Colchester 169
Scarborough 164
Scaresbrick, John 89, 181
Scaresbrick, Joyce 89
Scotland 56–57
Seacome, John 169, 173, 178
Seacome, Robert 95, 170
Seel Street 14
Selby 112
Seven Years War 20
Seymour, Sir Edward 178
Shambles 46
Sharples, Cuthbert 175–76
Sheffield 111, 112
Sheilds, Elizabeth 90, 125
Sheilds, Robert 90, 125, 170

shipbuilding 19, 23
Short, Edward 96–97
Short, Elizabeth 96, 99
Short family 96
Short, Mary 96, 99
Short, Michael 96–97
Shrewsbury 22
Sierra Leone 26
Sligo 153
Smith, Nathaniel 179
Sorocold, George 172
South Carolina 26
Southwark 112, 164, 174
South Sea Bubble 19
Speke 146, 169–70, 177
Squire, William 153, 156, 177, 181
St Christopher 16
St George's church 37, 62, 172, 180
St Helens 22–23, 55
St Mary Catholic chapel 55
St Mary's church, Walton 147
St Nicholas' church 139, 147
St Peter's church 34, 37, 154, 171, 179
St Thomas' church 37
St Vincent 26
Staffordshire 23
Stannage Park 95
Stanley, William, Lord Strange 5, 141
Steers, Thomas 24, 146, 172–173, 180
Stockley, Thomas 167
Stoke Bruerne 127
Stringer, Jacob 97
Sturzaker, John 152, 165
Styth, Robert 171
Summerset, Alice 89, 121
Summerset, Elizabeth 121
Summerset, Mary 121

Tarleton, Ann 123
Tarleton, Edward, junior 145
Tarleton, Edward, senior 95, 120, 123, 145

Tarleton family 100, 122, 124
Tarleton, Frances 122
Tarleton, John 120
Tarleton, Timothy 122
Tarvin, George 97
Tennant, William 121
Terling 109
Tithebarn Street 14, 34, 99
Tory 164, 168–70, 174–178
town officials, role of 140–43
Townfield 14, 35, 91, 129
Townsend, James 179
Toxteth Park 14, 125, 127
trading connections
  . Africa 19, 26
     Americas 15, 19
     Atlantic 1, 15, 20, 24
     coastal 17–18, 22
     Europe 8, 19
     internal 22–23
     Ireland 8, 15, 20–21, 24, 153
     North America 16, 26, 152–53
     West Indies 16, 19–20, 26, 153
trade
     in coal 16–17, 21–23, 153
     in indentured labour 20
     in iron 16–17, 153
     in livestock 16
     in manufactures 153
     in salt 15–17, 20–23, 152
     in slaves 19–20, 24, 26–27
     in sugar 15–17, 19–20, 153
     in textiles 16–17, 23, 26, 153
     in tobacco 15–17, 19–21, 26, 152
Trueman, William 167
trustees, appointment of 112–13
Turner, Robert 95
turnpikes 1, 22
Tyrer, Thomas 170, 175
Tyrer, George 141, 154, 156, 176,
     179, 180–83

Ulster 17
Upholland 125

urban growth 9, 14–15, 33–35,
urban government
     officials 140–44
     participation in 139

Valentine, William 119, 167
Vernon, Thomas 181
Virginia 26, 131, 152, 153, 184

Wakefield 132
Wales 15
Walles, John 152
Walpole, Thomas 164, 178, 183
Walsh, Catherine 109
Walton-on-the-Hill 53, 120, 140,
     171, 179
Warrington 8, 9, 22–23, 78, 123
Warwickshire 22
Water Street 25, 34, 61, 152
water supply 46–47
Watkinson, Cuthbert 94
wealth
     constituents of 107–08
     lifetime distribution of 119
     preservation of 108–10
     unequal distribution of 124–25
Webster family 98
Webster, James 98–99
Webster, Sarah 98–99
Webster, William 152, 176
Wentworth, Ruisshe 166
West Indies 18, 26, 56–57, 153, 184
Westminster 177–78, 183
Whig 164, 168–70, 174–78
Whig hegemony 178–83
Whiston 91
Whitby 173
Whitechapel 14
Whitfield, James 165
Whitfield, Robert 181–82
widows 109–10
Wigan 9, 22, 141, 156
Williamson, Anne 123
Williamson, Edward 166

Williamson, Margaret 91
Williamson, Robert 91, 112, 167
Williamson, Thomas 166
Willis, Thomas, 121
Windall, Richard 167–68, 170, 175
Winfield, Phoebe 89
Winsford 22
Winstanley, John 141
Winwick 54
Wirral 24, 57, 129
Witter, Francis 143
Witter, Thomas 143
women, economic activity of 88–93,
    121, 125, 129

Woods, Alan 97
Woolpack 97
Worcester 164, 179
Worcestershire 22
Workhouse 35
Worsley 22
Wright, Hannah 92

Yarmouth 173
Yewdale, Anne 90
Yewdall, Jeremiah 90
York 162, 164, 178
Yorkshire 22–23, 112